MW01709104

THE PARTY'S OVER

THE PARTY'S OVER

Diary of a Recovering Cocaine Addict

KATY HENDRICKS
(pseudonym)

Preface by Norman Denzin
University of Illinois at Urbana–Champaign

Foreword by Barbara Sherman Heyl
Illinois State University

KOD/NA
KODAK BRANCH
Sevier County Public Library System
319 West Dumplin Valley Road
Kodak, Tenn. 37764

The American University Press

Copyright © 1992 by
The American University Press
4400 Massachusetts Avenue, N.W.
Anderson Lower Level
Washington, D.C. 20016

All rights reserved
Printed in the United States of America
British Cataloging in Publication Information Available

Distributed by arrangement with
National Book Network
4720 Boston Way
Lanham, MD 20706

3 Henrietta Street
London WC2E 8LU England

"BADMAN'S SONG"

Words and Music by Roland Orzabal and Nicky Holland

(c) 1989 Virgin Music (Publishers) Ltd./10 Music Ltd.
Administered in the USA and Canada by Virgin Song, Inc./Virgin Music Inc.
International Copyright Secured All Rights Reserved
Lyrics reprinted by kind permission of the publishers.

Library of Congress Cataloging-in-Publication Data

Hendricks, Katy, 1963-
The Party's Over : The Diary of a Recovering Cocaine Addict / by Katy Hendricks.
p. cm.
1. Hendricks, Katy, 1963- . 2. Narcotic addicts—United States—Biography. 3. Narcotic addicts—Rehabilitation—United States—Case studies. 4. Cocaine habit—United States—Case studies.
I. Title.
HV5805.H38A3 1991
362.29' 8' 092—dc20 [B] 91-36057 CIP

ISBN 1-879383-07-1 (cloth : alk. paper)
ISBN 1-879383-06-3 (pbk. alk. paper)

∞ TM The paper used in this publication meets the minimum requirements of American National Standard for Information Sciences—Permanence of Paper for Printed Library Materials, ANSI Z39.48–1984.

Contents

Preface

Norman K. Denzin

The Party's Over: Diary of a Recovering Cocaine Addict is a powerful document. We have Katy Hendricks, Professor Waldeman (her sociology professor),[1] and Barbara Sherman Heyl to thank for its existence. Such works are not easy to produce. Written by a recovering female addict, with Professor Heyl's encouragement and comment, it takes its place in a long tradition of first-person, biographical texts that have detailed the brutal, self-destructive, self-degrading worlds of drug and alcohol addiction. Americans love recovery stories. They love stories about good people who get into trouble, are punished, and then get better. Perhaps it is the pull of the old "fall from grace–redemption" myth so deeply entrenched in Western culture that attracts us to the addict's tale. Perhaps it is that this person is like us, only they have felt life's pain more deeply than we have. In reading their stories we vicariously take their chances. And when they get better, we know that we could too, if we were ever to take it to the edge as they have.

In reading Katy's story, the names of many famous and not so famous drunks and addicts of the past immediately come to mind: William Faulkner's fictional Mr. Acarius; Fitzgerald's multiple versions of his crack-up; John Cheever's Mr. Wickwire; Malcolm Lowery's Consul; Don Birnam of *Lost Weekend;* John Berryman's drunken poets—and then there is Freud. Hollywood has given us our share of stories about such individuals. Who can forget the addicts in *The Man with the Golden Arm, A Hatful of Rain, Bigger than Life, Monkey on My Back, The Rose,* or *Lenny?* Or those larger-than-life screen alcoholics in *I'll Cry Tomorrow; Come Back, Little Sheba; Days of Wine and Roses; Lady Sings the Blues;*

Fat City; The Morning After; Arthur; Educating Rita; Tender Mercies; and *The Dresser?* Closer to the present, we have the figures of Charlie, the cocaine addict in *Clean and Sober* who never gets clean; the tragic husband and wife cocaine addicts in *The Boost;* and more recently, Meryl Streep playing Suzanne Vale as Carrie Fisher in *Postcards from the Edge*.

Of course, these individuals have not just been detailed in the pages of fiction. There is a long and rich sociological tradition focusing on addicts and alcoholics: Janet Clark, the heroin addict who told her story in taped interviews with Howard S. Becker in *The Fantastic Lodge* (Hughes, 1961); Manny, another hard-core addict (Rettig et al., 1977); and William Tanner, the drunk in James Spradley's *You Owe Yourself a Drunk* (1970).

There is another body of literature that speaks to experiences like Katy's. These are the fall-and-redemption stories found in Alcoholic Anonymous's Big Book (AA, 1939, 1976) and Narcotics Anonymous's White Book (1962, 1984). These works contain first-person stories of many different types of alcoholics and addicts. All of them are told from within the framework of AA or NA. These miniature recovery tales follow the classic model of the life story of a person who rises to the top, slips into addiction or alcoholism, and then—after suffering the pains of their addiction—recovers through the efforts of AA or NA. (The form of these stories hovers in the background of Katy's diary.)

In the past decade, another recovery literature has emerged. Here are the more straightforward recovery manuals that have become the stock in trade of a new branch of the publishing industry. They focus on personal health and recovery. The titles do not require elaboration: *Quitting Cocaine, Maintaining Recovery: Enjoying Life without Cocaine, Managing Cocaine Craving, My First Ninety Days*. These works often offer hands-on, personalized discussions of getting and staying clean and sober. Many employ the 12 Step model of Alcoholics Anonymous and Narcotics Anonymous.

Framing Katy's Story

The above storytelling traditions frame *The Party's Over*. This is a story of the fall from grace, but a fall particular to its historical moment. As Sartre reminds us, each individual is a *universal singular*—universalized by his or her epoch, but singular in his or her reproduction of that history. Few of the famous addicts and alcoholics of the past ever told a story of recovery. Many never made it into recovery. Katy has.

She symbolizes the women of her generation. She, like millions of other women, is single, attractive, and concerned with her appearance. She comes from a working-class family background but has fully internalized middle-class values. She makes her way through college and then finds herself in that unstable economic position that comes from pursuing a career in higher education, where seeking the Ph. D. forces one to live on the economic edge. She, like others in her situation, doubles up on jobs. She works as a graduate research assistant and as a waitress, while living a lifestyle in the fast lane where cocaine use becomes a mark of status and a means of escaping the stress of the very lifestyle that the drug defines.

The large-scale recreational use of cocaine became a national phenomenon in the United States in the decade of the 1980s. It quickly lodged itself as the drug of choice among millions of people. It could produce a quick high, giving the user an immediate sense of well-being and self-confidence. It would banish fatigue and hunger and reportedly increase sexual interest and performance. These effects would be short-lived, however: 15–30 minutes at a cost of $3–$5 per minute. For many, the high became obsessive; their frequency of use and their drug dosage quickly escalated. The "crash" from coming off the drug, accompanied by fatigue, depression, irritability, anxiety, and sometimes psychotic reactions, would soon erase the euphoria of the high (Gold, 1984, p. 3). And a regular user could become addicted in a matter of weeks or months. In order to remove the negative effects of the withdrawal from the drug, users take it again. This creates an immediate high and obviates the depression and fatigue that come from the crash. Addicted users take the drug daily, often building up a weekly habit that can exceed $500. (For example, in Katy's last 24-hour binge she used seven grams of cocaine, with a street value of about $700.)

Many of these users binge on the drug and seem unable to stop for as long as a month. Their lives become centered around it. They enter a new social world defined by illegal drug use, dealers, telephone numbers, beepers, contact persons, and interactions with others whose lives also center on the drug and its use. Addicts have been known to steal money from their employers, write bad checks, and go into debt to support their habit. Many lose their spouses, lovers, friends, and jobs; some attempt suicide; and more than a few have, at the end of their using careers, moved from snorting the drug to intravenous use and then to "freebasing" (in which the drug is rendered very volatile and smokable). By the mid-1980s, cocaine addiction had become a national social problem. One in three addicts was a white, middle-class woman.

This is where Katy's diary enters the picture. She had many of the above experiences. She is one of the lucky members of her generation, for she has found a way out of the world of cocaine addiction. Hers is a story of recovery written from the ground level—from the degree-zero of each day, where staying clean becomes a project to be pursued for one more 24-hour cycle. Her vision is narrow, her text grounded in the present. There is no overarching framework here, at least not in the beginning—just the daily pains of getting back to normal. There does not exist anywhere in the contemporary literature on addiction and recovery an account like this.

The Party's Over is driven by an urgency, a desire to write the self of recovery before it escapes or slips away. Consider its beginning. Katy writes in her Introduction, "On April 24, 1988, I surrendered to 12 Step recovery. . . . I have been clean since then. Recovery from drug addiction has been the most difficult thing that I have ever had to do, but it has also been the most rewarding. In recovery, I have often felt as if my world were going to fall apart. Other times I have felt just fine. The journal entries describe those experiences."

But the beginning doesn't start on April 24, 1988, or in the fall of 1986 when she first used cocaine. Katy begins her story when she was 16 years old and drank her first beer and became intoxicated. This was her entry into the world of drug use. From that point forward, pivotal features of her life will be defined by the social circles where alcohol and drugs flow freely. But these drugs work against her other images of who she is: a good student, an attractive woman, a promising scholar in the fields of sociology and criminology. The pressures from this world lead her back to the world of partying, where she discovers cocaine; and here, in the "cool" and magical universe that the cocaine high produces, she finds the social self she desired. It is all downhill from this point. It was only a matter of time before she would live into existence her version of the cocaine addict. Binges, bills, lies, and deceptions followed. She was hooked and didn't know it.

The Epiphanic Moment

Recovery begins with an epiphanic moment—a turning-point experience where the person surrenders to his or her addiction. This moment is often grounded in a mundane event, yet it often carries great symbolism. With Katy the symbols turn on a set of office keys and a conference at a prison. Her surrender begins with doing lines of coke while assembling a filing system for her professor. Too high to return the keys to her professor, she binges by herself, and then goes to a conference at a prison. High, and behind prison walls, she sees herself for who she is: a hypocrite—a person studying how to reduce the world's crime problems, yet doing cocaine, breaking the law, and contributing to the very problem she is committed to solving.

She retreats from the prison; but the prison follows her, for she is a prisoner of her own addiction. She escapes to her apartment, running from herself, the keys, and the prison walls. Thus begins the final 12 hours of insane binging, stopped only when her roommate comes home and sits with her through the final crash. Now the story begins.

Reading the Text

It is not a story in the usual sense of a story. Oh, it ends on December 31, 1989—20 months and seven days into her sobriety—and it began with that first drink at 16. But in between there is no plot, no consistent cast of characters, no real theme, no real beginning or end—just a series of overlapping middles, one day after another, journal entries on first this topic and then that topic. One day it is how terrible she feels; another day it is a discussion of loose ends, or lifestyles, or a meeting with a sponsor or a counselor, or what it feels like to be high, or to make sense of a dream, or a birthday party, or a vacation in Key West, or working the steps.

Three threads unite the text: the journal itself, the program, and who she is today. She writes on July 16, 1989, "Here it is the middle of July and I have yet to write in my journal. What a dumb fuck I am. I have chosen to make this month difficult for myself by not writing in my journal, by not calling my sponsor as much as I should, by not praying, and by not attending many meetings. Basically, I have been running a real shitty program lately and it is about time that I get back on track."

Talking to herself, she—like many recovering alcoholics and addicts in the early months of recovery—is obsessed with writing the recovering self into existence. But what is this self made of? It is made up of the talk it directs to itself, and this talk is mediated by the new social world of recovery that she has entered—the worlds of AA, NA, other recovering addicts and alcoholics, counselors and sponsors. The journal is her self-text—the record of who she is becoming.

Katy's diary brings the reader into the world of the recovering female cocaine addict. Its stream-of-consciousness tone records her daily experiences with the world of recovery. It documents her struggles to redefine herself within a new vocabulary and interpretive framework. It points to the shifting, illusive nature of the self (Who Am I?), and illustrates how the writing of a journal produces a new form of subjectivity. As she progresses into the world of recovery (gets further and further away from her last use of cocaine), her conversations with herself (and her dreams) raise issues that all addicts struggle with—namely, how to live a new form of selfhood into existence when the old self defines the inner structures of the self that wishes to change.

Now, many addicts keep diaries and journals, and her journal is like these; in this sense there is nothing new here. However, few addicts persist in these activities. This author has, and in her efforts she has produced a document that speaks to the universality of the recovery process. As a universal singular, her unique struggles with recovery illustrate the generic processes that all addicts go through. This is its strength and herein lies its importance; this inner side of recovery has seldom been recorded in such detail.

This, then, is a piece of feminist, autobiographical recovery literature. It needs to be read within this frame. It is also a class production, for the author is not lower class. She did not end up on skid row. She did not become an addict-prostitute, or an addict–welfare mother. She kept her station in life, pulled her life back together, and has gone forward to become the kind of woman-scholar she desires to be. Hence, this is a working- to middle-class story of recovery. In AA and NA terms, she was (is) a high bottom drunk-addict. She stopped before she lost everything.

Finally, it must be noted that Katy's diary is recorded under a specific set of epistemological assumptions. To wit: the camera theory of reality (and realism) asserts that the closer you are to an event, the more accurately you can record its details. Hence she wrote nearly every day, believing that, if she didn't record today's details, they would escape the camera's eye (or the grasp of the writing-computer hand). This assumption justified the daily journal entries. It presumes that an event not directly recorded cannot later be recovered and accurately written about. But suppose that the camera theory of realism is wrong.

Assume that an event is inscribed multiple times on the memory disk; and that each inscription is but another version of the event; hence there is no original—only multiple inscriptions (depictions, pictures, etc.), each with as much validity as any other. This is William James's theory of the stream of consciousness. This theory runs counter to the theory that structures this document. As a countertheory, it cautions the reader to pay attention to the critical moments in Katy's recovery story, especially when AA and NA enter her talk, when she begins to talk about counselors and sponsors and so on.

However, her text could have been written in no other way. The blank page of her journal, when written on, became a record of who she was that day. Without an entry she did not exist—that is, she did not exist as a recovering self. The recovering self must write itself into existence. If it doesn't write and record its thoughts, feelings, and emotions, it does not get better. So, no journal entry meant no recovery for that day. Hence the obsession, hence the diary.

This is what recovery is all about—becoming obsessed about a new obsession, becoming a new self by forming the new self out of the discarded waste of the old sick self. When recovery takes hold, the old life of using is gone, and the person lives in the present. The past becomes a foreign country where they do things differently. The recovering self comes to see that he or she has led two lives: the old life of destruction, and the new life of recovery. When this insight occurs for Katy (and it has), she will be able to answer like Raymond Carver, who when asked by an interviewer, "How long since you quit?" said, "June 2, 1977," and then, "If you want the truth, I'm prouder of that, that I've quit drinking, than I am of anything in my life" (Carver, 1983, p. 207). If she keeps on doing what she has been doing, Katy's answer will be Carver's. Only her date—April 24, 1988—is different.

Doing what she has done is difficult, the hardest thing a human being can attempt. When it works—as Carver puts it—it is pure gravy. And don't forget it.

Note

1. Both names are pseudonyms to protect Katy's identity.

References

Alcoholics Anonymous. 1976. *Alcoholics Anonymous*. (Known as the Big Book.) New York: Alcoholics Anonymous World Services. (First published, 1939.)

Carver, Raymond. 1983. *Fires: Essays, Poems, Stories*. New York: Vintage.

Gold, Mark S. 1984. *800-COCAINE*. New York: Bantam Books.

Hughes, Helen M. (ed.). 1961. *The Fantastic Lodge: The Autobiography of a Girl Drug Addict*. Boston: Houghton-Mifflin.

Narcotics Anonymous. 1984. *Narcotics Anonymous*. (Known as the White Book.) Van Nuys, Calif.: World Services Office. (First published, 1962.)

Rettig, R., M. Torres, and G. Garrett. 1977. *Manny: A Criminal Addict's Story*. Boston: Houghton-Mifflin.

Spradley, James. 1970. *You Owe Yourself a Drunk: An Ethnography of Urban Nomads*. Boston: Little, Brown.

Foreword: The Days of a Changing Self

Barbara Sherman Heyl

This book is the diary of a young woman recovering from a cocaine addiction. She began writing these journal entries two weeks after she came to the realization that she was addicted to cocaine and that her life was out of control. This turning point stemmed from an experience in which she had been unable to stop using cocaine as long as it was available. It was a terrible week of extensive cocaine use, toward the end of which she finally confessed her situation to her roommate. In the next few days she revealed her situation to a few other key people in her life, one of whom was a sociology professor who urged her to begin keeping a journal. She has written in her journal, often daily, since May 1988. This book covers only the first 20 months of this period.

This diary is a *journal intime;* it is in such documents that the days of a changing self and the meanings brought to that self unfold in and through time. This book and its author fit comfortably in a tradition of diarists who write intimate, "uncensored outpourings . . . either daily or at longer intervals," concerning their sense of who they are through their experiences and their feelings about those experiences (Allport, 1942:100). Such diaries shed light on basic human processes, such as ways of coping with life and its terribly embarrassing moments, financial crises, or even death. The diaries document the process of humans finding and sustaining connections to others and dealing with the loss of such relationships. Diaries can provide "fine texture" to the picture of such changes, as Paul Rosenblatt observes from a study of loss in which he used nineteenth-century, unedited diaries:

> This texture allows one to see more clearly day-to-day changes, long-term trends, and the effects of specific events. Diaries can provide not only more

> detail, but more accuracy, as well as reactions less distorted by subsequent experiences and thought. Diaries can give greater accuracy for dates, people, places, and events than interview accounts or oral history material, because the diarist is usually recalling events that are fresh. The accuracy of a diary account may also be relatively great because a diary can provide a less censored report of reactions, a record of feelings and events that would in retrospective accounts be considered too trivial or too embarrassing to mention, if they were even recalled. (Rosenblatt, 1983:5)

Throughout this century historians, anthropologists, psychologists, and sociologists have utilized diaries as resource material; and in the 1930s and 1940s the Social Science Research Council—representing all the above disciplines—published three volumes of work devoted to assessing the research value of "personal documents" (Blumer, 1939; Allport, 1942; Gottschalk, Kluckhohn, and Angell, 1945). Gordon Allport describes the power and value of the intimate journal:

> The spontaneous, intimate diary is the personal document par excellence. In it the author sets down only such events, thoughts, and feelings as have importance for himself; he is not so constrained by the task-attitudes that frequently control his production in letters, interviews, or autobiography. He is ordinarily more subjective in his reactions than he is in any other form of writing, and much less self-conscious. As a rule, he himself is the audience for which he is writing, or else there is some imaginary friend who, when told all, will understand all and forgive all. Whatever rationalizations enter into a diary are self-deceptions, and for this reason are of greater significance for the writer's personality than are the masquerades that may cloud his public utterances.
>
> In its ideal form the diary is unexcelled as a continuous record of the subjective side of mental development. . . . The turning points in a life are exposed to view, set, as they ought to be, in the everyday frame of unaccentuated routine. (Allport, 1942:xii)

For the purposes of publishing this intimate diary, the author calls herself "Katy Hendricks." Although she has chosen to keep her personal history in the background, I can tell you a little about her. She was born in 1963 in a medium-size city in Pennsylvania where she lived until she was 18 with her parents and three siblings. She describes her family as "working class," and she notes: "My parents always provided us with the essentials of life, but finances and money were always big concerns. We all knew that my father had to work overtime to make ends meet, and so my siblings and I were raised to not ask for things that cost money" (Hendricks, 1991).

Katy and her brother and sisters went to public schools, where Katy was active in extracurricular activities. In junior high and high school she played in the band, played sports, was an editor of the school yearbook, and was on the speech and debate teams. She wanted to go to college in one of the big cities, but was accepted only at a "branch campus" of the major university. She was very disappointed, but she decided to prove that she should be allowed into the main campus. She made the dean's list her freshman year and petitioned for early transfer. The petition was granted. As Katy describes it, "I was off to the big time, the big city, and in pursuit of the party. The big city was everything that I had imagined: fast, exciting, overbearing, and diverse. My undergraduate years were great! I found both the life in the big city and my course-work fascinating. I developed an incredible interest in the social sciences, for academia, and for professional research during my undergraduate years" (Hendricks, 1991). She graduated with high honors and was accepted into a highly ranked master's degree program.

She began this program in 1985 and finished her master's degree at the top of her class. Katy is now a graduate of a fine doctoral program, specializing in the study of sociology. She was midstream in her graduate studies when she became addicted; and when she hit bottom, one of the people she confessed her problem to was the sociology professor for whom she was working as a graduate assistant. The professor was shocked by Katy's revelation, but—moved by her student's expression of a commitment to stop using cocaine—the professor urged Katy to start keeping a journal of what she was experiencing in this moment of change in her life. When I became informed of the journal entries four months later, I too encouraged Katy to keep writing. The letter I sent her on September 17, 1988, included the following:

> I read your work [journal entries] immediately and could not put the pages down. What you have written brings the reader into intimate contact with your experience, and that is a powerful effect that most writers would love to achieve.
>
> I would urge two things: one, send me some more journal writings and, two, keep writing your journal, letting it continue to reflect as bluntly and honestly as possible what you are feeling and how you are living out this recovery process. The nice thing about keeping the discipline of journal writing is that as life goes on, which it does anyway, the more data you will have about what it was like for you.
>
> I have learned a great deal about this topic from your journal already, and that is a wonderful advantage to me in my own field of interest in sociology. It is important for others to learn also, so I commend you on your efforts to

> write it up. It is and will continue to be *work* for you, but it is well worth doing, [Katy]. For what you have is a document of survival, and in my opinion, nothing is more important.

I am not sure just what we sociologists thought the outcome of such a journal would be. I knew that notes taken at the time of an experience allow the writer to articulate the events in detail as well as express the feelings of the moment. Such notes also have the power to return the writer at some later point in time to those feelings and events. In my readings of autobiographies of house prostitutes and madams, I was impressed with a description that Carol Erwin (1960:183) gave of Clarence Darrow's telling her she would write a book one day about her life; he urged her to keep a notebook and write down just a few words a day on what happened. According to Erwin, Darrow said to her, "You'll be surprised how a few words will bring back all the details of the past when you need them. Don't fancy it up, my dear, just put down the bare facts. Promise?" She promised. The resulting book contains rich details of the changes in her life, including what it was like to operate small houses of prostitution in the Midwest during the Depression.

Norman Denzin reminds us that "no self or personal-experience story is ever an individual production. It derives from larger group, cultural, ideological and historical contexts" (1989:73). Some of these contexts of Katy's diary include her Protestant, working-class background with a strong personal drive to succeed in education and in life. Her belief in the importance of education, along with her own commitment to it, is a key factor in Katy's life. Indeed, her outlook on life reflects a solid dose of American values. The impact of the feminist movement on this young woman is also part of the cultural, ideological, and historical influences. Additionally, her writings are no doubt influenced by her study of sociology at the undergraduate and graduate level. Katy's sociology professor and I were periodically given whole chunks of the diary to read. Our responses were at a general level, often in the form of "Great Stuff! Keep Writing!" It can only be speculated what, if any, specific impact this had on the content or style of Katy's writing. Katy maintained she never wrote with us or any other specific reader in mind. Still, this diary is a work that Katy has produced against a backdrop of a myriad of general social influences.

Regarding more specific social influences, Katy's diary entries begin with more of her own personal voice than where they end, which is closer to the language and interpretive formats of the 12-Step recovery programs, such as Cocaine Anonymous and Alcoholics Anonymous, of which she gradually became a part. The diary allows us to watch Katy's description of herself and her personal experience move along this continuum, toward the strong influence of a group-taught format of how to tell her story of addiction and recovery (Denzin, 1987; 1989:69–77). Thus, the chronological order of the diary enables the reader to glimpse not only the experiences of the day as Katy describes them, but also the change in her description of self.

The diary also interprets what each day is like—a day that she has to get through in order to get to the next day of a cocaine-free life. In the diary, Katy copes with her past and a self of that past that she evaluates negatively, while trying (with help) to build a new positive self for the future—all during a present that finds her in precarious financial and emotional circumstances. It must be noted that this diary covers only the beginning months of the recovery process. But as the reader can appreciate, it is exactly such months of drug-free existence that must be accomplished in order to permit a future drug-free life. Thus, as Howard Becker (1963) noted in his classic study of marijuana users, we must understand a person's early experiences on a path in order to explain the later outcomes of having walked down that path. To be drug free for three or five or 20 years, one must have first been drug free at some point for a year! These are Katy's first 20 months of recovery. She describes using the diary as therapy—a place to pour out her feelings about what happened to her each day and sometimes to assess where she is now relative to where she was and where she wants to be. It does provide us with a window to the recovery process, grounded in the nitty-gritty of each day's experience.

This diary, then, should have value to a wide range of audiences—anyone interested in a story of survival, of abandoning a destructive addictive lifestyle. This would include anyone who has experienced an addictive lifestyle themselves, including those with alcohol or drug problems, eating disorders or sexual addictions, or those who have come out of family backgrounds of violence. There are many people today who are wondering whether the conpulsive coping patterns they have developed from old wounds left over from long ago can be restructured to allow for living a calm, centered, productive life free of destructive addictive behavior. Katy's book not only says yes, but provides a glimpse into how this restructuring begins. Then too, not only people wondering about how to change, but also those people currently involved in recovery programs of various kinds will find that Katy's journal reflects their own daily struggle, as well as affirming the positive outcome of that struggle. Two other interested audiences will be the professionals who work with such people and the significant others and families of these people. The large number of people active in Al-Anon groups attest to the prevalence of this latter group and their desire for information about addiction and recovery.

Students and scholars of a variety of disciplines will find the diary a rich resource. Feminist scholars interested in the woman's statements about herself and her changing life will find here a strong personal document in a woman's voice (Stanton and Plottel, 1984; Spacks, 1977). Researchers from the social sciences are rediscovering the diary (Stewart, Franz, and Layton, 1988). Personal documents are enjoying at the moment a new era of respect as the work on life histories increases in the social sciences today (Bertaux, 1981; Bertaux and Kohli, 1984; Faraday and Plummer, 1979; Kaplan, 1982; Kohli, 1981, 1982; Plummer, 1990; Watson and Watson-Franke, 1985). Katy's diary contributes to the renewed interest in using such personal statements to illuminate specific social worlds and the changing lives within those worlds.

Katy's diary also fits with the current interest in the drug addict. Kaplan (1982) describes a project of gathering sociological life histories of heroin addicts in the United States and Germany. He also elaborates a number of explanations for the rise in popularity of the life-history method noted above. He cites, for example, the impact of this method on both the sociologists and the interviewees; the parties are involved in negotiations, "resistances," personal insights, and ultimately a joint outcome that "creates 'extraordinary' people out of ordinary people" (1982:48). Such projects allow these people's voices to be heard. Kaplan quotes from Inowlocki and Mai's introduction to the life story of a German heroin addict: "Drug addicts themselves are not being listened to in a way which lets them relate what they experienced and what happened to them in a thematic sequence and a language of their own" (1982:48). Although Katy's diary is not a life history produced jointly with a sociologist (although sociologists figure in the background, including Katy's own "becoming sociologist"), it does allow her to be heard in her own language.

The argument that the diary is particularly valid is based on the immediacy with which the experiences of the day are recorded by the person who has just lived through those experiences, and includes his or her subjective appraisal of the events and reactions to them. This is not to say that the author's description of the events is equivalent to the events or even to how she lived those experiences. But there is a power in such description. The diary of Carolina Maria DeJesus (1962) describes her daily struggle for survival on the streets of São Paulo in a way the reader will never forget. Katy's entries, too, allow the reader to hear the compelling concerns that occupy her thoughts—how to explain the addiction, how to repair family ties and broken trust, how to cope with a collapsed financial situation, fears about relapsing, struggles with the cravings for cocaine, nightmares, and living through problems at work and in her "program" and with friends, while at the same time documenting the accumulation of "clean" days and the construction of her new self.

After Katy had been writing for about a year and a half, I was invited by her and her sociology professor to meet with them about what we might do with the now bulging manuscript. We eventually sent a description of the diary and sample entries to numerous publishers. When The American University Press showed interest, we contacted Norman Denzin about writing a preface.

The book itself is Katy's; and when the publisher stipulated a limited number of manuscript pages, she made the decision to include only those entries up to 20 months of recovery. She felt that it was much easier, and also truer to the original document, to cut out whole journal entries after that point—as well as a few within that time period—than to try to "edit down" individual entries. Thus, neither her sociology professor, who remains anonymous to protect Katy's identity, nor I have edited the manuscript. Rosenblatt (1983:10–12) notes that in his research he avoided edited diaries because one could never be sure what material had been edited out, leaving the document reflecting an unknown bias. What bias is here is Katy's and not one imposed from the outside. This should make the document of special interest to grounded theorists, historians, sociologists, and psychologists, for it contains what might be seen as "raw data" on a changing self. These researchers can compare their theories about such change with the diary entries; and as Rosenblatt notes,

> Diary material has the potential to change the way those theories are eventually understood and used. Rich diary material may provide less support for the selective vision that is both beneficial and harmful when one works within a given theory. Vivid documentation, such as diary material, when used in conjunction with a theoretical framework, may inevitably lead to regions that have been ignored. (Rosenblatt, 1983:7)

The chronological format of the diary means that we do not know what theme will be addressed in the next day's entry. The body of this book, then, does not follow the typical biographical format that tells the reader where the author came from, how she got to where she is, and where she is going—a format that is considered to be linear, masculine, success oriented (Clough, forthcoming; Stanton and Plottel, 1984:5–22). We do not even get the traditional recovery format of the fall, repentance, and redemption. We get instead, on any day's entry, whatever topic has preoccupied Katy that day. It resembles, then, the way that we all live, responding to whatever confronts us in our daily lives *that* day. Yet we do also see the growth and the gradual accumulation of days of sobriety. The poststructuralists would remind us that it is not the young woman's life that we are seeing through her diary. But the truth is, she *is* living her life, and her diary represents her own efforts to put into words her experiences and feelings. Now they are accessible to us, and they are well worth reading.

References

Allport, Gordon W. 1942. *The Use of Personal Documents in Psychological Science.* New York: Social Science Research Council.

Becker, Howard S. 1963. *Outsiders: Studies in the Sociology of Deviance.* New York: Free Press.

Bertaux, Daniel. 1981. *Biography and Society: The Life History Approach in the Social Sciences.* Newbury Park, Calif.: Sage Publications.

Bertaux, Daniel, and Martin Kohli. 1984. "The Life Story Approach: A Continental View." *Annual Review of Sociology* 10, pp. 215–237.

Blumer, Herbert. 1939. *Critique of Research in the Social Sciences.* Volume 1: *An Appraisal of Thomas and Znaniecki's 'The Polish Peasant in Europe and America.'* New York: Social Science Research Council.

Clough, Patricia T. Forthcoming. *The End(s) of Ethnography.* Newbury Park, Calif.: Sage Publications.

Cohler, B. J. 1982. "Personal Narrative and Life Course." Pp. 206–241 in, *Life-span Development and Behavior.* P. B. Baltes and O. G. Brim, Jr. (eds.), New York: Academic.

DeJesus, Carolina Maria. 1962. *Child of the Dark: The Diary of Carolina Maria DeJesus.* New York: New American Library.

Denzin, Norman K. 1989. *Interpretive Biography.* Newbury Park, Calif.: Sage Publications.

———. 1987. *The Recovering Alcoholic.* Newbury Park, Calif.: Sage Publications.

Erwin, Carol. 1960. *The Orderly Disorderly House.* New York: Doubleday.

Faraday, Annabel, and Ken Plummer. 1979. "Doing Life Histories." *Sociological Review* 27 (4), pp. 773–798.

Gottschalk, Louis, Clyde Kluckhohn, and Robert Angell. 1945. *The Use of Personal Documents in History, Anthropology, and Social Work*. New York: Social Science Research Council.

Grele, Ron. 1979. "Listen to Their Voices." *Oral History* 7 (1), pp. 33–42.

Hendricks, Katy. 1991. Original version of author's preface to *The Party's Over*. Unpublished document.

Kaplan, Charles D. 1982. "Addict Life Stories: An Exploration of the Methodological Grounds for the Study of Social Problems." *International Journal of Oral History* 3, pp. 31–50.

Kohli, Martin. 1982. *Biographical Research in the German Language Area*. Presented at the 10th World Congress of Sociologists, Mexico. 26 pp.

———. 1981. "Wie es zur 'Biographischen Methode' kam und was daraus geworden ist. Ein Kapitel aus der Geschichte der sozialforschung." *Zeitschrift für Soziologie* 10, pp. 273–293.

Plummer, Ken. 1990. "Herbert Blumer and the Life History Tradition." *Symbolic Interaction* 13 (2), pp. 125–144.

———. 1983. *Documents of Life: An Introduction to the Problems and Literature of a Humanistic Method*. London: George Allen & Unwin.

Rosenblatt, Paul. 1983. *Bitter, Bitter Tears: Nineteenth-century Diarists and Twentieth-century Grief Theories*. Minneapolis: University of Minnesota Press.

Spacks, Patricia M. 1977. "Women's Stories, Women's Selves." *Hudson Review* 30, pp. 26–46.

Stanton, Domna C., and Jeanine P. Plottel. 1984. *The Female Autograph*. New York: New York Literary Forum.

Stewart, Abigail J., Carol Franz, and Lynne Layton. 1988. "The Changing Self: Using Personal Documents to Study Lives." Pp. 41–74 in Dan P. McAdams and Richard L. Ochberg (eds.), *Psychobiography and Life Narratives*. Durham, N.C.: Duke University Press.

Watson, Lawrence C., and Maria-Barbara Watson-Franke. 1985. *Interpreting Life Histories: An Anthropological Inquiry*. New Brunswick, N.J.: Rutgers University Press.

Acknowledgments

I want to express my appreciation to the following people for their encouragement and support in this effort as well as their role in helping me stay clean and sober: Professor Geraldine Waldeman, my family (mother, father, Beth, Paul, Christopher, and Kellie), my sponsor (Karen), two of my friends (Ben and Sandy), and those friends not mentioned in the book—R.K.S., G.A.Y., A.V.H., and Dr. C.P.H.

Introduction

Before presenting the first 20 months of my recovery journal, I wish in the following paragraphs to offer a retrospective interpretation of my fall from grace, or the events in my life that helped me realize I was powerless over cocaine and needed help to stop doing it.

My "career" with drugs and alcohol started long before I did my first line of cocaine in the fall of 1986. I began experimenting with alcohol and pot when I was 16. The first time I drank alcohol (at a field hockey party with the other kids when I was 16 years old), I consumed nine 16-ounce cans of beer, got drunk, passed out, threw up for hours, and had a major hangover the next day. It was horrible!

I thought I hated it until the other kids told me how great I was. Everybody was talking about me and was patting me on the back for getting so damn drunk. I became the center of attention and was more popular. It made me feel wonderful.

Basically, I had a love/hate relationship with alcohol back then. I didn't really want to drink again after that horrible incident, because I didn't want to get sick again. I hated being sick! On the other hand, I wanted to hang out and be cool with the rest of the "jockettes," so I ended up drinking again and getting sick again. I didn't get sick all of the time, and I certainly didn't drink all of the time. Eventually, I started to like the taste of beer and wine. I considered myself an occasional drinker after that first experience with alcohol, until the cocaine in 1986.

I was a freshman in high school when I first smoked pot, and I really didn't like it that much. Actually, I thought it was rather boring. Everyone was making such a big deal about it, but all it did for me was slow me down and make me silly. And I had no tolerance for anything that slowed me down and made me silly. I was in a hurry to excel, achieve, and go beyond everyone else. I wanted to be respected, admired, and praised.

And as far as I was concerned, pot didn't fit into any of that. All the potheads in school cut class, got bad grades, grew their hair long, wore terrible clothes, and were considered "less than" my little group—a group of kids who stayed after school to play sports, write for the school paper and yearbook, and compete in the speech and debate club.

I belonged to this "popular" group and liked it very much. Often I was elected to responsible positions like team captain or student council president, and I gained the respect and admiration I longed for. At the same time, I was quite the class clown. Teachers and coaches regularly reprimanded me for being loud and obnoxious in class and on the field. Given this conflicting behavior, teachers, friends, and family members had difficulty taking me seriously. And I resented that right away. I resented having to prove things to people. I just wanted them to take me seriously and accept me for what I was or was going to be.

And that conflicting behavior and those resentments followed me into later years with drugs and alcohol. During my undergraduate years, I worked very hard to get the best grades possible. I studied my buns off during the week and then would unwind on weekends with alcohol and occasionally pot, getting stinking drunk or incredibly high. For instance, one weekend during my freshman year, my roommates and I bought a half ounce of pot and smoked it in two days. I took complete charge of the whole deal. I rolled all of the joints and decided when to light up another one. That weekend, I drank a lot of rum and coke, smoked a lot of pot, watched Mr. Bill on *Saturday Night Live*, and laughed like I had never laughed before in my life. Pot was not boring that weekend.

During my freshman year, I got drunk at least once every weekend, but I thought that was normal because everyone was doing it. Besides, my grades were okay. I got a 3.0 and a 3.6 my first two semesters. Still, I wanted to do better. I wanted to be better. And being better meant raising my grade point average. It also meant changing from a big, cute, and immature girl into a smaller, pretty, and sophisticated woman.

Alcohol and drugs had no place in any of that. So, during the next three years I didn't drink much and I did no illicit drugs whatsoever. My obsession with my grades, weight, and exercise prohibited excessive drinking and drugging. But in order to stay in the center of things, I "sacrificed" one night a week to socialize with my friends on the bar scene. The bar scene stressed me during those years because my calorie limit would only permit two light beers. After I drank those two beers, it was time to go home. And I rarely closed any bar, because I had work to do the next day.

The conflicting behavior that I talked about before disappeared during those three years. I devoted all of my time (weekdays and weekends) and energy to my schoolwork, job, diet, and exercise. No one doubted that I was serious about any of those things. After all, I was at the right weight and was in wonderful cardiovascular and muscular shape. I succeeded in paying for my own college education and living expenses during those four years, and I ended up graduating magna cum laude in a double social science major (criminology/sociology). Consequently, I did not have to prove much to people anymore—just to myself.

I came to Washington, D.C., in the fall of 1985 to begin a master's degree in one of the social sciences. Immediately, I felt challenged by my new setting and wanted to achieve all I could in as little time as possible. I continued to obsess about my appearance and grades (mostly my grades) during the first year of my graduate education, because there was a new group of people to impress, new goals to attain, and new challenges to meet.

The first year of graduate school went very well. Early in the first semester, I distinguished myself from my colleagues, excelled to the top of my class, and was recruited by the dean of my program (a well-known sociologist) to be her research assistant. Yet I managed to have a social life too. I remember going to Friday-night happy hours at Yuppie-type bars with roommates, but I seldom got drunk and certainly never did any drugs. Besides, my graduate stipend (about $650 a month) was not going to pay for a night out in Georgetown (where domestic beer cost $3.00 a bottle). Basically, the drinking was isolated to weekends and was like during my freshman year of college—a reward at the end of the week for long, hard work.

Soon things changed, and resentments and conflicting behavior resurfaced. I got tired of living on $650 a month and worrying about how I was going to pay for all the wonderful things around me that other people had. I wanted them desperately and thought I deserved them. As far as I was concerned, my days as a poor, struggling college student were over. It was time for me to enjoy the "good" things in life. And that included partying on weekends, shopping at expensive stores, and dining in posh restaurants.

So, I began working in a restaurant as a waitress during the fall of 1986 to supplement my income and to secure enough money to finance my increasingly expensive lifestyle. At the time, I thought my waitress job was the perfect combination with my graduate work, because it gave me things that graduate school couldn't: a lot of money in a short amount of time without using my brain, a "cool" set of friends who replaced my "boring" colleagues on campus, and the best social life I ever had. I moved back and forth between those two very different worlds for the next two years and thought my life was complete.

Shortly after I took the job in the restaurant, I became friends with two women, Rebecca and Leslie, who worked there. They introduced me to cocaine. That first cocaine experience is still vivid in my mind. Four of us (Rebecca, Leslie, my roommate Meg, and I) decided to have a ladies' night out on a Friday. That day at work, Rebecca said, "Boy, I sure do wish we could cop some 'toot' for tonight." I looked at her in total surprise, stuttered, and then tried to sound cool and experienced by saying, "Yeah, me too."

She made a phone call and got the stuff. I gave 25 bucks for it and didn't even know if I really wanted to do it or not. But the others did, so I went along with it. From the start, it was secretive, cool, exciting, and fashionable. I got high on the first couple of lines and immediately fell in love with it. And there was no hangover or getting sick with cocaine. There was just instant and powerful feelings of superiority, uniqueness, warmth, and endless energy. I felt special doing cocaine. I felt privileged to be a part of this cool group that did this posh drug. And I chased that feeling for the next 20 months.

After that first incident, the "fabulous foursome" (Rebecca, Meg, Leslie and I) would cop cocaine every Friday night before we went dancing. Wayne, my boyfriend at the time, became very annoyed about this. At first, he didn't know about the cocaine. He just complained about me not being at home with him. Finally, a few months later, I told him about the coke and showed him the amount I usually bought—a quarter gram. He made some nerdy and stupid remark like, "You mean to tell me that you pay $25 for that? There's nothing there." I looked at him with what must have been an intolerant facial expression and replied in a very condescending fashion, "You just don't understand." We broke up shortly after that.

As far as I was concerned, everyone in graduate school had Wayne's attitude. So I put them in this "nerdy" and "uncool" box and refused to associate with them outside of class. In fact, it was all I could do to even participate in discussion with those jerks in class. By the beginning of my second year in graduate school, I did my work as fast as possible and then ran to the restaurant for money, fun, excitement, and friendship. The conflicting behavior was back stronger than ever and was becoming difficult to manage.

Around this time, I was living in a very nice apartment in Northwest Washington with Meg and another friend. Meg and I spent a lot of time together because we were both graduate students and we both liked the posh nightclub scene and cocaine. Our other roommate wasn't into any of that. Typically, we would each buy a half gram of cocaine for $50 on Friday night and then would go out to a nightclub in Adams Morgan or Georgetown to dance, drink, and "toot" all night long. Sometimes I had a few lines left over for the next day, and I really appreciated that since I had to work Saturday night at the restaurant. I usually needed a couple of lines to pick me up right before work.

It went on like that for about a year, with the amount of cocaine and the frequency of use steadily increasing. We were copping cocaine through the beeper system (dealers with telephone beepers) at the time. It was a real drag, and I became frustrated. I was tired of beeping numbers that were out of order, dealing with irresponsible and young dealers with severely cut (i.e., adulterated) cocaine in bad parts of town, and being unsure I was going to score dope for the night. And that's what pissed me off the most. I wanted to be sure I was going to have cocaine that evening. After all, everyone else was counting on me. But you could never be sure of anything with this system.

Eventually Rick, a member of our cocaine group, introduced us (the fabulous foursome) to Ricardo—the responsible dealer. Ricardo made things very simple for me and the rest of my cocaine buddies. He called me three times a week to see what my friends and I needed and then arranged a place to meet. He always showed up. He was never late. Most importantly, he had lots and lots of goods, clean cocaine that wasn't too badly cut.

Ricardo stored his cocaine in a safe, carried a briefcase, and kept track of his transactions in a ledger. And since he did not want each of us calling his house at all hours of the night whenever we felt like scoring some dope, he requested that Rick suggest a contact person. After the two of them discussed the matter, I was chosen to be the contact because they thought I was the most intelligent and responsible of the group and was the least likely to get in "trouble" (hooked) with the stuff. I was flattered and impressed that I had been chosen.

Being chosen as the contact person to Ricardo and moving with Meg to a two-bedroom apartment in Silver Spring, Maryland, were two turning points that greatly affected my life with cocaine and alcohol. The first turning point—the move to the new apartment—enabled Meg and me to have uninterrupted cocaine parties with our buddies. Four or five of us got together to snort cocaine and drink alcohol. We talked about solving the world's problems and actually believed we had real solutions. (Actually, they were just cocaine delusions.) The parties usually began Friday night before we went to the posh nightclubs, but then they started happening during the week. Later, we never left the apartment to go to any of the clubs. Those posh clubs were history! Instead, we chose to spend our money on cocaine and our time doing all of the lines we possibly could.

The other turning point—being selected as the contact person with Ricardo—was the most dramatic. The relationship between Ricardo and me started as a business, but soon turned into friendship. It was never sexual. We talked about sex and flirted quite a bit, but those discussions and thoughts passed as soon as we got high. We really liked one another and had a lot in common: computers, music, bike riding, intellectual thought, academics, cocaine, cocaine, and more cocaine. I loved it as much as he did. And I remember the first day that he and I partied together, because it changed the way I partied from then on.

I invited him to dinner one Friday night in November 1987 and impressed him with my cooking. After eating, we went to get a few six packs and came back to my place to party, which is why I invited him over in the first place. We stayed up all night snorting lines. We did an eightball (3.5 grams or $250 worth) that night and I got anxious about how much money he would want for it. I expected to give him $125, but hoped he would treat me. He did. He charged me only 50 bucks for the dope and accepted a check. I was greatly relieved! Relieved that I had found a responsible dealer who was generous, fun, safe, and practical about money (i.e., he took checks).

I drove him to his place in the morning and then went back home to sleep because I had to work from 6 p.m. to 2 a.m. that evening at the restaurant. I tried my hardest to fall asleep, but was unsuccessful. So I decided to do some studying. I studied some, but all of the members of my party group kept calling me on the telephone to see how my night went. I told each of them what happened and they were awestruck. They were also very jealous that Ricardo and I spent the night together doing cocaine, because they wanted a piece of the action—the "free" action. But Ricardo was only just so generous with his dope, and he kept his club closed—closed to all but him and me. And that made me feel special. It was intoxicating.

I went to work that evening, did a few lines with Rick and Leslie on the way, and went home at 2 a.m. Sunday morning after making about $150 at the restaurant. I collapsed in my bed and slept until noon and then got up to do some studying. I studied all day and went to bed early, because Monday was the beginning of another long, hard week.

I can remember thinking, after this first cocaine all-nighter, that I had really pulled it off. I partied hard with the "man" at almost no expense, made a bunch of money at the restaurant, got my studying done, and even did some running. I was impressed that I had pulled it off. After this, I thought there was nothing I couldn't do. I remember thinking I must be the most special person in the world to pull all of this off. After all, I was at the top of my master's program, was doing wonderful work for Dean Waldeman, was queen of the party scene, and was admired, respected and envied by everyone. Or at least I thought I was. I thought I could run back and forth between my worlds (the two most wonderful things in life: a career and a social life), and keep it all together and under control. I thought I had it made!

If it were possible, I would still freeze my life at that moment. What can I say? I'm an addict and I still like cocaine. I wish sometimes that my life would have stayed that perfect way and never changed. At times, I fantasize about being able to party hard with cocaine on weekends and keep the rest of my life together. But that's impossible for me because I'm an addict. That "perfect weekend" was a one-shot deal. There were no perfect weekends after that. Things changed for the worse and my addiction escalated.

By this stage in the game, I used cocaine to bridge the gap between my worlds (which were becoming more fragmented as the days passed), to fill gaps and holes inside me, and to make me feel okay about myself and others. Basically, I began using it for everything. I used it to study all night, to work all day, to party with friends, and even to go running at times. For instance, in November 1987 I ran my second marathon high on cocaine. I took four muscle relaxers and six Advil and snorted six lines before the race started at 9 a.m. I did another four lines at both the 13- and 20-mile marks and finished the race in my best time ever. I went home that afternoon, sat in a bathtub for a while snorting more cocaine, and decided to shift my training priorities from running to weight-lifting. (I was concerned about the pain in my heart, but never considered giving up cocaine.)

Time passed and I found I needed more and more cocaine to get the same high and needed to be in an intoxicated state to deal with my life and myself. Cocaine was in every part of my life. I did lines before, during, and after work at school and at the restaurant. I went to class high, did lines during breaks, left class early to get high, or simply didn't show up for class at all. I spent my days thinking about cocaine, doing cocaine, or trying to get enough money to buy cocaine.

Finally, I started to question whether I really had it all together and wondered if I had a cocaine problem. By now, I knew I could not stop doing it after the first line. I knew, for instance, that if I started doing cocaine at the restaurant, I wasn't going to be able to wait on any customers. I was going to have to run up and down the stairs to the bathroom in order to keep my high and avoid that dreadful crash. And I knew if I got high before class, I would not be able to concentrate on anything besides cocaine, I would leave class to find a safe bathroom to toot in, and I would be paranoid about what my colleagues would be thinking about me. Basically, I knew there was no bridging the two worlds anymore. It was one or the other.

And this is when things started getting out of hand. My binges with Ricardo were happening twice a week and lasting between 16 and 48 hours each. I can't estimate how much cocaine I did on each one of those binges or how much money I spent. I did cocaine with Ricardo until he decided to stop. I did not care about the money. I did not care if my heart was beating a mile a minute. I did not care about chest pains or bloody noses. I didn't care about work, friends, colleagues, professors, or family. I didn't even care if I had showered, exercised, or had sex in days, weeks, or months. I just didn't care about anything other than cocaine.

The binges kept getting more destructive. Two are still very painful for me to talk about. The first one happened around my twenty-fifth birthday and involved my family members. I talk about it in a few journal entries, so I will not discuss it in great length here. I still cry when I think about it. I definitely knew I had to stop doing cocaine after that binge, because I didn't want things to get any worse. But I could not stop. I could not control the cravings. I couldn't control anything at all. And so I kept doing cocaine for another two and a half painful months.

The last binge, or series of cocaine-filled days, started about a week prior to April 24, 1988. I went in on an ounce (28 grams) of cocaine with Ricardo. My cut was 14 grams for $700. I intended to do seven grams myself and sell the other seven so I would break even. My plan failed as usual. I sold two lousy grams and did the rest myself in less than a week (12 grams in six days). The night we scored the ounce, Ricardo and I rented a motel room and stayed up snorting lines from 10 p.m. until noon the next day. We checked out of the motel, but were not finished partying. We decided to continue partying at a nearby park. I overdosed in the park, recovered, and kept doing lines until about 8 that evening.

That binge was filled with tremendous amounts of paranoia, fear, and guilt. So I decided—for about the hundredth time—to get my act together and chill out for a while. I promised myself I would stop. But I had made and broken that promise many times before. And so it was no surprise to me that I was doing cocaine by the end of the next day.

After crashing hard from that binge with Ricardo (which was the last one I had with him), I found myself craving the drug in a matter of hours. I gave in to it and dipped back into my diminishing supply. A few nights later—Thursday, April 22, 1988, to be exact—I went on a cocaine binge by myself that lasted from 8 that night until midnight the next day. I snorted seven grams of cocaine during that time and probably would have snorted more if my roommate hadn't stopped me. This binge brought me to my knees and forced me to seek help.

Thursday evening, I started using while working late in Dean Waldeman's office. I was trying to get a filing system together for her—a system I had been promising to finish for weeks. I remember being pissed off that I had to do this. I couldn't understand why I, Katy Hendricks—the top doctoral candidate and computer hotshot—was constructing a filing system. After all, yesterday I was doing all of the statistical analyses on her research projects—and today I was organizing her publications into a filing system? How unfair, I thought. What a waste of my valuable skills and time.

I did not want to be there. I just wanted to go get high with Ricardo. On the other hand, I knew Dean Waldeman was very angry with me for not finishing this a while ago, and I wanted to keep my promise to her this time. But the cocaine in my pockets weighed a ton and soon I reached inside, pulled the bag out, cut some big fat lines, and snorted them up. And then everything seemed much lighter and I felt much better.

By the time I finished the filing system, I was extremely high. I called Dean Waldeman on the telephone to tell her I had finished her stupid filing system, and I can remember rushing her off the phone. After all, I was in no condition to talk to her. She wanted me to drop her keys by her house that night, but I made up some excuse not to do it because I didn't want her to see me in the condition I was in. I just wanted to party. Still, I had her keys, so I had to make arrangements to get them back to her. I promised to drop them off at her office by noon the next day, but I had no intention of keeping that promise.

Then I called Ricardo to see if he wanted to party with me. He turned me down and even told me to chill out. That was the first time he ever did that. Boy, was I pissed! I went home to party by myself. When I got home, I picked up the phone to call a few friends to come party with me; but then something came over me that made me want to be alone with my quarter ounce, so I decided not to call my friends. Whatever the reasons were, I didn't want to share that night. I just wanted to be alone. And so I proceeded to stay up around the clock, doing cocaine by myself.

I started writing a paper that was due on Monday, but I lost my concentration as usual and never finished it.

Friday morning, I was supposed to go to a prison conference with a colleague. I tried my hardest to get out of going, but I couldn't think of an excuse. Reluctantly, I got myself together and went to the conference. I did cocaine in my car while following my friend. It is at this point where it all gets very painful for me to recall.

When I arrived at the prison, I was very high. I had been snorting cocaine for 12 long, hard hours. I did not want to be at the conference, but I wasn't able to finagle my way out of going. By this point, all of my rational thinking was gone and I concluded that I would have to take cocaine into the prison, because I could not be without it for any period of time. I walked through those gates with about four grams of cocaine in my pockets and was terrified. I was sure that someone, anyone, and everyone would catch me.

I felt terrible inside the prison. I felt fear, paranoia, guilt, and self-hatred all at the same time. It was all so heavy and it became heavier and more painful because I could only think about when I was going to do more cocaine. The inmates were serving us breakfast, and one came over to me and offered me a muffin or something. I looked up at him and said, "No, thank you." And he just walked away with a smile on his face.

And that was all it took. I simply fell apart. I sat back in my chair for a while and thought to myself that there was only one difference between the inmates here and myself: They got caught and I didn't—yet. I realized that I had just spent seven years studying how to reduce the world's crime problems, yet here I was doing cocaine, breaking the law, and contributing to those problems. What a hypocrite I was! I just couldn't stand it anymore, so I made up some excuse to leave the conference and I went home—home to party alone.

I spent the next 12 hours in a totally insane state. I was not thinking or functioning at all. I didn't drop off the keys at Dean Waldeman's office, I didn't show up at the restaurant for work that night, and I didn't take my rent check to my landlord. Instead, I isolated myself from everyone and continued using. I ran from my colleagues, my friends, and my family. I simply ran from everyone, because I wanted to be by myself and I didn't want anyone to see or talk to me. When someone came to the house, I got in my car and drove around doing cocaine. All I did that day was run and get high. I ran from everyone and everything in my life right into the arms of that high.

What was I running from? Myself, I guess. I couldn't stand myself anymore. I felt ashamed of what I was doing and terrified of what I was becoming. Because it wasn't a party anymore—it was my life. My world had been reduced to cocaine, and I was simply a slave to it. Cocaine had all of the power and control in my life, and I knew it.

That binge ended when my roommate Carolyn (who worked in the hospital's detoxification unit) came home around midnight and asked me if I was okay. I said I was fine, but then she asked me again. Right at that moment, I threw up the white flag. I turned to her and said, "No, I am not okay." I told her I couldn't stop doing cocaine. After this, I placed all of my trust in her. I listened to everything she said and did everything she told me to do.

Carolyn sat with me for hours while I crashed. She talked to me about addiction and listened to what I had to say. She helped me through the most painful crash I had ever experienced in my life. Carolyn saved me that night and I owe her to this day. I often wonder if I ever would have entered recovery if she had not been there for me.

I used to think I surrendered on April 24, 1988, because of Carolyn and that painful last binge. I now think that those events played a big role, but I no longer think they were the main reasons I surrendered that day. What I realize today—and what I knew in my heart back then—is, I surrendered that day because deep down inside me I knew the party was over!

On April 24, 1988, I surrendered to Cocaine Anonymous, a 12 Step offshoot of Alcoholics Anonymous. I have been clean since then. Recovery from drug addiction has been the most difficult thing I have ever had to do, but it has also been the most rewarding. In recovery, I have often felt as if my world were going to fall apart. Other times I have felt just fine. The journal entries describe those experiences.

The bottom line is that recovery takes work for me on a daily basis. It may be difficult one day and not so difficult the next. But I don't have the power to predict or control any of that. I just know I will stay sober today if I don't pick up any drugs or take a drink. I also know I will never be fully recovered from the disease of addiction. My recovery comes one day at a time.

PART ONE

May 6 through September 9, 1988

During the first four and a half months or so of my recovery, I focused on not doing cocaine and not drinking. (I stopped drinking on June 11.) I also dealt with rapid mood changes, lots of tears and euphoric recalls, and what seemed like endless, horrible dreams. At first, I bragged about how easy it was going to be to stay away from cocaine, but soon I found it was not going to be so easy after all. The cravings were more than I could bear. The dreams more devastating. I fell into a black hole of despair and confusion. I was reliving my active addiction, and this was very painful.

There were a lot of questions running through my mind during this time. I wanted to know why I was an addict, how many of my problems were tied to cocaine, how much I had damaged my relationships with others (family, friends, colleagues), and what was going to happen next. I realized I was an addict, but still did not want to accept that fact.

I also realized I had to make several immediate changes to stay clean and sober. The first and most painful change was to let go of some friends who were threatening both my recovery (Leslie, Ricardo, and other members of my cocaine group) and my sanity (my best friend Rebecca). Another change I had to make was to quit my restaurant job and find one that would structure my day better. I got my first professional, nine-to-five, job during this time.

MAY 6, 1988

Today is the first day that I begin writing in my journal. The purpose of this journal is therapeutic—that is, this is supposed to help me deal with my cocaine addiction. I guess I feel pretty good today. It is 2 p.m. and I have just finished a shower after a seven-mile run in the rain. I forgot how much fun it is to run in the rain. My running is really improving. I am almost back to where I was before I started heavy use in January. The people at Narcotics Anonymous [NA] and Cocaine Anonymous [CA] say the addict must develop some "Higher Power" that is stronger than cocaine. For most people, it seems as if this Higher Power is God. My Higher Power seems to be running right now. My running gets me high, it alleviates my stress, it makes me feel good about myself, and it helps me look better. I can truthfully say that I have been replacing the cocaine with running.

I would like to change the topic of today's journal entry right now. Ever since I've been going to NA and CA meetings, I have been confronted with this issue of religion. Both NA and CA are very religious programs and it seems as if most of the people that go to the meetings claim to be born-again Christians. A common statement at the meetings is that "I really felt like using today, but then I prayed to God and he helped me get through the day." I don't know about too many other families, but my parents and my religion taught me that it is not right to "use" God only in times of trouble and out of desperation. God is something that exists in every moment of your life, and through constant prayer, church attendance, and "good" behavior, one will be saved. I suppose that's Protestantism talking to me.

I guess I'm trying to say that I am the one who has fucked up this time and I don't feel it is right for me to call on God to bail me out. I have not been praying, going to church, or behaving good for the last year or so. I feel I have no right to call on God right now, but have to clean myself up first and then I may deserve His love again. My religion teaches that God's love is unconditional and that He will love you regardless of what you do and how you sin. All I can say in return is that I do not feel worthy of His love right now and will not until I get my life back in order. In the meantime, I guess my running will have to be my Higher Power. It's working. I have been clean for two weeks. I guess I can thank God for that.

MAY 7, 1988

Everything was going great today until I started thinking about my friendship with Rebecca. I had a great leg workout with Nadine today at the gym between 1 and 2:30 p.m. Nadine is a lot of fun. She has some really young ideas; however, we always seem to have a great time together. Rebecca and I used to be workout partners, but she has Jim now. After I finished working out, I went for a five-mile run, which was also very good. I am in the best shape I have been in, in six months. I just wish my mental shape was progressing as rapidly.

It really doesn't seem fair. I have invested so much in this friendship and am getting nothing in return. I can't bear it anymore. I'm not emotionally stable enough to deal with this. She actually said that the problems between us were due to the cocaine. BULL SHIT! These problems existed before I began heavy use, and they still exist now after being two weeks drug free. Leslie, Mary, Joni, and everyone else who know us can attest to that.

Rebecca loves to look for excuses to crises. She loves to run from problems, tossing them off as if she had absolutely no part in them. I have put up with this shit for over six months and I keep saying I am making progress on the friendship when in fact I am not. Who am I trying to kid? You know, admitting defeat with this friendship is harder for me to do than admitting I am a cocaine addict. What in the fuck am I supposed to do? I really wish I had some answers, but I can't seem to find any.

The truth is that I don't want her lending her sympathy to me because she thinks I am sick. I can take care of my sickness by myself, without her; and even if I did let her help me through this, she'd go right back to treating me in the same lousy way she has been over the past six months after she thought I was "cured." The really sad part about it is that I live closer to her now than I ever did, but am spending less and less time with her. Jim is definitely responsible for some of this, but I can't put all of the blame on his shoulders. Much of it is Rebecca's doing. I guess she is not the friend I thought she was.

All I know is that I hurt. I miss her so very much and I need her so much right now. I am too tired to call on my Higher Power right now and it is too late to call anybody to listen to me. I do know that cocaine will not help me through this. I must go it alone. I just wish that my best friend was there with me. I just wish that my perfect Saturday would have remained as such, but I guess that's how the ball bounces.

Listen, I am starting to mess up my writing so I am going to go to bed. I am selling flowers tomorrow and am working in the kitchen at the restaurant again. I really dread working at the restaurant, but am looking forward to selling flowers. I am going to try to prevent tomorrow what happened today. It is not fair to have such a great day ruined by dwelling on a useless cause. I'm tired of beating my head against the wall. It hurts too fucking much.

MAY 8, 1988

Today is absolutely gorgeous! There isn't a cloud in the sky. The sun is shining and it is at least 75 degrees outside. If this weather keeps up today, I'll be sure to sell a lot of flowers on Mother's Day. I feel a lot better today, but it's only 9 a.m. There is only one thing that bothers me about today so far. I have to work at the restaurant tonight, which means I will miss a CA meeting. I haven't been to a meeting since last Wednesday evening. I need to talk to someone soon because the pressure is mounting. I had at least three coke offers last night and I am sure to get a few more tonight.

As of now, I don't seem to be having a problem saying no to the drug. I found out Friday night that members of my "party" group are still hanging out, and that pisses me off. It just doesn't seem fair. Fair to whom? I wonder about the answer to this question. I guess all I can do about their use is hope they stop because their lives are still in jeopardy. It's really amazing just knowing how many people are doing cocaine these days. The saddest part about it is that most of these people will end up in a situation like mine, or one that is even worse.

If I got on the cocaine subject, I could talk forever. That drug makes me feel all kinds of emotions with such great intensity. It tricks your ass into thinking a lot of shit that just isn't true. An example of this is how I have been feeling about my value to Dean Waldeman. For the past eight months, I have been thinking that she has been giving me shit work because she doesn't think I can write or am smart enough to work for her. All of that kind of thinking is the cocaine talking. I must be absurd to think that. If she didn't think I was worth something, then she would just get rid of me.

And to think that she has given me another chance. A second chance to start my life in D.C. over again. A chance to get it back to where it was when I first moved here in 1985. A second chance at my career after I fucked it up so badly. I said it before I came to the university and I'll say it again. The woman is God! She gave me a swift kick in the ass last Thursday, and that bruise is going to stay with me until I get tenure. It will probably stay with me for the rest of my life.

What I am trying to say is that I do not intend to blow this second chance. Everyone who is in my life has given me another chance. I have a chance to clean up my act and to find the old Katy who first came to D.C. in 1985. I will not blow this opportunity to redeem myself or to gain back the respect I lost. How could I screw these wonderful and caring people over again? I can't, and I'm going to try my hardest not to. That's all for today.

May 10, 1988

Today was a great day! From the moment I woke up this morning, I have had nothing but a good time. It feels so good to have days like today. I only wish that every day could be like today. I just came back from Chrissey's house, where we had some pizza and a few beers. Today's journal entry will be primarily about Chrissey and the cats.

I met Chrissey when Meg and I were apartment shopping in September of 1987. Chrissey was our leasing consultant and subsequently leased us our apartment in Silver Spring. I rarely spoke to her last fall and certainly never bothered to develop a friendship with her, but I knew that she was very nice and a good person. I began to develop a friendship with Chrissey when I walked into the rental office in January looking for a few guest parking passes for my friends one weekend. It was at that time (after Meg had moved out) that Chrissey asked me if I wanted two kittens. One of Chrissey's cats just had seven kittens and she was looking for homes for them. I guess I was in the right place at the right time.

I always wanted kittens but Meg never did. My new roommate at the time, Eydie, was an animal lover and she agreed to take the kittens. To make a long story short, I developed a friendship with Chrissey because of the kittens. I grew to love the kittens, and my friendship with Chrissey grew as well. When I moved into this townhouse, my new roommates agreed to take me as a package deal with my kittens; but after I came back from my hometown, they decided they did not want the kittens living here anymore. I am in a terrible position right now and I am not sure what I am going to do about it.

Chrissey and I had our first argument last Saturday, and that argument really upset me. I guess the fight made me realize how important Chrissey has become to me. I value the friendship that I have with her very much and I am excited about us becoming closer. I don't know how much of the development of this friendship is due to my problems with Rebecca. In fact, I'd rather not think of it in those terms. Tonight, Chrissey and I straightened things out and reached an understanding with one another. I feel really good about being able to do that with her.

After the conversation I had with Dean Waldeman today, I have come to realize that I do not need or have to compromise any of my standards or strategies in establishing and maintaining a friendship just because someone may think they are unreasonable. On the contrary, what Dean Waldeman taught me today, and what Ricardo has been telling me for months, is that I am a wonderful person and friend. I cannot change Rebecca's definition of a friendship to suit mine, and I don't have to compromise my definition of a friendship to suit hers. Rather, I must come to the resolution that she is not the friend I thought she was and I should just let her go. I should spend my time with people like Chrissey, instead.

The solution to the Rebecca problem is clear: Let her go and get on with your life, Katy. It's going to be awfully hard to do this. My relationship with Billy [Rebecca's son] really complicates this matter, but right now I really need to be fair to myself. I hate to say this but Billy may have to suffer for a little while because I cannot deal with his mother right now. I need to feel good about myself and not bad, and she makes me feel lousy. The cocaine has fucked my life up and I need to concentrate on keeping it out of my life and getting my life back in order. This process will be accelerated and assisted by investing time into good friends who define friendship the way that I do. These friends will be there for me when I need them; they will keep me in line when I get out of hand; they will be able to spend time with me and call me on the phone. But most importantly, they will *appreciate* the friendship that we share. One of these types of friends is Chrissey. She is wonderful. I am really growing to love her.

I firmly believe that Chrissey and I have a friendship that transcends the kittens. Tonight's discussion is proof of that. I have promised myself that I am going to become a better friend now that the cocaine is out of my system. I have a lot of work to do this summer; but if I give 100 percent and accomplish all of the work that I have in front of me, I truly believe I will become a better person for it. I love my life, my friends, my family, and myself. I choose not to put an order to the things I love because I feel it is inappropriate. It's time to get back to doing the good things. It's time to look out for number one again and to look out for those people who care about me. If I had to construct a list of the people who care about me and the people who define friendship in the same fashion that I do, the list would be long. For this I am fortunate. If I had to construct a list of the people in my life who don't really care and don't define friendship in a similar fashion, that list would probably not include more than one name—and we all know what name that would be. In other words, Chrissey is definitely on my good list, and we all know where Rebecca is.

The next discovery will be to find out where Katy is. I think I am on the road to recovery. Sometimes this road will be rocky and other times it will be smooth. The meetings, the therapy, this journal, and my friends on my good list will help smooth out the rocky road that lies ahead (so will my family). If I spend my time and energy on those people who are on my bad list, that rocky road will flatten my tires and will hinder my destination to become the best person that I can be. I owe it to myself and to others to become the best person that I can be. I guess I really do know what I have to do.

May 11, 1988

I spent today in my hometown with Joni, looking for a car at a friend's car dealership. I got to show Joni a little bit of my hometown, but not as much as I would have liked to. I guess I can take her up home again sometime. Needless to say, I had a wonderful day at home with Joni, my Mom, and my Dad.

My parents have a lot of questions about my plan of action with treatment here in D.C. This week I start the outpatient program [at the hospital] in Potomac and am really looking forward to it. I can't wait to tell my side of the story to people who truly understand what addiction is all about. I still don't tell the people closest to me all of the dirty details of my cocaine lifestyle because I am ashamed of many of the things I did while I was using. I'm sure I will become more comfortable discussing the details with people in the future.

Sometimes it seems as if things are going too easy for me. I have not really craved the drug, and that really seems odd to me. I still have the dreams and often wake up in the middle of the night sweating, but I have not wanted to get high for about two weeks now. All of the talk that you hear is that you will crave the drug tremendously and it is this craving that can torment you back into using. Maybe I'm an exception to the rule or maybe it's just too soon to say these things, but I really feel that it is not going to be that fucking hard to give up this drug. All I am hoping for is to continue to stay clean and that abstinence is always this easy.

Still I often find myself crying or having tears in my eyes when I think back to all of those times I was doing coke. Everything is so fucking clear in my mind. I can't determine whether the tears are self-pity or not. All I can do is cry sometimes. Just writing in this journal arouses a lot of emotions inside of me that I didn't feel an hour ago. Sometimes writing brings a smile to my face, and other times it brings tears to my eyes. The only thing that seems to be consistent is I always look forward to writing in this journal. It seems to be the only place where I can truthfully discuss everything. Thanks go out to Geraldine for suggesting this to me.

Not to change the subject so drastically, but I had a conversation with Billy tonight (when I returned Leslie's phone call) that is bothering me. Billy sounded really glad to hear my voice, which I thought was a bit unusual. However, what struck me as extremely strange was he told me he loved me before we ended our conversation and before I even told him the same. It was like he really went out of his way to tell me he loved me. What's going on here? I find this strange because Billy never tells me that he loves me on his own account. In fact, I don't know if he has ever told me he loves me, although I have always known he does love me very much. Why is he offering this information to me now? Something is going on with this little boy, and I want to know what it is.

I really wish I could talk to both him and Rebecca to see what is happening in their lives, but I feel I can't. I have come to the resolution to let Rebecca go and I am not sure how I can maintain a relationship with Billy, knowing the position I am going to take with his mother. I love that little boy so much and I really miss him. I really do want to spend time with him, but I don't know how to do it without exposing myself to her and leaving myself wide open for more pain. Does anyone have any suggestions, please? I guess this is another one I have to figure out by myself. Isn't life a bitch sometimes? Good night!

May 12, 1988

Today, Joni, Sue, Paul, and I went to Baltimore for the evening. I began the day with a wonderful nine-mile run. I am still sore from the hamstrings workout that I had on Tuesday. After I came back from running, I lay out in the sun with Joni, Sue, and Paul and then we had a cookout. We left for Baltimore at 4 p.m.

Joni insists that my party friends and I think she and her friends are nerds because they don't do coke. I feel awful knowing that I may have given her that impression when I was tooting, because I certainly didn't intend to do so and I surely don't believe that anyway. Subsequently, she spent most of the day trying to show me that "nerds" can have just as much fun as "coke heads" and also that people don't need drugs to have a good time.

I know that. I've never even tried to defend the position that doing cocaine is superior to all other things and that those people who do it are better than others who don't. Wait a minute. Maybe I did think that doing cocaine was superior to many other things. I know for a fact that, in the beginning of my cocaine use, I thought I was cool as shit when I was doing coke. Coke has always been a big status symbol for me. Picture it as such: You throw a gram or two out on the table for everyone in the room to snort. Each person in that room knows how much money that coke is worth. In their minds, you must be pretty well off to be able to toss out a couple grams of coke for everyone in the room to share. After all, there is probably much more where that came from.

Time and time again I used to say to those around me that I hated to party alone. My motto was, if you want to party and don't have as much money as I do, it's okay if I spend more on coke than you because we both want to share the high together. Well, this kind of thinking was okay if we were each spending only 50 bucks; however, when it got into the hundreds, things started getting pretty messy. For example, I took four grams of cocaine to *my* birthday party. I knew a couple of people wanted to party, and there was a general consensus that each of us would chip in for the four grams. That four grams went before 11 p.m. Consequently, we had to get more from the man.

We got more alright and stayed up until 6 a.m. snorting cocaine. When it came time to collect the money for that night's party expenses, I received a lousy $150 for five and a half grams of cocaine. Boy, did I get screwed! You should have heard everyone bitch when I asked them for money. I said to one friend, "How in the world can you expect to put in $25 and party all night long? You must have done at least a gram yourself [$100], and you only want to give $25? Where do you think the money is coming from to pay for the rest of the stuff? Damn right! I know you think I can take care of it—and will, because I always have in the past. Bullshit!"

Looking back on it all makes me sick to my stomach. My friends were always taking advantage of the cocaine I had. As a matter of fact, they took advantage of everything. I was the one who made the connections for us, I was the one who drove to get it, I was the one who put the money up front, and I was the one who "had" to secure more when the supply was finished. But most of all, I was the one who always put the most money into it and got the least amount of coke for that money. I can't believe how many times I shared that extra gram from the eightball [3.5 grams for the price of 2.5] with everyone, when they had absolutely no right to it. They always expected me to share it—every single, fucking time. How could I have been so stupid!

A sad picture is what I have painted for myself, and now that picture is staring me in the face. I guess I did all of those foolish things because I was so seduced by that fucking drug. It took away my logical thinking, my intelligence, and my pride. I was doing just about anything to get that drug—but I never thought I was doing it just for myself, but also for everyone else. I guess that was just the cocaine talking to me. Every time I claimed I was making the hookup for us, or getting the best deal for us, it wasn't for anybody other than myself.

Hey Joni, look at the picture I have just painted of myself. Who is the idiot? Who is the jerk? Who is the one who is uncool, and who is the one who lost her sense of self? It surely isn't you or your "nerdy" friends. It's me, babe, and don't I look ugly. I guess being a nerd is rather attractive after all.

MAY 14, 1988

Rebecca actually called me today at 11 a.m. She sounded so cheerful on the telephone. I loved it when she sounded as if she was interested in what has been going on in my life. Her interest in my life is only due to her concern about my cocaine addiction. I don't want her concern about me now. As a matter of fact, I don't want any part of her.

I went to my first group session today. My only reaction thus far is, WOW! The meeting was so intense. Those people don't let you get away with anything. I told them I had a dinner date this evening with my dealer and I asked them if I should go or not. I proceeded to answer my own question by saying I have been clean for two weeks and feel really good. If I go out with him tonight, I am afraid I will want to use again—and I really don't want to do that. When I came home from group, I called him on the phone and told him I had a meeting tonight and couldn't go out with him. I know he is probably mad right now, but I guess I gotta do what I gotta do.

Today has been going very well. I had a great run and I spent some time with Nadine at the gym. I am getting ready to go out with a few people from the gym. We plan to go dancing later. Joni wants to go to Baltimore again instead of going dancing. I want to go both places. Decisions, decisions!

Listen, tonight's journal entry is going to be short because I am short of time. I'll write more tomorrow. There surely are tons of things I could write about. My life is okay today. When the sun comes up tomorrow, I hope I feel like I do right now. Shit, I hope I feel for the rest of the evening as good as I feel right now. I have confidence that I will.

MAY 15, 1988

Where do I begin tonight? I wish I could have had my computer in front of me the entire day today. Why? Because I went through so many emotional states and mood changes, many of which I could have written down in this journal. It's kind of hard for me to recapture now the feelings I experienced earlier today. I guess I'll just start with where I am right now.

Loose ends. There are nothing but loose ends in my life right now. What do I mean by loose ends? Loose ends are things that need attending to, things I have left open, responsibilities I must now face, and pieces of my life puzzle that need to be put back together if I am going to make it. Where in the fuck do I start? Which piece goes where, and which one do I attend to first? It's all so much, so confusing at this point that I don't know what to do. Everyone in my life is a loose end, and everything in my life is a loose end. Guess who gets to tie them all up? You got it: It's *me*. I am not looking forward to this job but I certainly asked for it.

Part of me just wants to be miserable right now, and part of me wants to be happy. The problem is that my happiness just doesn't seem to last as long as my sadness. I used to be such a happy person. What has happened to me? Is all of this due to the cocaine? I start out feeling happy at dinner, or at the club, or with friends; and shortly thereafter, I find myself miserable. I'm angry, sad, frustrated, dejected, humiliated, and bitter all at the same time. On the other hand, I am happy and cheerful at times as well. It just so happens that the good times are much less frequent and shorter in duration than the bad times. What to do, what to do.

How fucking long will I go on like this? How long will I feel lonely, unloved, sad, angry, and all of the other negative adjectives that one can use to describe oneself? I simply must shake this mode I am in, but I just can't seem to do it. I just can't shake it. I just can't. How long will it be before I'll be able to tie all of the loose ends back together and get the pieces of my life puzzle back in their proper places? Do you think I will ever accomplish this?

The bottom line is this: I'm sick of talking and thinking about how I feel. I wish there was someone I could really talk to, but there isn't anyone. As I told Leslie today, I can talk to certain people about certain things, but not about everything to one person. The worst part of it all is, when I do talk to people about what's going on in my life or what I'm feeling, I rarely tell them the whole truth anyway. What good is telling a joke without delivering the punch line? Not much fucking good, huh? It really only leaves you unsatisfied and in a worse position than you were before you started the conversation.

I want to start another journal entry tonight. This one will be really brief. I'm going to call it "What It Feels Like."

Do you know what it feels like to do coke?
Do you know what it feels like on your tongue, gums, in your nose, down the back of your throat, in your stomach, and on your teeth?
Do you know what it feels like to be so high that everything else is beneath you?
Do you know what it feels like to be less high than you were ten "lines" ago?
Do you know what it feels like to try to get back up there?
Do you know what it feels like to try and try, line after line [of cocaine], to get back up there—only to find that you can't?
Do you know what it feels like when it's all gone?
Do you know what it feels like when the party is over?
Do you know what it feels like to start coming down, and down, and down?
Do you know what it feels like to take that big crash that you have been trying to postpone for hours or even days?
Do you know what it feels like to not be able to fall asleep?
Do you know what it feels like when sinuses collapse?
Do you know what it feels like when the coke starts to burn?
Do you know what it feels like to have the headaches?
Do you know what it feels like being hot one second and cold the next?
Do you know what it feels like when you can't seem to get that one last line up your nose because it's so clogged?
But do you really know what it feels like to not be able to stop?
Do you know what it feels like to not be able to stop doing cocaine?

I hope and pray that you don't know any of these things and have never felt any of them; but if you have, than you are an addict and it's time for you to deal with that. You know the list could be much longer. What do you feel like now? I feel like a goddamn cocaine addict—and let me tell you something, it doesn't feel too fucking good!

May 16, 1988

Can you believe that I don't feel sorry for myself today? I've spent a good part of this past week brooding over everything possible and feeling so sorry for myself. Well, today was an exception to this week's rule. I feel absolutely wonderful today—the best I have felt in a long time. The good feelings lasted all day today. Not at one moment did I feel shitty or sad or lonely or any of those other adjectives that I used to describe my feelings last night. I am on cloud nine right now and I'm here without any cocaine. I guess I'm rediscovering what that natural high is all about.

Do you want to know what really amazes me? *People*. I have been trying to figure out for three weeks now how amazing people really are. What do I mean? Cocaine addicts don't need people when they are doing cocaine. As a matter of fact, they don't need anything other than their next line. I am one of these cocaine addicts, and when I was doing cocaine, I didn't need anyone or anything. All I needed was cocaine and more and more of it. Coke addicts forget their friends, they forget the people they work with, and they even forget their families. The only people who exist in an addict's life, while he is using, are the imaginary people he believes are watching him and are out to get him. The psychological terminology for this is "paranoid delusion."

These cocaine addicts had people in their lives before they started to use, but they don't have those people in their lives now. Coke addicts abandon the people they love and the people who love them. Addicts can try all they want to be good friends to others, good relatives, or good working partners, but soon they discover they have to let all of those people go because the drug is more important. Coke addicts become selfish, irresponsible, indifferent, ungrateful, disobedient, critical, and abusive to all of those people who are in their lives. In other words, coke addicts fuck all of the people in their lives over for a drug. They fuck the people over who care about them, respect them, and love them. Coke addicts become real shitty people.

But do you know what is amazing? The people in the addict's life, who truly love the addict, don't change. They don't change anything about the addict's place in their hearts. They continue to love the addict just as much as they did before and during his addiction. Now something seems wrong to me here. If someone fucked me over because of his obsession with a drug, I don't know if I'd feel the same about that person anymore. My rationale would be this statement:

> Man, you have been a real jerk to me lately. You tell me that you love me and cherish what you have between us and then you selfishly forget that, because you are so fucked up on cocaine. And I am supposed to be comforting now and understanding of your addiction? You're the one who didn't show up for the appointment and left me in a bind, you're the one who never showed up when we planned to work out, you're the one who always left us at the bar, party, or at dinner to chase your drug, you're the one who fucked me over—and now I'm supposed to be kind, caring, supportive, and understanding? Fuck off!

The point I am trying to make is, I have treated the people in my life terribly for quite some time. I have been a terrible friend, sister, daughter, colleague, and worker for at least eight months. I have screwed so many people over, and these people should be reacting to this in a similar fashion to that I described above. The amazing thing about it all is that they are not. People are pissed, but they still care. People are angry at me, but they still love me. And here's the one I find most amazing: People are disappointed, but they still respect me. I don't think I deserve any of this. These people are so wonderful and I have treated them terribly. I don't deserve to have such people in my life. I don't think I am good enough for them.

The amazing thing about it all is that they think I deserve this. These people think that I am still worthy of their love after treating them so horribly. This is truly amazing. I just really had to write about this tonight because it has been on my mind for a while. Katy Hendricks, you are one fortunate young lady. What more could a person ask for? I need to pay really close attention to what I have just written, because there is a valuable lesson in it.

MAY 17, 1988

He said that he wanted to meet so we could talk about what has happened. Well, we met this evening and he didn't listen to a word I said. I told him I had a letter all ready to give him, but he insisted that he wanted to see me and did not want any letter. The conversation went basically as I predicted. I told him exactly how I felt about it all; and when things started to hit too close to home with him, he changed the direction of the conversation.

The important thing about seeing my dealer tonight was, I finally confronted him with the truth even though he was reluctant to hear it. He spent most of his time trying to alleviate his own guilt for my situation and also trying to rationalize his cocaine use, which he claims is coming to an end. More than once, he told me he hasn't been doing it and is really getting into being healthy again. He also told me he is dropping out of the business as soon as this batch of cocaine is gone.

I guess it doesn't matter how much of his talk I believe or not. The bottom line is that he is not being realistic about all of this and I am. He's kidding himself, and he's trying to kid me as well. He still refers to us as "social" users. Can you actually believe that? According to the cocaine progression chart at the hospital, he and I are way past the social-use stage and are in the chronic stage. You should have seen and heard his reaction when I told him I was in the chronic stage according to the chart.

Something phenomenal happened tonight. I have made a tremendous discovery and it has shed a new light on my life. I was in a social situation tonight with every one of the people I used to party with. Not for one single second or moment did I feel the slightest inkling to do any cocaine. Being around my party crowd tonight was not uncomfortable for me at all. In fact, I handled it pretty damn well! I can't believe I actually didn't feel the urge to use tonight. I even saw him pass some on to Rick, and I still didn't want to do any.

What does this all mean? I think it means I don't desire the cocaine lifestyle anymore. Maybe it's too soon to say this, but I feel very strongly about it. I don't want to have anything to do with the drug or the people who use it. I am ready to live a drug-free life. I'm not denying the fact that it's going to be hard. I know damn well it is going to be very difficult to stay away from cocaine. I also know it may be too soon in my recovery to be talking about this, but I'm going to do it anyway. I feel really good today knowing I made this major discovery: I don't desire the cocaine lifestyle anymore. I'm ready for it to be a part of my past.

MAY 18, 1988

I wrote this one last December [1987], during finals week. I was fighting with Rebecca and doing cocaine at the time.

How is it that we come to these points in our lives where all
seems gloomy, dark, and dismal?

How is it that we can give all we have to give and
still have it rejected?

How is it that I'm writing today about something I thought
yesterday would never be?

Mother always told me nightmares never came true. Why
did she lie?

What was written in this poem six months ago still holds true today. You can see from the poem that the cocaine was beginning to affect my life at this time. Why couldn't I have seen it then? I had a cocaine problem then and I couldn't see it. If I would have realized and admitted my problem in December, I would not have found myself in such a terrible position today. I am really pissed at myself right now. Man, am I angry at myself.

LATER, THE SAME DAY

Let's do some cocaine together. Here is the best way (well, Katy's way) to party your brains out. (I'm going to go straight through this without interruption.) Take the mirror and put it on the table. Pull out your packet of coke and open it up. Be careful to open the bottom flaps of the packet carefully and keep the packet pointing upward so none of it spills. The packet should look like a triangle right now. Unfold the triangle and bring the opposite ends of the triangle, the packet, together so as to gather your coke right in the center of the packet. Now pour some out on the mirror. How much? Pour out as much as would cover a nickel I guess. Take out your blade. Make sure that your blade is not too rusty and is clean. Why? You don't want any dirt in your system, do you? And you certainly don't want to lose any of your cocaine because your blade was moist, now do you? Gently begin to chop up the cocaine on the mirror. Make sure you chop up all of the rocks so it looks just like sugar or baby powder. Remember, rocky cocaine is harder to get into your system because it sticks to the side of your nose. Waste not, want not. Keep chopping. That's right. Does it look like sugar? Well, I believe it's time to cut up some lines. My strategy is a takeoff from many other serious partiers. This strategy is guaranteed to get you as high as you are going to be during the party within the first three minutes of your party session.

Listen up, rookie: The amount of coke that you put out on the mirror—once the size of a nickel—is probably larger now because you chopped up the rocks. Cut yourself four lines. When I say "cut lines," I mean go to the pile of coke with your blade and section off four separate lines of about one-half inch long and an eighth of an inch wide and line them up beside each other away from the pile. This is where it pays to have a sharp, clean blade. You may want to carry several blades on you. I always did. Pull out your straw. Don't use a dollar bill because it is dirty. Your straw should be about two inches long. I always liked to do the right nostril first, so let's begin there. Put the straw about a quarter of the way up your right nostril and bend over to the mirror. Push your finger against your left nostril and snort two lines. Immediately do the same with the next two lines; however, this time put the straw in the left nostril. Tilt your head back and inhale again to make sure that the coke gets up there. Quickly cut yourself another four lines. Wait about 30 seconds and snort these four the same way that you did the previous four.

It is important to keep some water with you so that you can keep your nose clean. After each set of lines, you should take some water and drop it into your nose, with your head slightly tilted. This method helps keep your nose clean and also helps the coke to penetrate your system better. How do you feel? Good, I bet. I'm going to sign off now, but you just keep right on tooting. Make sure you keep tooting every few minutes. This strategy will help you maintain your high and prevent that big crash that you will soon get to know. If you're anything like me, then tomorrow at 7 a.m., when I wake up, you'll still be doing lines. Have fun and enjoy! And remember, if you find it hard to breathe and you feel your heart pumping a mile a minute, keep right on tooting. You do want to be the best partier, don't you?

MAY 18, 1988, AGAIN

What does it feel like to be high? I never realized how difficult it would be to verbally describe the high until I started to try. I have been sitting here for at least 20 minutes trying to decide where to begin. I think that I have an idea.

Let's go for a walk. I stand up and begin to move my legs. All of a sudden I feel 20 pounds lighter than I was a few minutes ago. It's like my arms and legs are small sticks that are so easy to move. I can't believe how much easier it is to move around than it was before. And look at how quickly I am doing things. I can move swifter, faster because I am so light on my feet. I want to do another line. This is great. Let's play around some, okay? Watch how quickly I can wash these dishes. I look down at my hands and I see a blur. Only I can't feel them moving. I do feel some movement, but my hands certainly can't be traveling as rapidly as they appear to be. Oh my God. Have I finished that large stack of dishes already? Time for another line. Ahhhhhhhhh!

What can I do next? My head is moving from one side to the other, back and forth and back and forth. Left, right, left, right as I look for something to do next. I keep moving my lips in and out. I must look pretty funny. Look at all of the funny faces I can make. Wow! I'm laughing and I can't seem to stop smiling either. It seems as though my face is locked in this position. Not too bad having a permanent smile fixed on your face, is it now? Now what is my mouth doing? What are my teeth doing? I'm clamping my teeth together and am moving them back and forth as they are pressed together. Look how much strength my jaws have. I can press my teeth together with such strength it feels like I am going to push the top teeth right up through my gums—or will it be my bottom teeth down through my gums? I'm going to keep doing this so I can see what happens. Wait, it's time to do another line—or should I do several? Yeah!

I'm back. Boy, those last two lines were a bit small. I better cut a few more. I bet I can get even higher. Let me wipe my nose a second. I have an idea. I'll go get a wet paper towel and will inhale some water. I saw a few of my friends do this. Sniff, sniff. I tilt my head back and I feel the water go up my nose. Wow, along with the water went some coke. Man, does that taste good! My friends were right. What a rush! I don't believe I have ever been this high. I can't feel my head at all right now. I better touch it to see if it's there. It's there alright. What a drug!

Finger dancing. As the music is playing in the background, I'm moving my fingers to the beat. I used to play the trumpet, so I know which finger should go down for each note in the music. Let me go get another tape because this music is too slow. Okay, I'm ready to finger dance to Prince. My right hand is on the table waiting for the music to start. Here we go! My fingers start moving. The tune is familiar, so I know when the verses come and when the choruses come. I know each little melody and each little harmony. Look at that. I can move my fingers so rapidly and with such coordination I can tap out both melodies and harmonies with one hand full of fingers. I got my feet going now. This sure is a lot of fun. My feet are the drums, tapping out each beat. My right hand is the lead guitar, of course, because I'm right handed. My hands are dancing to the music, while my feet are tapping out the drumbeat, while my head is moving all around singing the words to the music. I'm a one-woman band!

Aw shucks. The song is over. That's okay—this one-woman band stuff is getting boring anyway. Man, am I thirsty! Let me do a few more lines and then I'm going to have to go get a glass of water. I just noticed I am gritting my teeth together again. I don't know if I like this anymore. I know—I'll go get a piece of gum. Perfect solution to that problem. Wow, I'm really chewing the fuck out of this gum. Wonder who's outside. Let me get up and go check. Look at all of those people down there. They look so tiny and they are moving so slowly. Look at that fat woman with her two kids. Wonder if they'll grow up to be fat too? I can't see why people have to eat. I never get hungry. My stomach is all caved in. My ribs are even sticking out. Look at that Puerto Rican over there with the greasy hair. My man needs to wash that shit. Bet you he has a slew of kids that are not fat. That chick over there must think she's hot stuff. I'd bet $100 she got her whole outfit at Mariannes or Casual Corner. I know for a fact she didn't get it at Ann Taylor. Wait a minute—Hold the phone Joan—I've seen it all now. Here comes an older couple dressed in leather. Spare me! Look at how teased her hair is—and of course it's not gray, but rather ten shades of blonde. Hubby has gray hair though. However, he's got plenty of gold around his chest to divert the attention away from his head. You can tell they bought their leather outfits in the U.S. because they have seams—that is, the pants pieces of leather are sewn together. Real leather pants, jackets, et cetera from Europe or Canada have seams, but are not sewn together as panels like American leathers are. Leather goods from other countries are the best in the world. These two are screaming new money, which usually implies a lack of class. Their outfits validate my point. What a shame!

What to do next. How could I be so stupid. It's time for a few lines. Yes, that's right—make sure to chop up that coke and make those lines nice and even, thick and long. Blow your nose, Katy. You don't want any of your precious drug getting caught up in your snot, do you? I'm going to do these four really fast. Boom, Boom, Boom, Boom. And up they go. Ummm. Burned a little bit this time. Guess I should expect that, after the first hour. God! Damn, damn, damn. I'm humming. My eyes are wide open. It's like my eyelids have left my face. I can't even feel them anymore. My face is so tight. The skin on my face feels like it is so tightly stretched across my jaws, my cheekbones, and my forehead. I just noticed a runny nose and a headache. Better go get a tissue and a few Tylenol. On second thought, I'll just get the whole box of tissues and the whole bottle of Tylenol.

I'm talking to you now and I'm straight. The above scenario is a brief description of what I experienced within the first hour or so of snorting cocaine. You must remember that things change as the hours pass. It's not that there are definite stages that you pass through during a session with cocaine. It's just that the experience can be so cyclical.

MAY 19, 1988

Tonight I have to work at the restaurant, and it figures that I would have to close my first Friday night back. I had such a great time working there on Wednesday with Rick, Leslie, Mary, Pat, Joe, and Jay. It really feels good to be back there. I feel absolutely no tension. I feel quite comfortable.

I want to talk about Rebecca for a minute right now. I'm not upset or anything. I just want to talk about her. I saw her at the gym last night. She was there working out with Jim. We spent an hour and a half inside the same two rooms without even uttering a word to each other. As a matter of fact, we didn't even make eye contact once. Is this what we have come to? It was uncomfortable for me. I wonder if it was for her? I'm sure she felt some discomfort, but probably only temporarily.

I have really forgotten what it is like to have a good time with her. I can't really remember the last time we actually had fun together. It must have been some time in January. Don't get me wrong. I am not sitting here brooding about what is happening between the two of us. I am just trying to reminisce.

A little while ago, I was not able to reminisce because doing so would have meant that the friendship was a thing of the past. A little while ago, I was not willing to admit that the friendship was a thing of the past. Now I am willing to do so and I have. I can't lie and say I don't ever want her in my life again. I just know I can't be friends with her right now and that we may never be friends again. After last night's behavior in the gym, I realized things have to be this way for me. I can't let her bring me down anymore. I am a good person and I need to start feeling that way again.

So I find I can think back to the good old days when she and I used to have so much fun together. I can think about them and smile. And although the reminiscing is possible, I still find it hard. It will become easier. Do you know why? The answer is that I'm keeping the reminiscing in the past and am no longer trying to make it a part of the present. Rebecca is a friend of the past.

MAY 21, 1988

Questions. I have so many unanswered questions running around in my head. To top it all off, I feel miserable again. Group stirred up a lot of feelings inside of me today. The group had a good session, but I don't think I did. I don't know why I can't share in the meetings and at group, but I just can't do it. Consequently, these questions of mine never get answered. As a matter of fact, I'm finding the list is only growing longer as the days pass. What are the questions I have? I think I really do need to list them right now. I need to write down the questions I have so I can refer to them when I search for answers.

Questions

1. Why am I a cocaine addict?
2. Why don't I feel this overwhelming need to do cocaine right now?
3. Why am I pissed that I can't drink?
4. Why do I have the dreams?
5. How can I stop the dreams and the flashbacks?
6. Why can't I share at meetings and in group?
7. Why has my friendship with Rebecca fallen apart?
8. Why does her absence in my life hurt so much?
9. Why did I keep doing lines after I almost had a heart attack three times?
10. Why am I drowning myself in pity?
11. Why don't the good moments last as long as the sad ones?
12. How do I control mood swings?
13. How come the only reason I am not doing cocaine right now is because I am afraid of that crash and how I'll function and feel afterwards?
14. What happens when I'm not afraid of the crash anymore?
15. Why do I hate myself right now?
16. How important is a man to me?
17. Why did I take cocaine into the prison with me?
18. How do I get my life back in order?
19. How do I find happiness again?

This list is not even a good list. This afternoon in group I assembled a good list with all of the questions I have been asking since admitting addiction. I can't seem to recall that list. All I do know right now is, even if I find the answers to these questions, I'm afraid I will still be unhappy and will not be at peace with myself because I think there is some really big fear in my life that I can't seem to see. What I mean is, I think there is something in my life that I am very afraid of, but I just can't seem to place it. It's somewhere in my subconscious. I guess that is the big question I have and need answered most. I'll talk to you tomorrow.

May 22, 1988

I have yet to write about how I feel about the meetings. The meetings I want to talk about tonight are the Sunday-night CA meetings at the hospital. I have attended four of these meetings, hence I have been clean for four weeks now. Let me just say that 30 days clean or four weeks feels absolutely great! I picked up my 30-day chip tonight at the meeting. Everyone applauded me and cheered me on for more abstinence. What great camaraderie!

Back to the Sunday-night CA meetings. These meetings are my favorite meetings. I really look forward to going to these meetings each Sunday night. I feel so good when I leave them. I have only been attending these Sunday meetings and my group on Saturdays. I thought to myself on the way home tonight that I have only been going to meetings two days a week. Maybe this has something to do with why I feel so lousy during the week. Look, if I came out of tonight's meeting feeling so good, why can't other meetings give me the same feeling? I need to start attending more meetings. They make me feel good.

Why are Sunday CA meetings my favorite? I could sit here and construct a very long list of answers to this question, but the most obvious answer is the people. I like everything about the people who attend these meetings. It's very hard to explain why I'm so fascinated with the people at these meetings; however, one person at the meeting tonight provided an explanation for me. He said that he never really looked at himself while he was using and, therefore, he didn't know what he looked like. He proceeded to say that only after coming to CA meetings did he actually come to see what he really looked like. He said it was like looking in the mirror when he listened to the people tell their stories, that essentially these people were in fact telling his story. I can truthfully say I feel the same way.

Do you know what it is like to have this disease? Before you surrender and admit your addiction, you feel all alone in the world—that there is no one out there for you, who can listen to your problems or even relate to you. You certainly can't tell any of these people about your addiction because you don't think you have one; and if you do think you're an addict, you have to keep your addiction hidden from others. Consequently you are alone. These feelings follow you right through recovery. I have been feeling more lonely as days pass. I have felt so many emotions and have changed moods and states so much since admitting addiction, my head is spinning. Things are very difficult right now for me.

The world does not have to end here. When I go to meetings, I feel as though I am in a room full of people who are just like me. I can relate to everything these people say, and they can do the same with me. Do you know what it feels like to be able to find someone who really understands you and what you're going through? God, it is all so wonderful. It's like every person in that room is telling my story of cocaine addiction. Sharing your experiences in these meetings is rewarding for everyone who is sitting in that room. It is the sharing that can be very crucial in one's recovery.

Atmosphere. You can only appreciate the atmosphere in these meetings by attending one. It is hard to explain. Some of the adjectives I could use to describe the atmosphere are supportive, understanding, caring, intense, casual, and cool. What I find amazing is, I feel totally rejuvenated when I leave them. I often feel shitty going to the meetings, but I always feel great when I leave them. I try to maintain the feelings generated in the meetings for the rest of the evening, and I usually find I can do so.

Tonight I picked up two people's phone numbers. I have never asked for a number and have never given mine to anyone before this evening. Why did I do so tonight? Tonight I finally shared at a meeting. Tonight I talked about the dreams I have been having. I cried out for help, and so many people responded. Do you know what that kind of caring is all about? I can't believe people can be so wonderful. These people really know me, and they really know what I'm going through right now. I am so fortunate to have these people and these meetings. All you have to do to get this caring is go to the meetings and share—share your experiences, share your problems, or talk about what's on your mind—and people will listen, they'll respond, and they'll even try to help you. All of this caring and understanding for just opening your mouth? Some meetings, huh?

I never want to miss one of these meetings. I know when the semester starts back up and when the pools open this summer I will probably find it harder to attend these Sunday-night meetings. God grant me the willpower and the discipline to never miss one of these Sunday-night CA meetings at the hospital. I really need to attend every one I can. They are very crucial to me at this point in my life, and they probably always will be. Good night.

MAY 23, 1988

Here's what it feels like to be high:

It feels so soft and cushiony up here. That's what they told me walking on clouds was like. Everything is so wonderful up here. I feel no aches, no pains, no troubles. I feel like I'm walking on air with all of my worries behind me. I can look down from my cloud and see everything and everyone beneath me and it all makes me feel happy because I am no longer down there, but am rather up here. I can move so much faster up here. I'm like a fly, just buzzing around. I can fly here and there with the utmost swiftness. And I can just keep on buzzing around. I have all the strength in the world. I never seem to tire. Life is so wonderful up here. I am so happy up here. Why doesn't everyone come up here? If they would come up here they would see how wonderful it all is and they would never want to go back. They would feel like I feel.

MAY 24, 1988

Today, I was thinking that, when it was just a quarter a week or a half gram every other week, I never had any guilt and I never had any dreams. Things are quite different now. I began having guilt dreams last September. Meg and I had just moved into an apartment in Silver Spring. Before Meg and I moved to this apartment, our cocaine use was curtailed by a third roommate who didn't party. This third roommate didn't follow us to Silver Spring; therefore, Meg and I were alone to do our coke together with no interference from anyone.

It was at this time that my guilt dreams began. I can remember one dream in particular. All of my friends and I were sitting around a table, passing around a mirror with lines of cocaine on it. When the mirror came to me, the lines turned into a red jelly-like substance. I took the mirror and said to my friends. "What in the fuck is this? Where is the cocaine, guys? It's my turn, you know." My friends replied, "These are your lines, Katy, so just snort them." I replied, "How in the fuck am I supposed to get these up my nose? There is no way that these lines are going to go up my nose." I remember getting pretty irate about it all. I proceeded to demand my lines from my friends.

When I woke up the next morning, I realized what the dream had meant. It was a guilt dream, for sure. I was beginning to think I was doing too much cocaine, but I didn't want to let anyone know I thought that, and I sure didn't want to admit how much I was doing. Essentially, the cause of the guilt was concealing my cocaine use from others. The red lines indicated that everyone knew I was doing too much cocaine and should stop.

I didn't stop using cocaine after that dream. In fact, I had many dreams like this [for a while], but soon they disappeared. [Then] I had absolutely no cocaine dreams whatsoever. I thought the guilt had passed —the guilt I subconsciously felt for doing the coke. Looking back on it all now, I realize that there was a definite reason why the guilt dreams stopped. I began living the dreams. My cocaine use kept escalating as the weeks passed. The guilt dreams disappeared, but the guilt didn't. I began living the guilt.

We all know the story of the cocaine addict. Coke addicts begin to lie, they miss appointments, they are chronically late, they shirk responsibility, and all of that other gross stuff. I became an addict and did all of the above. It was the irresponsibility with all aspects of my life that created the life of guilt for me. I was constantly worrying about what excuse to use this time, how to pretend to be sober when I was high, and how to explain to those who knew about my addiction that I didn't have one. However, the most troublesome and painstaking thing during it all was that, even when the lies worked and even when I fooled people into thinking I was sober and not high, the feelings of lying and cheating others made me feel so guilty. I constantly felt guilty about fucking people over. You see, then, I didn't have to dream about the guilt because I was living it.

The ironic part of it all is that it was the guilt that saved me. I just couldn't deal with it anymore. The lies began to get larger and occur much more frequently. I began shirking responsibility not only in my schoolwork, but also for Geraldine and Ben as well as the restaurant. The guilt was so powerful that I even felt it while I was doing the cocaine. I have never experienced that much guilt before in my life. It actually was very painful and debilitating. The culmination of the guilt came when I went into the prison with the coke in my pocket. I couldn't even look Pat in the face. I sat beside her for three hours and didn't even look at her. The guilt that I felt inside the prison was so overwhelming that I had to leave just a few hours after the conference started.

The guilt definitely saved me. I had reached the line I wouldn't cross where the guilt was at its maximum. During that last weekend, I lied to my family, my friends, and my employers and co-workers. I shirked responsibility at the conference, at the restaurant, and for both Dean Waldeman and Ben. I just couldn't bear it anymore, and so I came out with it all and admitted I was a cocaine addict.

Again the word "amazing" comes to mind. You wouldn't believe how good I felt when I first admitted it to Pat. It was like the weight of the world had been lifted from my shoulders. The guilt just disappeared. I felt at peace with myself. However, 30 clean days later I find that the guilt is still haunting me. I feel awful for the things that I did to myself and others. I feel really guilty about it all, but it's okay now because the guilt is therapeutic. It's a healing guilt and not a using guilt. I think I can definitely live with that type of guilt in my life.

MAY 26, 1988

I relapsed last night in my dreams. And now I find I can't stop thinking about last night's dream. It's all so vivid in my mind right now. I am totally preoccupied with it. So much so that I'm finding it debilitating. Maybe if I write about it I'll be able to ease the pain.

Last night's relapse was basically a reenactment of my last cocaine binge that began on a Thursday evening at 8 and ended the next day at 11 p.m. During this 27-hour binge I snorted between five and seven grams of cocaine—that is, $500–700 street value. The last binge that I had was preceded by a three-day binge the week before. I think that I snorted somewhere between seven and eight grams in those three days. Why am I discussing these two binges instead of last night's dream? These last two binges were reenacted in my dream last night.

I purchased half an ounce of cocaine the Wednesday before my second-to-last binge. I had every intention of selling seven grams or more to my friends and doing mine for free. In other words, I laid out $700 for 14 grams of cocaine. All I had to do was sell seven grams of the half ounce to break even and then I would be able to do seven for free. This was the first time I had done this, upon recommendation of my dealer. Consequently, it didn't work out the way it was planned. I ended up doing about nine of the grams myself; I sold two, and gave the rest to Rebecca to flush down the toilet. The number "14" was very significant in last night's relapse dream.

Last night's dream began with Leslie following me around. She must have known I was going to relapse. I had 14 grams of cocaine in my pockets, each gram in its own little packet. All throughout the dream, I can remember, I had seven packets in each of my front pockets and I couldn't keep my hands out of my pockets. I just kept playing with the packets, passing them through my fingers. I kept opening packets up and doing the cocaine myself. Finally I confided in Leslie. I told her how much coke I had and that I planned to do it all. I told her I planned to relapse but wanted to hide it from everyone. She told me she wouldn't tell anyone I was doing the coke.

Leslie and I began to do it together behind everyone's back. I can't remember if she asked me for any cocaine; all I do know is that she kept following me around wherever I went. When I began sharing my cocaine with Leslie, I had already gone through three grams, leaving me with 11. Flashback! I started my second-to-last binge alone on Thursday. When Rick joined me on Friday, I had 11 grams left. I guess that 11 grams is significant for me somehow.

Back to the dream. Leslie and I kept running to different rooms doing cocaine behind the backs of people I know. I remember my mother asking me where I was going and why I couldn't sit still, I remember Ben in the dream, and I remember both Joni and Chrissey constantly looking at me. I also remember almost getting caught several times because of Leslie's carelessness with the paraphernalia. She kept leaving the straw, mirror, or blade out in front of others—almost on purpose. I kept telling her to be more careful with it, and she just ignored me.

What I remember about the dream the most was how I couldn't seem to satisfy my craving for the coke. I was constantly starving for lines. That's why my hands were constantly in my pockets feeling the packets of cocaine. I couldn't get enough of it. The part of the dream I remember the most, and the part that woke me up three times last night was the guilt. It hurt so much. I was back to doing my cocaine behind everyone's back. I was back to lying and hiding. In fact, I was back to being a junkie. To top it all off, I was absolutely helpless. No one could have helped me last night. No one could have prevented me from relapsing, and no one could have stopped me from doing all the cocaine I had in my pockets last night in that dream.

I am so scared right now. Why? I am scared right now because I woke up wanting to use today, and I can't seem to get rid of the craving. When will this all end? I can't go on like this much longer. I am having such trouble sleeping. I keep having flashbacks. All I did last night while I was running was stop in a Roy Rogers restaurant to go to the bathroom and I had a flashback to my last binge when I tooted in that same Roy Rogers's bathroom and parking lot.

Today I have come closer to wanting to relapse than ever before. And I still want to do cocaine. I thought the cravings would pass as I remained abstinent!? Why won't these cravings go away? Why are they getting stronger? I am so afraid I am going to relapse soon, I can't seem to function right now. The problem is that right now I want to do cocaine and I want to get high, but I can't. I can't deal with the lifestyle of the junkie anymore. It's too painful. I experienced both pleasure and pain in last night's dream. I saw the good and bad sides of doing the coke. But what makes me scared is, I don't know which side is going to win. All I do know is that they [the two sides] are tearing me apart.

May 27, 1988

Yesterday's craving for coke disappeared as soon as I went running and to the gym. Working out is definitely my Higher Power. I'd like to talk about last night's outing in my journal entry today. A bunch of us from the restaurant went to Perry's for sushi and then on to Dakota's to dance. I can't remember the last time I had so much fun.

Rick and I spent some time talking about my addiction and our friends' cocaine use last night. This discussion was the first one I had with Rick since admitting addiction. I remember just a few weeks ago I never wanted to speak with him about it, but things have slightly changed. I can't talk to him about what goes on in the meetings and in counseling or even what I am personally going through right now, but I can talk to him about things in the past. I feel comfortable enough to talk about these things.

Rick and I had a very good conversation last night, but I must confess I am a bit worried about him and Leslie. If Rick only does as much coke as he tells me, and if he was honest last night, then I don't think he has a problem with cocaine right now. The only thing that concerns me is, he feels this compulsion to assure me he doesn't have a problem.

One of the first indications that someone is having difficulty controlling their cocaine consumption is when they begin rationalizing their use to themselves and to others. In other words, they start explaining to you why they don't have a problem with cocaine. As time passes, the rationalizations mount because the guilt and lying increase as well. I instructed Rick last night not to discuss why he uses coke and why he doesn't have a problem with cocaine because doing so is indicative of a problem in and of itself. He agreed with my point and consented to conceal his discussion of it from others.

Another thing that concerns me about last night's conversation with Rick is that he was really shocked when I told him I have been clean for five weeks. He couldn't believe that five weeks had gone by since I admitted addiction. I'm not trying to insinuate that Rick is having memory problems [I certainly started having them], but I am suggesting it is strange that he is so shocked about my five weeks of abstinence. All I can think about is that he probably has never been abstinent for so long and can't imagine being so. This concerns me.

Another topic that concerns me is Leslie. I could write forever on Leslie; however, I will make it brief. Leslie definitely has the cocaine personality, and she certainly has many of the signs of addiction. The only thing that puzzles me is that she hasn't been getting any cocaine lately from the man. I wonder if she has found another dealer. If she *has* found another dealer, she is in big trouble. She will be strung out in no time at all. Leslie has already lied to both Rick and me, as well as to many others, about cocaine use or about cocaine-related topics. On top of this, she is into denying that she is doing certain amounts of cocaine, and she is trying to persuade me that she is keeping clean. I am concerned about Leslie because her behavior is very suspicious.

Getting back to last night, I just want to mention that I had a wonderful time with everyone. Not for one moment did I wish I had any coke with me so that I could get high. I didn't need the coke to get high last night: I had such a great natural high. I haven't danced that much in years and haven't laughed that much in months. The best thing about last night was, I felt extremely comfortable in a familiar scene that had often featured cocaine, without the drug. I think last night proved to be a very positive and important experience for me.

I have to get ready for work now so I'll write more later when I get home this evening. Good afternoon.

MAY 30, 1988

Today my parents, grandmother, sister, and nephews came down to visit. We had a cookout with tons of food as usual. The weather was perfect, which proved to be an added bonus on the day. Everyone loved the house and continued to rave about it all day. We all had a very nice visit together.

There is only one thing that bothers me about today's visit. Every time I looked at my mother, she had a look of worry on her face. Don't get me wrong—I know she had a good time with all of us today, but I could just tell that she was preoccupied with worry about me and my addiction. It really hurts me knowing I am causing her so much worry and possibly pain. All of me just wants to take her aside, hug her, and assure her that everything is going to be okay, that I'll never do any more cocaine, and that I'll never fuck my life up again. But even if I could tell her these things, and even if they do happen, I know she will constantly worry about me.

So now I find I feel terrible in another respect. I haven't only fucked my life up, but I have damaged my parents' lives as well. To know that they will be living with this as long as I will hurts me so very much. I can hardly stand to look at my mother to see the pain and concern on her face. What have I done? I don't have any right to make them go through this. It's too late now. They are consumed with worry about me. I'm sure that a day doesn't go by that they don't worry about me getting back into cocaine. What a burden I must be for them! It just doesn't seem fair. How could I have done this to them? How could I have done this to me?

How long will it take for all of this to go away? When will I be able to look at her face and see the worry gone? Beth told me that this was my probation visit. She said that, after their visit on my birthday in March, my mother said she would never come down to visit me again because of the horrible day we all had. That day was truly horrible. No one had any idea I had been doing cocaine for ten hours. In fact, I did my last line as they were pulling into my driveway.

I remember feeling so miserable that day. I was totally preoccupied with my runny nose, my lack of sleep, keeping away from the cocaine that I still had, trying to hide it all from my relatives, and trying to have fun with them. It was a total failure and it hurts like hell when I look back on it. Someday I'll have to fully discuss everything that occurred on my twenty-fifth birthday with someone who will be able to help me to understand what happened then, because every time I think of that day I just break down and cry. Too many parts of my life during the past year are so fucking painful. When I think of times like my birthday—where my relatives were involved—my heart starts to ache, tears begin to fall, and soon I find I am so upset I can barely do anything but sulk. And it's like the end of this tunnel of pain is so far away.

There are constant reminders everywhere. When I turned on the computer for [my nephew] Phillip today, I opened the top drawer of my desk—only to see remnants of coke in the drawer. I know that Phillip didn't know what this white stuff was, but I did. When I saw those coke remains, a sharp pain went right up through my chest and I gasped for air. This kid thinks I am the most wonderful person. Phillip absolutely idolizes the ground I walk on. He is very intelligent and he wants to be a scientist. He looks to me as a role model because I will soon be a "doctor." What kind of role model is a coke addict? You see, I don't mean to change the focus of this journal entry from my concern for my family members to myself, it's just that all of my emotions are mixed together and it's really hard to separate them. When I start talking about how lousy I feel about the pain I have caused others and the shit I have done to others, I get so upset I soon find myself sitting on that pity pot. I just don't know how to handle it all.

So, Phillip didn't notice the coke remains and I did. I coped with that particular occurrence by suppressing my feelings and by paying a lot of attention to my buddy Phillip. I taught him about WordPerfect, I played tennis and baseball with him, and I listened to the stories he had to tell. And I soon found I didn't feel like such a bad aunt after all. It took a lot of effort today, but I felt like Katy around my family. I hope that my mother thinks I passed the probationary period, and I hope she'll come down again. I hope they all come down again.

I know the pain is not going to disappear overnight. It only hurts me to know how much I have hurt them and how difficult beating this thing is going to be. I guess one of my biggest incentives for staying clean is my family. I will never be able to get rid of the pain I feel for my birthday and for knowing I almost chased my family out of my life. The pain exceeds these two issues because there are many more painful issues and occurrences where these two came from. I just hope one day the pain will become manageable instead of debilitating.

May 31, 1988

I began today with tears. The tears were for the pain I saw on my mother's face yesterday. I called Dean Waldeman when I was thinking about it all today and she invited me to go to the health club with her. I'm glad she invited me to go along because it made me feel much better to be able to talk about my mother with her and to also get my mind on something else. Consequently, I feel much better now.

Music. I'd like to write about the significance that certain songs have in my life right now. Various songs by many different artists have significance with my cocaine addiction. One such artist is Steve Winwood. So many of the lyrics in his songs can be easily tied into my cocaine addiction. I'm not saying that Steve Winwood wrote songs that pertained to cocaine use and addiction; all that I am implying is, I can relate parts of my cocaine life to his music.

Some artists have written about cocaine use, et cetera. These artists include Eric Clapton, who glamorized its use in his song "Cocaine," and Stevie Wonder, who recently told the real cocaine story in his song "Skeletons." It is Stevie's song "Skeletons" that I want to discuss tonight.

Stevie even made a video of the song. The video includes all different kinds of people with their own problems. One woman has a regular job during the day and is a nymphomaniac at night. Another man is a businessman during the day but likes to dress as a woman at night. Another is a homosexual, and another is an alcoholic. The person I could relate to was a very good looking male athlete who was a cocaine addict. The video showed his relatively normal lifestyle during the day, but it also showed him running around behind everyone's back doing cocaine. The people around him were becoming aware of his cocaine addiction, and you could tell by the video his life was becoming chaotic because of the drug.

This song and video send shivers up my spine every time I hear them or see them. I can remember doing all of the things this coke addict did and how terrible it all was. Looking at that coke addict in Stevie's video was like looking in the mirror. Even though the coke addict was a guy, he looked so much like me. This guy was an all-American. He was good looking, athletic, and fun loving. All of his friends liked him. He was a popular guy. Probably no one suspected he was doing cocaine, given the type of person he was. Throughout the video, however, people around him started becoming suspicious of his cocaine addiction. His efforts at hiding this addiction were beginning to fail. His lies were just not working anymore.

Very few people in my environment knew I was having a problem with cocaine. Near the end, however, many people started catching on to my problem. Some people were absolutely shocked to discover I was doing cocaine, and certainly no one even imagined that I had an addiction to the drug. Think about it for a moment. I am a doctoral candidate getting my Ph.D. My master's degree was in the social sciences and so was my bachelor's degree. I do fairly well in academia and have some decent accomplishments. In addition to excelling in academia, I have a tendency to do the same with athletics. I run marathons, ride my bike long distances, and lift weights. I am good in racquetball, basketball, softball, and field hockey.

Most people, I think, would consider me a popular person. I have a lot of friends and always seem to have an easy time making new ones. I guess I am a likable person. My favorite people are kids under 12 or 13 and adults over 21. I absolutely adore children and they usually find me pretty entertaining. I guess the point I'm trying to make is that, given all of these accomplishments, talents, and personality traits, most people never would have guessed I was a coke addict. In fact, many people probably would have laid money on the bet that I had never even tried the drug. What I have come to learn over the past few months, however, is that many more people knew about my cocaine use than I thought.

People were beginning to notice behavior changes such as quickness of temper, short attention span, and restlessness. In fact, many people that I talk to about my addiction today say that they began to see a different Katy emerging and that this Katy wasn't the Katy they previously knew. Many of my friends didn't like this new Katy, and most of them wished that the old Katy would come back.

So, just like that guy in Stevie's "Skeletons" video, I was a well-respected person with tons of friends and lots of talent, but I had this incredible monkey on my back that was changing me for the worse as the days passed. I look at that addict in the video and then I look at myself. We both look pretty ugly, and this is what sends shivers up my spine. The video reminds me of what I did to myself and to others. It is all I can do to sit through the video without crying. I keep seeing a horrible nightmare that just ended a few weeks ago. And a nightmare that I will be living for the rest of my life. And all I can do when I hear this song or see this video is to think about myself. It is these thoughts that make me cringe with disgust and hatred of myself. However, it is also this song/video that keeps reminding me of what life was like as a user—which is currently scaring the shit out of me. The song brings on such strong feelings about doing cocaine, it makes any cravings for the drug disappear. I'm glad I have the tape. Thanks for a wonderful song, Stevie.

JUNE 1, 1988

Today was absolutely fantastic! I began the day with Chrissey in running class at a local college. The class is a bit slow, but I think it will be worth it to attend. If anything, the class will ensure I do some running by 9 a.m. I need to get back on that schedule.

After running class, I came home to write in my journal. I then did something I hadn't done in such a long time. I rode my bicycle to campus and back. It was like I never got off my bike. This is the first time since last year that I have ridden my bike, and the first day I rode 26 miles. Not too bad for a coke addict! I had a good day on campus with Ben, Mary, and Dean Waldeman. I can feel my academic desire coming back to me. Right now I feel out of place at school, but I feel confident in saying that it will only be a matter of time before I am back in full swing.

I rode back home after meeting with Dean Waldeman, made dinner, and went to the gym with Leslie. I guess the topic of the next few paragraphs will be Rebecca once again. Leslie and I saw Rebecca at the gym this evening while we were working out. I used to tell Leslie how, for the past few months, Rebecca has treated me while we were at the gym. Leslie saw it all this evening. She could not believe how much of a bitch Rebecca was to me tonight. Rebecca could not even say hello to me. I did not attempt to start any conversation with her, but I certainly was congenial. At the very end of my workout with Leslie, Rebecca walked over to me and said she saw me riding my bike on Connecticut Avenue this afternoon. I slowly turned my head to acknowledge what she said and just looked at her. She then said to me, "I don't know where you get the energy, girl." I simply replied quite slowly, "Yeah. It's amazing, isn't it?"—and proceeded to exit the gym.

I realize that my reaction to Rebecca's attempt at conversation was pretty cold, but I don't care. I have every right to be cold to her. With all of the fucking around that she has done to me, she deserves to get some of it back. And boy, let me tell you, I'll be more than happy to give it to her. I saw that look in her eyes tonight. She misses me: I can see it written all over her face. She looks as if she is actually afraid to talk to me, and knows how unfair she's been to me and feels so guilty about it. I think the analogy with how Rebecca feels about fucking me over is very similar to how I feel about fucking my co-workers and colleagues over during my cocaine use. I know that cocaine was the reason I did what I did, but I sure as hell do not know what Rebecca's reason is for doing what she is doing.

All I do know is that she has lost her best friend, her roommate, and her job within the past few months—and she's not even doing any drugs. I heard her mention she is going to go back to school now to study whatever. When is this woman going to stop pretending to be 23, and when is she going to wake up and act 33? Don't get me wrong—I think going to college is wonderful and I think Rebecca could do well in college, but I don't think her heart is in it and I want to know what she plans on doing for food for her son Billy.

One of these days my concern for her life will probably disappear, but I'd be lying if I said I didn't care what happened to her. I know she has been so rotten to me, and everyone else knows the same. I don't know what it is about that woman, but I still love her and care about her a lot. This letting-go business is certainly difficult. I know it will get easier. I can feel it getting easier already. I am just not fully prepared to have her out of my life yet. That day is coming, though. Finally, I can feel the rope loosening and the tension ease. I'm not hanging myself with the rope any longer, but it is still around my neck. I think I can live with that right now. Good night!

JUNE 2, 1988

I never really got to finish what I was saying about the role music has had during my addiction. Songs like "Skeletons" by Stevie Wonder accentuate the lifestyle of the addict. I illustrated the relevance that this song has for me in yesterday's journal entry.

Other songs by different artists also have relevance to my addiction. Many of these songs are written by Steve Winwood. Winwood's new tape entitled *Chronicles* is a collection of his best work over the years. I guess the main reason for liking his songs on this tape is because the man and I used to listen to this tape constantly. I refer to my drug dealer, Ricardo, as "the man." One of these days I will try to describe my relationship with him, but not right now. It's all too soon and much too painful right now. There are three songs in particular that symbolize certain things about my addiction. These songs are called "Spanish Dancer," "Help Me, Angel," and "Talking Back to the Night." Each of these songs represents a different stage in my addiction and ignites a separate mood and different emotions.

The first song that I want to discuss—and the one that is the most difficult—is "Spanish Dancer." The man introduced this song to me as his favorite Steve Winwood song. The music in this sets the stage for using drugs. The song has that typical seventies style to it: whiny guitars, smooth bass, and soft lyrics. The song really sounds like it came out of the 1970s drug era, which is probably true. The song always put me in the mood to do coke while I was using; and now when I listen to it, it takes me back to that familiar drug scene. I feel very mellow and relaxed when the song plays. The melody of the song is conducive to this relaxed mode. I can relate the drugs to the style of the music [the instruments] as well as the lyrics.

Some of the lyrics in "Spanish Dancer" sound like a coke trip to me. The music and lyrics to this song are so powerful in suggesting that cocaine high for me. My reaction to this song, however, has changed since admitting addiction. Before addiction, I loved to listen to the song while I was high because it set the mood for the party and was soothing. Now all the song does is remind me what that mood felt like and how miserable the memories of reliving that mood really are. There have been several times recently when I have found myself crying during this song. It's hard to explain how powerful the song is in bringing back all of those memories about using.

The next song I want to discuss is "Talking Back to the Night." I may be a bit off on this one, but I think Winwood wrote it with the coke user in mind. Why do I say this? A very heavy bass beat carries this song. The song is fast paced and climactic. What I am trying to say here is that the music itself is indicative of the fast-paced city and nightlife and a cocaine trip. The nightlife usually features drinking, dancing, and drugs. With the swingy sax, the loud bass, and the escalation of Winwood's voice, "Talking Back to the Night" paints a picture of what people do to keep up with the nightlife, how much people need this nightlife, and what goes on there. All of this suggests cocaine use to me.

I don't feel any particular emotion or mood when I hear this Winwood song. What the song does for me is to paint that all-too-familiar scene of the nightclub filled with pretty people doing cocaine in the bathrooms. I remember those good old days. That's when my addiction was in the recreational stage. I'll have to admit that there are times when I actually try to put myself back in this scene when I listen to the song. When the song plays, I actually fantasize about being out with my friends, looking good, dancing in an exclusive club with all of the pretty people, with plenty of coke in my pockets to keep me up long enough to enjoy the evening's events. "Fantasize" is the key word here. What I have written about above is nothing but a fantasy.

I can't do coke recreationally anymore. I haven't been able to do it like that for a long time. Sad as it may be, I actually do miss that scene at times. The first thing that popped into my mind last Thursday evening when we all went to Perry's and Dakota's was to swing by the man's house and pick up some toot for the evening. In the past, all of that would have qualified for a perfect evening. Today is quite different for several reasons. I can't do coke recreationally anymore because I am addicted to it now. As a matter of fact, I can't do coke at all. Therefore, that quest to pick up a gram from the man would have proved futile because I can't do the drug anymore. And even if I did, I wouldn't have enough money to do the amount I would have needed and wanted. Can you see how very important it is for me to be able to go out these days without cocaine, like last Thursday, and have a good time without the cocaine? I think it's a major accomplishment.

I still see the same scene when I hear the song by Winwood, but it doesn't impress me anymore and it certainly doesn't excite me. Rather, the scene I see painted in the song is one I don't want anymore. I have been there and back, and all I can say is no thank you. I don't need the posh nightclub scene with the coke. I'll settle for the nightclub dancing with my friends. I feel sorry for all of those other ninnies that think they need the coke to make the scene complete. I hope they don't learn the hard way like I did.

The last Winwood song I want to discuss is "Help Me, Angel." "Help Me, Angel," believe it or not, is my song of hope. It is where I cry out my problems to a Higher Power, who—in this case—is an angel. This is the song I identify the most with right now. Sometimes I sing it as a cry of helplessness, and other times I sing it with determination and hope for permanent abstinence. "Help Me, Angel" is such a powerful song. It has a very simple but strong beat that often leaves the listener humming the melody in his head for the rest of the day. I love the way Winwood matches the music with the lyrics in this song. I think the music perfectly illustrates what Winwood is trying to say.

What I find really important about his song—and quite therapeutic—is that it allows me to ask for help and it offers me hope for beating this addiction. It might very well be that I place the song in a different setting every time I hear it, but the important thing is that the song makes me feel okay. I really can identify with it. I can cry to it in many different ways. The crying is for sadness, determination, and hope. Not too bad for one song, huh?

June 5, 1988

I think I have just come to a resolution this evening. Tonight's CA meeting facilitated this resolution. What is the resolution? I have come to grips with the real reason why I have stopped using cocaine and why I had admitted addiction. I have not voluntarily decided to give up cocaine. I have not chosen to abstain from the drug. On the contrary, that choice has been made for me by the responsibilities in my life. On April 24, 1988, I was forced to admit addiction and give up cocaine because I had gotten myself in such a mess that I was unable to undo the damage. It's like I was finally caught. I did not choose to come out of the closet with my addiction and admit my problem to others, seek counseling, and adopt a new identity. I had no other explanation to give for my actions that weekend of April 24, 1988; therefore, I had to admit addiction.

If you can't tell by now, I am really angry. I came out of that meeting steaming tonight. I'm supposed to come out of those meetings feeling good, but tonight proved to fuck that ideology up. Tonight's meeting topic was "Honesty." That one simple word has stirred up so many powerful feelings inside of me right now. I wanted to share in the meeting about how terrible I have been feeling about Leslie's getting fired from the restaurant for stealing. After thinking about how I felt about this situation, which deals with honesty, I began to try to be as honest with myself as I possibly could. At this point, I decided I have not been honest with myself for a long time. Tonight's journal entry is going to be long.

Leslie. The woman was caught pocketing money from a check that she should have keyed in on the documenter at the restaurant. Leslie and I have been doing this for quite some time now. Both of us have been turning over buffet checks, handwriting checks for food and drink, and a few other things in order to pocket a few extra bucks here and there. Leslie and I did this together on Saturday evenings at the restaurant. I can remember Leslie on occasion saying she better fix herself up with 25 extra dollars tonight so she could pay for that quarter gram of coke she already did. I was the same way.

Well, Leslie got caught for it and I didn't. Leslie was punished for stealing from the restaurant by being fired. I was punished for missing work because I was doing cocaine for two days by being suspended for a month from my job. What the people at the restaurant don't know is that I stole from them just as Leslie did. And although it was not a lot of money [$25 here and there], and although I don't do it anymore, it was still very wrong. How can I sit back and let Leslie get fired for the same thing I did? I don't feel too good about that. I deserve to be fired as well. Honesty. It seems that, when the conversation at the restaurant gets to Leslie, Katy has a hard time trying to find that word. I feel this need to be honest about what I did, yet I find I can't.

What else can't Katy be honest about? I still find I can't be totally honest about the details of my cocaine use. I'm still hiding a lot of the truths. I have often told people some of the truths about some of the things I did, but I always get a fucked-up reaction from these people that makes me feel uncomfortable and guilty. My only recourse to this is to keep a lot of the gory details to myself. The problem then becomes my internalizing the things I need to discuss. I get more and more fucked up when I internalize things. Half of the time I say I don't know how to be honest about the things I did, and the other half of the time I am asking myself to be honest, too. Consequently, I am all fucked up.

Another issue I need to be honest about is my addiction. Tonight's meeting made me realize the true reasons why I gave up cocaine. I didn't give it up because I wanted to. I gave up cocaine because I felt I had to give it up. I had fucked up so badly during the last binge that the only way I was going to get out of all the mess I had gotten into was to admit having a problem with cocaine.

Knowing I didn't voluntarily give up coke—but rather felt forced into doing it—scares me a whole hell of a lot. Other people in my group and other addicts at the meetings have discussed this same point. Some of my

KODAK BRANCH

friends in group have confronted me with why I stopped using; and when I explained my reasons to them, they seemed quite ambivalent about my desire for help. Many people think I have not had enough of my addiction. They are insinuating that I am going to go back out there to use and adopt the dope-fiend lifestyle once again. Tonight's meeting brought all of this back to me, and now I am sitting here trying to analyze it all.

Part of me actually does believe I haven't had enough of my addiction yet. I still want to party at times. And although I know these cravings are normal, the strategies I use to suppress them are not quite correct. I mentioned to another person last week that, if Katy wasn't a good enough reason to stay away from cocaine, then my family was or Dean Waldeman was or some other person was good enough reason to do so. I guess what I am trying to say—as honestly as I can—is, I am not keeping clean today because I want it that way. I am not doing what I'm doing today for myself. Instead, I am doing it for everyone else in my life.

Amazingly enough, this strategy is working for me right now. It would absolutely kill my parents and family if they found out I was doing coke again. I would greatly disappoint everyone at school who has afforded me a second opportunity to redeem my standing there. I would let each one of my friends down who has listened to me when I needed to talk and who has helped me when I've had a problem. The bottom line to all of this is, if I would relapse and begin using cocaine again, I would hurt so many people in such a horrible fashion. If I were to relapse tomorrow, I would do irreparable damage to just about everyone who is in my life today. I guess it is pretty clear why I am in treatment for cocaine addiction. I have a big responsibility for recovery on my shoulders, and I am in no position to shirk that responsibility.

This is what scares me. I should be seeking treatment because of me and not for others. I should be staying away from cocaine because it is harmful to me and not only because I will harm others if I begin using again. I do believe that being held responsible for answering to others is functional and good for me. I willingly ask for this responsibility and want to always be reminded of it. However, I only wish that my primary reason for seeking help with my addiction was for my well-being and not for everyone else's—because what in the fuck is going to happen to me when and if these people don't make me answer to them anymore?

I'm scared. I'm being quite honest when I say that my life and my well-being are not worth my staying away from cocaine. It is the guilt I feel today about hurting others that is keeping me away from cocaine. When am I going to start doing this for me? When am I going to start seeking help for my very own benefit and not everyone else's? If I don't soon realize that I am the most important person in the world [to me] and that my life is worth living, I fear I will soon be back out on the streets doing cocaine. I have got to start doing things for myself and not just for others, and I have to do this before I go back out there and use.

Only one thing is going through my mind right now. I do not love myself enough to stay away from something that is likely to kill me. Sad as it may sound, right now I feel that, if there were no one to answer to and if there were no one to make me feel guilty about using, then I would be right back out there using until I severely fucked up my health. I might even use until I had a heart attack or something. I'm sitting here with tears in my eyes right now because I realize how little I care about myself. I don't love myself right now, and I haven't for quite some time. The old Katy used to love herself. What has happened to that Katy? Where did she go?

JUNE 7, 1988

Today I spoke to Carolyn about last night's meeting and journal entry, and she didn't seem surprised at what I had to say. As a matter of fact, it was actually no big deal to her. Carolyn shed a little light on my dismal outlook. She said many of the people that come into her program at the hospital feel the same way as I do. Most people don't give up cocaine because they really want to; rather, they do it for something or someone else in their lives. The main point that Carolyn proceeded to show me was it really doesn't matter why you choose to seek treatment and why you admit addiction. I'm not exactly sure what her rationale for this is, but it has something to do with the fact that, even if you enter treatment for addiction for someone other than yourself, you will eventually come to seek that same treatment for yourself. I guess what she meant to say was, treatment will help you learn and want to do things for yourself and not just for others. I'm placing all of my trust with her right now. I hope this is what happens with me. I want to love myself again real soon. I want to do what I'm doing for myself as well as others. I really want to believe all of this. Hopefully I will understand it all with time. Needless to say, I feel a lot better today.

JUNE 7, 1988, AGAIN

I started the new job today down at the agency. I like it. Heidi, my supervisor, is leaving the office and vacating her position. Consequently, a new opening is now available on the project as well as in the office itself. One of the "big" supervisors was in to talk to me yesterday about my position. He first offered me Heidi's position and essentially asked me to name my price. He also told me that, with Heidi leaving in a few weeks, my responsibilities on this crime project will now include writing as well as data entry and programming. I guess I am excited about being able to write and publish, but I am a bit cautious about the amount of time that all of this will take. I have a lot of work to do this summer and I don't need any extra work I can't handle. I have time for about 20 hours and no more.

Despite this, I did have a good day at the office. I actually felt I had quite a constructive day. I believe this job, along with all of the other stuff I have to do, will help me stay away from the drugs. I know that just being at the office yesterday made me feel good about myself again. I feel confident when I say that, although it will take some time, I will come to like myself again. I can't wait until it happens. I can truthfully say I like myself more and more each day. Make no mistake about it—I do have my share of ups and downs, ins and outs, bad moods and good moods. But despite all of this I can feel the love for Katy grow inside me more and more each day. Who's to say I won't end up a better person because of this? The future doesn't look too damn bad, after all. Wonderful things are coming with abstinence. I just have to remember to think about those wonderful things, give them all of my energy, and not let the shitty stuff bring me down. What a journal!

JUNE 7, 1988, YET AGAIN

I didn't think he would, but then again I didn't think he wouldn't. I sort of expected Ricardo to call me again after the conversation we had at Rick's birthday party, but I sort of knew he wouldn't. He hasn't called and I can truthfully say I am glad. I am glad he hasn't called because it is making abstinence much easier; however, I am also glad he is not calling because he doesn't understand me and I don't think he will any time soon.

He was the one who said we could remain friends even if I chose to give up the drugs, yet he has failed to call me or make any effort to stay in touch. I guess I have all the answers I need. What a shit he turned out to be! I bet he's partying more now than ever. I know he is staying with a friend and not his mother. His mother was always a big obstacle to our partying. I guess he has removed himself from that obstacle. His girlfriend was another obstacle, but I heard she left for Europe the other week; so now I guess he is alone to do his blow. I pray to God that he doesn't die or get busted by the cops. He is so intelligent and is such a wonderful person. Why is he throwing his life away on cocaine? I just want to tell him to get out of it before he loses everything he has, including his life. Who am I kidding? He won't listen to me because I'm an addict and he isn't. Right!!!!!

Today I had a flashback to the time the two of us were in the park studying and doing cocaine. The weather was really nice that day. I can remember sitting with him at that picnic table talking about how nice it was outside. We must have arrived at the park around noon. We had been partying all night at a motel room and now we had to face the day, try to do something constructive, and eventually go to class. This was the evening we cut the ounce of coke. This was my second-to-last binge. It is over two months later and that incident is so clear in my mind. Scary!

We left the park an hour after we got there. I remember not being able to concentrate too well. We got in the car to leave and I asked him to drive. The plan was that he'd drop me off at school for work and class and then he'd come pick me up later that evening. Man, it really hurts right now. I feel sick all of a sudden. An incredible feeling has just overwhelmed me. Can you believe I am actually feeling that high today, right now? God, does it hurt. My stomach hurts, my head aches, I can't sit still, my skin is wet with perspiration, but I feel so cold. I have the chills, yet I'm sweating. What's happening to me? The sweat is pouring from my body. I feel this incredible nausea in my stomach and it makes me feel like I want to throw up. But I can't throw up because I can't breathe. My heart is coming out of my chest. My chest is burning up. It feels like it is on fire. I feel faint. Why can't I breathe? The air has escaped my lungs and I can't seem to take any in. My chest hurts so fucking much. I'm having chest pains right now and can't breathe. Oh my God! The pain is so severe. I want to barf but I can't. I'm panicking. I'm flipping out.

"Relax," he says. "Take a deep breath. Breathe slowly and open your window." I listen to him and wait for the pain and discomfort to pass. It soon does. I can breathe again. I'm not sweating anymore and the nausea has disappeared. I guess I can do another line now. And I proceed to do lines for another four hours, but not so frequently.

I just want to cry right now. That was a heart attack, Katy. You just nearly had a heart attack. You just relived the heart attack you almost had that day in the park. How fucked up are you? You almost had a heart attack and you kept doing lines afterwards!? This is what scares me about cocaine right now, and I think it always will. So close to death and so willing to die—and for what? Another fucking line. It wasn't the only time either. There were two others. How sick and demented can such a drug make you to risk death for more of it? God, that's what cocaine does. Can't you see, Katy? That's what happened to Lenny. Lenny Bias died of a cocaine-induced heart attack. I didn't die, so I guess I am lucky.

Ricardo was with me each time this happened to me. He never prohibited me from doing another line. I don't even think he knew what had actually happened. Do you know what? I probably would have been the same way with him. I probably wouldn't have really understood the severity of what was happening to him because I was so fucked up that I wasn't thinking rationally. I wasn't really thinking at all. All of this just validates my point that cocaine is an evil drug. It allows you to risk death and it allows you to sit there and watch another person risk his life as long as the party goes on. Thank God I am out of it. Thank God I'm alive today.

It's really painful for me to discuss what I have written above. The despair and pain are so overwhelming every time I try to write about incidents like these. I usually end up doing what I'm doing now: crying. I'm not ready to let anyone else know about these incidents, and I don't know when or if I ever will. It takes all I have to just write about these times without falling apart for the rest of the day. Maybe someday the pain will subside, but I actually hope it never does. Funny how it has turned out this way. For a drug that makes you feel so happy and on top of the world, I feel so low right now. The only thing I can remember about my partying days right now are the bad times. I can remember no good times or fun at all. How dare that drug make me feel so good while I use it and so horrible when I don't. I certainly have spelled out the meaning of addiction tonight, haven't I? Good night!

June 8, 1988

I just got off the phone with Jenny. Jenny is a member of my Saturday group. We went to a meeting way out in Maryland tonight, but she couldn't stay because her kids were in trouble. She told me to call her later and I did. We have been talking on the phone for the past hour and a half. I think the conversation the two of us had this evening was absolutely wonderful. She is so together with her addiction. It feels really good talking to her. I can just hear the wisdom about addiction and the confidence she has about her addiction in her voice. I guess I can really relate to her. I'd like to ask her to be my sponsor, but I'm going to wait until the time is right.

Jenny told me to talk about the three times I almost had a heart attack.

When I described these three events to her this evening, do you know what she said to me? She said I overdosed. OVERDOSED! Get the fuck out! Isn't overdose when you die from too much of a drug? I'm alive. How could I have overdosed? Jenny explained it all to me tonight: You had taken in all of the cocaine your body could handle; you had crossed that physiological line, and the only thing that was going to happen was respiratory failure and death. She claims I overdosed. The symptoms I described above were actually an overdose. I told her it couldn't be. I said that, if I had overdosed, why am I alive today!? She said I was just plain lucky. She also said that thank God you were as healthy as an ox. Your body was able to recover and you didn't die.

I'm fucking speechless right now. What can I possibly say? So many things come to my mind—but where do I begin? The first thing that comes to my mind is that I'm alive. I actually lived to tell about those three overdoses. What in the fuck saved my life? Why didn't I die? I'm only realizing now, two months later, how close I actually came to dying. It is earth shattering for me to realize this. I really do believe I could have died. Say it to yourself again, Katy: You almost lost your life to cocaine. You overdosed doing cocaine.

The next thing that comes to mind is—how in the fuck could I have been so blind not to see what was happening to me while I was overdosing? I didn't think I was having a heart attack at the time, and I sure as hell didn't think I was overdosing. How could I have been so ignorant? And to think that this happened three times, and each time I continued to do cocaine after the symptoms disappeared. There is nothing normal about this. This behavior is quite demented. I risked my life three times after overdosing. I overdosed three fucking times and continued to do coke afterwards. I'm definitely sick.

OVERDOSE. Is this a word I have to put in my vocabulary? Is this a word I have to get used to saying? This is a junkie word. This word is for real drug addicts, not for me. Wait a fucking minute. Jenny just told me I overdosed. Therefore, I must be a drug addict. I must be a fucking dope fiend. There is no other explanation. You're out of excuses, Katy. You better just join the crowd and accept the fact that you are a dope fiend. I've been denying this for so long now. I have been denying it even during recovery. I am a drug addict. Katy Hendricks is a drug addict. WOW! Well, do you know what? I don't like being a drug addict. I'll write about this tomorrow. Good night!

JUNE 9, 1988

No, I do not like being a drug addict. I don't like the image it connotes. I don't like the responsibilities it entails. I don't like the other people who are addicts. I just don't like anything at all about being an addict. Addicts have a special vocabulary that I find unacceptable. My vernacular is in no way compatible with theirs. Wait a minute. That is not entirely true. We often speak some of the same words but in different fashions. This is all bullshit. The reason I don't like being called an addict is because I still think I am above all of those "other" people and am better than they are. I do know this is not true, however. But I still have doubts.

Irrespective of what I may say about how the profile of the drug addict has changed, I still think that drug addicts are sleazy, low-down bums who have no intelligence, self-control, or self-esteem. I basically think they are the scum of the earth. Addicts are right down there with psychos and bag ladies and exhibitionists and all those other social deviants. They aren't as bad as hardened criminals, but they are pretty disgusting. It's so damn hard to place myself in that category, although I know I have to do it. I know I am an addict, but I just don't want to believe it. I'll continue this later. It's time to go talk with Rebecca.

I'm back and am in tears once again. Why in the fuck did I think it would turn out any differently? I'm inside my head right now. I can't seem to get out. If I stay here I'll cry all afternoon and night. How much damage have I done? We yelled and screamed and we didn't get anywhere. I expected this to happen, but I didn't expect to be in tears right now. Part of me wants to sit here and sulk about it, and the other part wants to get rid of it all. Face it, Katy—there is no resolving the friendship. It's gone. Just accept the fact that it is gone and there is no getting it back.

On the way back here, I thought to myself, "What if we started from scratch?" What if we tried to start a new friendship and pretended we had never met. What if we tried to start over? I'm so pessimistic right now about it all. Nothing will work for Rebecca and Katy. It's sad that it all had to end this way, but it has and I have to deal with that now. Rebecca has to deal with it too, but I won't see how she fares.

How much of this is due to the cocaine? How much of what she said is actually true? What is the explanation for our situation? Why do the questions continue? If I did fuck up our friendship because I was doing blow, and if she moved away from me because my personality changed because of the coke, then I think I fucked up much more than I think. Yesterday the answers were so clear to me, and today they have escaped me. Is this the drug? Can't someone help me find the answers?

I am trying to read a book that will help me write one of the papers I need to finish, but I can't seem to concentrate. Rebecca is on my mind.

The conversation we had is on my mind. That conversation was very ugly. I don't like thinking about it; as a matter of fact, I wish I could just forget it. I am going to try to put it out of my mind and not think about it anymore. I hope I am successful in doing this. I don't seem to have much patience in writing today either. Right now I am at the point where I don't know what I want to do. I would just like to spend the day at home here, curled up with my books, with the computer at my disposal for whenever I feel like writing.

Can't seem to make much sense of my life these days. I let so many things bring me down. I don't know where I am in my addiction. I don't know what I want to do about it and how I should go about dealing with it. The main problem that I seem to be having is not being able to determine how much of everything that is going on in my life is due to the cocaine. I am still denying the impact that this thing has had on me. I still am unaware of how it has affected me. I still have questions without answers. This shit is getting out of hand. There is no getting back to the old Katy. I have got to do what they tell me to do at the meetings and in the 12 Steps. I have got to grow. I can't turn the clock back and I can't spend my time and energy trying to recapture my old self prior to the coke. The same philosophy extends to my friendship with Rebecca. There is no getting back to square one. That friendship is long gone. There is only my future and her future. And neither of us are in one another's future.

Do you know what? I am boring myself with all of this self-pity right now. I am sick and tired of writing like this. I sound terrible and feel terrible. Stop living like this, Katy. Shape your ass up. Get on with your life. I guess today has been a pretty fucked-up day. Man, do I have my work cut out for me.

June 11, 1988

Tonight's entry will be about what went on in group today. Today was my session. The group and I spent most of our time discussing my problems. Allow me to say up front that, even though a lot of feelings surfaced at group today, and even though the group was very intense today, I felt great as soon as I left it. I poured out a lot of shit at group today, and they helped me deal with it all. They helped me deal with my denial of addiction, and they even helped me deal with the pain I am experiencing with Rebecca. Most importantly, however, they helped me to identify the major fear in my life—which I have kept hidden from every other person.

I don't like being an addict; therefore, I find it difficult to identify with the people in my group because all of them are serious addicts. I am going through a lot of denial problems right now. I don't want to accept the fact that I am an addict and a dope fiend, and I certainly don't want to adhere to the lifestyle it entails. What do I want? I want to stay coke free. I don't want my cocaine lifestyle back, but at times I find I'd still like to party. I also don't want to give up alcohol, but the group insists that this is necessary for a host of reasons. I will trust their judgment on this one and will do what they ask. I don't want to relapse. I do not want to experience any relapses during my recovery. I want to be clean for the rest of my life, but I have to learn to take it one step at a time, which means one day at a time. I want to grow. I don't just want to be sober—I want to grow. I want to be able to deal with my addiction and move on. I want to be at peace with myself.

There are many things that I want from other people and many things I want to do for other people, but right now I need to focus on doing everything for myself instead of just doing it for others. I have got to want to stay clean. I want to do it all for me.

So, group helped me recognize the denial I am going through, and they helped me deal with it. They told me what I have to do, and they let me know how to do it. It was like talking to experts. I have given them my total trust in advising me on how to deal with my addiction. They are all doing so well. I want to be like them.

JUNE 12, 1988

I haven't identified that big fear in my life yet, have I? I wrote about denial above, and I also have a great fear of rejection. Right up there next to rejection—slightly above it—is my biggest fear of all: FAILURE! I want that Ph.D. so badly, yet I am so afraid of it. Getting that Ph.D. means playing ball in the big leagues. I'll be out on that job market next year, competing with all of the promising young professors in the world for any job possible. This is all very scary to me. I have been a student for the past 20 years, eight of which are at the collegiate level. I'm not going to be a student anymore, but a real professional. I won't be able to hide at school and play the student role anymore. I'll be in the big time with all of the other professors in the world. I won't be doing anyone else's research but my own. I'm going to have to do the studies and I'll have to do a lot of good ones, too, in order to get tenure. All this work that I have done so far—and the competition is only going to start when I finish school.

I want it, but I'm scared of it. I'm not scared of the work, but am only scared of how good I'll actually do out there. I want to contribute and I want to make a difference. I want to educate the youth of America and the rest of the world about crime and other social issues. I want it very badly. I am just so afraid of not being good enough. I am afraid of not being the best. Intuitively, I know I will never be the best in my field; but I want to be an expert, I want to be well known, and I want lots of people to read my stuff. I want to do important work to make a name for myself like Dean Waldeman has done, but I also want to do this for others and not just myself. Simply put, I want to save the world, but I want the world to know that I did it. How egocentric, grandiose, and ideological! I bet I sound absurd right now.

Maybe the reason I am so afraid of becoming an academician is because of these expectations I have imposed on myself. When I was up at Montreal, I noticed that everyone was doing good work and that everyone was trying to make a contribution. What's wrong with that, Katy? I call it settling—settling for something that is okay, but not fantastic. I feel as though everyone else in my life has these expectations for me as well, and I will let them down if I don't do things before a certain age. I guess I am a bit confused about how much I expect from me and how much others expect from me. I actually do not like the word "expect." I can't ask anyone for reassurance about how good or bad I am going to do when I finish school. I have to do it all myself. I am on my own in determining my success, and this is what scares me.

I can't run from the pressure anymore, and I can't find something to hide the fear anymore. The cocaine will no longer help me. I don't have the cocaine in my life anymore to prevent me from dealing with the fear and to help alleviate the pressure. I am on my own this time; and if I don't keep it that way, I may end up dead. I need to find a happy medium because my life is too precious to me. Later!

June 30, 1988

It has been a week since I last wrote in my journal. I feel kind of bad about this, but I think my reasons are legitimate. I have been doing a lot of work on my incomplete grades, have been working a lot downtown, and have been running quite a bit. What I want to discuss this evening is my social life. I have been quite busy with work and these papers; therefore, my social life has suffered.

Social life. I used to think I really knew what that was. Social life was hanging out with all the "right" people (my friends), going to expensive restaurants and clubs, and dancing all night long. It was all one big constant party. I used to think I deserved to have this kind of fun every so often because of all the good, hard work that I had done. I also thought I deserved to do cocaine as well.

Thinking back to my days at main campus really makes me angry with myself. I was so disciplined back in those days. I lived on $30 a week for a social life and small-time expenses. I hardly ever went shopping; and if I did, it certainly wasn't to Ann Taylor or even the Gap, but was to stores that didn't even have popular names. I went out one night a week—Friday—and studied every other night of the week. I never felt as if I missed anything by not going out more often, but I always felt cramped for money. I scuffed and scraped my way through main campus and did very well. I graduated magna cum laude in a double major.

The financial constraints I lived with for four years were alleviated when I came to D.C. to do my master's work. For the first time in my life I didn't have to pay for my education. I worked two jobs and soon found I had plenty of money to do as I pleased. Soon I got my share of credit cards and began living the "good" life. It was about this time that I started getting into cocaine.

To make a long story short, cocaine had become a part of my social life—a very big part. Now it's gone. Drinking became a part of my social life, and now that's gone as well. Even though I was never a big drinker, my social life always seemed to involve alcohol. Some of the people I did coke with are fading out of my life. One day they will be entirely out of my life; therefore, my social life is affected once again. What I am getting at is this: I used to have a great definition of what a social life was all about. It used to work very well for me. Many people referred to me as the social director for the lot of our group, but those days are gone. I have to find a new meaning for "social life." My previous definition of it is no longer a reality, but rather just a past phase of my life.

I am looking to make a clean start now, and that means doing a lot of things differently. My social life has to change. I can no longer do coke, drink, and hang out with those so-called friends who did coke with me. I have to find a new type of social life. The idea of discovering a new way to have a social life without causing too much harm is quite difficult for me. It is a task I am not looking forward to mastering. It's not that I am so depressed about giving up the drugs and the booze; it's just that I have a hard time parting with the people. I don't know which ones to say goodbye to and I don't know which ones to hang onto.

You know, I was thinking about what my group said to me last Saturday. They asked me why I wouldn't let them in [why I wouldn't let them get to know me and love me]. I replied that I was too afraid of being hurt again like I was with Rebecca. I thought about that question tonight while I was running, and I came up with another answer. It takes a lot of energy to make new friends. Times like tonight I just ask myself—why invest so much time and energy into making new friends when they will only turn around and hurt you just like Rebecca did? I realize this is a cynical, pessimistic, and defeatist attitude, but I think I am just all tired out right now.

It would be very easy for me to find that new, functional social life right now if I just spent time with the people in group and at the meetings, but that means making a whole new set of friends. I know there are plenty of advantages to making these new friends, but all I can think of right now are the disadvantages of doing so. My social life wouldn't be so complicated if I would just decide which way to go. The problem is that I don't want to have to choose; I want to be able to keep everyone in my life, with only two exceptions. I'm confused.

JULY 2, 1988

Where to begin? Today was spent in treatment. I have devoted Saturdays to treatment. I have group at 1–2:30, private counseling at 4 p.m., and a meeting at 8:30 p.m. Thinking about it all makes me tired. I have to get used to this Saturday routine. Today went very well; therefore, I think I will adjust well to this schedule. It's funny that I began this paragraph with "Where do I begin?" because, after today, I feel as though I am just beginning my recovery. Today is the first day that I can truthfully say I feel in the "fellowship."

When I think about all of the shit I have gone through these past two months by myself, it makes me want to kick myself for trying to go it alone. The fellowship was there all along for me to turn to when things got really bad, but all I could do was run from it. Oh yeah. I said shit like "Well, I can't go tonight because I have to run or work on my papers, but I'll go tomorrow." It's really funny that tomorrow only came on Saturday when group met, and the only reason I went to that group was because I was paying for it. I am also very religious about attending Sunday meetings at the hospital, but this weekend treatment of mine has got to end.

I have got to make time to get to meetings during the week. I have got to consummate friendships with people in the fellowship. I have got to start working on my addiction. I have got to start getting better. It's all really dormant now. Inside I am standing still, making no progress on getting better. The only thing I am doing well right now is not drinking and not drugging. It's really easy to just not drink or drug. What I seem to find difficult is dealing with this addiction thing. Reggie told me today that drugs are just the symptom of some crisis that is going on inside of me. Shit! That's all I need to hear right now. I thought that the drugs were the problem. Do you mean to tell me that there is more?

What is this underlying problem? When will I discover what it is? When will I begin treating it? When will it go away? It's just like Donna said in the car tonight: "You want to be cured right now and you want the answers right now, but it takes time." Naturally, I want to know *how much* time. What is my big fucking hurry? You know, everything I do has to be done as fast as possible. I take no breaks, no time to rest, and no easy way out. The only breaks that I took were to do cocaine. I am constantly running. Running as fast as I possibly can without knowing exactly where I am going. What in the fuck am I running from?

You know, the only answer that pops into my head when I ask that question is this: Katy. I must be running from Katy. Who in the fuck is Katy anyway? I don't think I have slowed down long enough to address that question. I sure as hell don't have an answer to it. Who am I? Sounds like something out of a movie, all corny and shit—but just who am I and what do I want from life anyway? I may not be able to answer it all tonight, but there are a few things I do know right now. I want to be loved and I want to share my love with others. I'd like to begin with my family and move on from there. Funny how I could sit here and list tons of things I want, only to realize the list would never end. I probably would get so caught up in listing the things I want that I would forget about finding out who I really am.

I know I am a drug addict and I know I am a doctoral candidate—but who am I really? Someone tell me, or point me in the direction so I can make the discovery myself, because I'll never be at peace with myself until I find out who I am.

JULY 6, 1988

The days are getting much better. I seem to be enjoying life more and more as the days pass. Each day over the past three weeks has been a good day; many of them have even been great. What's happening here? Am I putting this experience behind me and moving on to better days? I certainly hope so. This recovery bit isn't too bad. I'm beginning to like it.

I can remember all too vividly the first two months of my recovery. I did very little but cry. During those two months, my moods changed faster than a disc jockey changes records. I was utterly miserable. I must have spent at least ten of every 16 conscious hours thinking about my addiction. To top that off, I was dreaming about my addiction in my sleep almost every night. It would be quite a task to sit here and list out all of the emotions I felt during those weeks. The only phrase to sum it all up would be that I fell apart into a million pieces and felt I would never become whole again.

Darkness and despair are all I remember about the first two months of recovery. I was living in a black hole where there was not even a glimmer of light. It seemed as though the hole had no bottom because I just kept falling deeper and deeper into it. Every time I thought I could get out of that hole, something would remind me what I had left outside and would push me back into it. I hated that fucking hole. It ate me up for two months. The worst part of it all was that I gave up the fight to try to get out. So many efforts I made to regain my sanity only proved fruitless. And so I fell deeper and deeper into the hole; mind, body, and soul in a state of utter confusion.

Today, I am 73 days into recovery and I am beginning to see a light at the top of that hole. Day by day I find myself climbing out of that hole and regaining my sanity. Things outside are still trying to push me down into the hole, but I am fighting back now. I'm winning the battle. I have been clean from cocaine for 73 days and haven't had a drink in six weeks. I am gaining my self-esteem back and am feeling really good about myself again. I'm starting to like Katy; and when I try to cry out about all of the shit I did during the months of my usage, I find it hard to do so. The pain is going away. What a fucking relief! I have a lot of work to do, but I am ready and willing to do it now. I am no longer resisting my addiction. I'm no longer allowing myself to let that hole swallow me up.

Who and what gets the credit for this turnaround? Many people and many things are responsible for helping me beat this disease. I feel responsible for making progress in my recovery; however, I know many people have greatly helped me make this progress. My group gets the majority of the credit in helping me turn my life around. They have taught me all about the disease; they have listened to me when I was troubled and have helped me get rid of that despair. But most importantly, they have given their love to me and have asked for nothing in return. They have shown me that a light does shine for me and will lead me out of the hole. I love them dearly and I hardly even know them. Thank God for each and every one of them. I don't know what I would do without them.

Family and friends get a good bit of the credit as well. My family has been nothing but wonderful to me during my recovery. I have never felt closer to them and have never loved them more than right now. I just need to always remember that they will always be there for me, and I need to go to them when I need them. Sometimes I tend to forget this, and I really shouldn't. They deserve the best and I'm going to give it to them. The same holds true for most of my friends—old and new.

July 14, 1988

I am one week away from 90 days and I can't believe the turnaround I have made during that time. My life is pretty close to wonderful right now. It's like something has fallen out of the sky and into my lap. Something so wonderful and beautiful, making me happier as the days pass. Tears just come to my eyes right now when I think about how happy I am. I can't even begin to tell you how wonderful it is to have tears of joy in my eyes, rather than tears of sorrow. I thought my happiness was gone; however, it's coming back to me now.

You know, I can sit here and think about why I am so happy today, and I keep coming up with one answer. Drugs are no longer a part of my life. Ironic as it may sound, when I gave up the cocaine, I found happiness. I actually thought for the past two years that cocaine was making me happy. I was too blind to see that it was tearing my life apart. Wrong! Wrong! Wrong! I spent 20 months of my life trying to find happiness through a drug, only to discover I was an addict. During those 20 months I lived in utter despair and emotional turmoil. My life became unmanageable, and my world fell apart. All I have done during the past three months is say no to drugs, and I find my life is wonderful again.

It wouldn't be honest of me to sit here and say that pursuing that happiness has always been easy. I spent the first two months of recovery crying. There have been times when I thought I wouldn't make it through the day, but I have made it through almost 90 days now. Not too fucking bad, huh? When I was running tonight, I made up this stupid little song and kept singing it to myself. It went something like this:

> You make a slip and you take a step back. You make a slip and you take a step back. Back, back, you take a step back. You take one step forward, you take another step forward, you take the third step forward, and if you say yes, you take one step back. It pushes you one step back. Back, back, you'll go one step back. You made progress today, you'll make progress tomorrow, but if you say yes, you'll take one step back.

Over and over this song went through my head like a drill team singing a rap. And it just all makes perfect sense. I'm making progress today. I've come a long way since April 24th, but it would take only one line to push me one step back. I've taken steps in the direction of recovery—and if I said yes and did another line, I'd just be taking one step back to the road of despair. One step back is one step too many. One step back with coke could be death.

I know things are going well today. I know things will continue to go well for me, but only if I stay clean. It would take only one line to chase away the happiness and lead me back into insanity. So I just have to be humbled by all of this. People may think I am nice, smart, good looking, productive, compassionate, and I may even think the same. But just when I think I am hot shit and think I can just celebrate this one time, I'll be taking one step back—and next thing I know, I will be back to April 24th. I don't ever want to be there again and so I'll keep going to meetings, keep working hard, listen to those who love me, and stay on top of this thing. I will remain humble knowing who I really am and knowing how I must live. I'd place all my money on this strategy in bringing me happiness. It's working thus far.

July 16, 1988

Joni scheduled me for Saturday night this weekend instead of Friday night, and now I'm pissed off. I don't want to work tonight. I have a picnic to attend and I have group and one-on-one with Art. I really don't want to rush it all and work tonight. I could do so many things today if I just didn't have to work at the restaurant.

All excuses aside, I guess the bottom line is I really don't want to work at the restaurant anymore. I'm tired of waiting tables; I have very little fun there anymore; all of the people I like to work with are gone. But most importantly, I just like having weekends off. I can't believe I once said I didn't like the nine-to-five routine. I absolutely love it! I can do everything I like to do in a day with this work schedule. I feel really good when I work it. I really need this constructive environment right now. I get up at 7:30 a.m. leave for work at 8:30, get to work at 9:30, and leave the office between 4:30 and 5 p.m.

Maybe all of this has something to do with liking my new job right now. I like the people I work with, and I like the job I do. My hours are pretty flexible, and my work affords me the opportunity to have time to work on my own projects. This will be especially helpful when I begin working on my dissertation. The point is this: I finally have a real job that I enjoy. This job has come at a perfect time in my life. Everyone is supporting me in taking the job on a full-time basis; therefore, I have announced my desire for the position. The restaurant just doesn't fit into any of this. I don't want to work there anymore. I need to get out of the restaurant business, and I need to do it now.

Things are going very well for me right now. As a matter of fact, they are going extremely well. There are so many more reasons to leave the restaurant than there are to stay. I won't deny that I've had a great time working there these past two years, but the time has come to move on. The restaurant has been very good to me, and for this I am very grateful. I am finally ready to throw myself fully into my career. This is what I both need and want to do, and I'm going to do it. I feel so good doing things this way now. No more cheating, no more partying, no more life in the fast lane, and no more illegal activities. I want to stay clean and I want to lead a good life. Leaving the restaurant will help me achieve this.

JULY 18, 1988

Today was good while I was at work, but turned out to be bad as soon as I left. The reason things turned out so poorly was because of a conversation that I had with Ben. Ben left a message on my machine today, and I returned his call.

You know, I used to have a very good relationship with Ben the first year I lived here in D.C. I was assigned to him as a research assistant where we worked on building the data archive. He has taught me most of what I know today about statistics and quantitative research. I don't know where I would be without him. He is my mentor. I hope one day to be just half as good as he is. To top all of that off, he is quite a wonderful person. He took care of me when I came out about my addiction. I don't know what I would have done without his and Sandy's assistance.

Something is wrong between Ben and me, and I'm not sure what it is. I know he is upset because I haven't sent out the paper I presented in

Montreal. I care to offer no excuse for this. I just never got around to doing it because it always fell very low on my list of priorities. I'll admit I was negligent with this paper partly due to my addiction and my unfortunate trait of overloading. I want to publish this paper, but it seems as though the time is never right.

I'm not going to sit here and make excuses about why I haven't sent the paper out yet. All I want to do is talk about how terrible I feel about my relationship with Ben. My life is pretty fucked up right now. I've been fucking it up for the past year now. Things are finally coming together for me. My head is almost back on straight, and my life has taken a turn for the better. However, I am nowhere near where I want to be. I have so much work to do. I can't do it all right away. Beating this thing takes time, and it has only been three months.

I cried for the first two months and was an emotional wreck. I just can't handle lots of stuff anymore. Some things have to be put on the back burner. One of these things is the paper I presented in Montreal. I do want to send it out, but have to complete other papers first. I also feel it is more important for me to be working on my journal right now, instead of this paper on female crime. I can only assume this is what Ben is upset about.

Maybe he is unhappy with other things I am doing or not doing. I guess I won't know until I talk to him about this. Another confrontation coming on—and all of a sudden I feel like running. Three months into recovery and I am still running from responsibility. I'm not running as much as I used to while I was using, but I am still running too much. I have to close for today.

JULY 22, 1988

I told Sarah about my addiction today. It wasn't a great time and place to bring up the topic, but I felt as though the situation almost demanded it. Initially, I felt better when I told her I was an addict. She even told me that she has a relative who is combatting the same problem. However, since I left work this evening, I have been doubting whether I should have told her or not. Here is my assessment of the situation.

When I told Sarah I was an addict, I began to cry. This is a familiar reaction for me. I wish I could change my reactions, but I can't seem to contain the emotions when I tell someone I am an addict. She sympathized with me, and she even gave me all of the responses to my announcement that I anticipated. She promised confidentiality and support, and expressed respect for my obtaining treatment and trying to get my life back together. I told Sarah I didn't decide to confide in her because I needed someone at work to discuss my problems with. Instead, I told her because she is becoming a good friend; therefore, I feel I must be honest with her. She replied that she was touched I felt I could confide in her and was pleased to know we were becoming good friends.

Somehow, I still feel as though she is not happy with knowing this about me. I guess I need to relax. I have barely given her time to take all of this in and try to understand it. I have the utmost respect for her. I think she is a wonderful person; I am proud to have her as a friend and feel privileged to be one of her friends. I just don't want this to change anything between the two of us.

You know, you should never underestimate the power of addiction. Addiction is something you live with every hour of the day, every day of the week, and every week in the year. I want so badly at times to not be an addict, to never have had this experience that has torn me apart. The reality of it all is that I am an addict and I have had this devastating experience. More important than that is, I will always have to deal with situations like the one I experienced with Sarah today. I hope and pray that I will be able to handle these situations the best way possible in the future. I hope and pray that my strength to handle this addiction increases as time passes, and I hope I will always be fortunate enough to experience friendships like the one I am developing with Sarah.

AUGUST 2, 1988

This weekend was fantastic! I spent all day Saturday with Sarah. We went for a 65-mile bike ride and then struggled to the restaurant for dinner. I think we will both do fine on our trip up home. I hope she enjoys the ride and visiting my hometown.

Today's entry is primarily concerned with the Sunday-night CA meeting I attended at the hospital. I really do love that meeting quite a bit. I always feel so good when I leave it. I like the people that go there and I always seem to like the speakers. This past Sunday at the meeting, the subject of helping others to beat their addiction came up. A good bit of the meeting was spent discussing this topic.

One of the ladies at the meeting said she was having a very hard time watching the people around her destroy their lives on drugs. When this lady shared, everyone at the meeting listened and did so in a very attentive fashion. Many people shared similar experiences after this, and the meeting went on to finish on the same topic.

You know, helping other people is one of those very natural things in life. Somewhere along the road of growing up, most of us are taught the virtues of kindness and caring. It only seems right to help other people in times of need. They in turn usually return the favor. Drug addiction is one big problem that demands a lot of attention. Drug addiction is a disease that is permanent and progressive. Drug addicts have great potential to harm both themselves and others. It is for these reasons that drug addicts need help.

I may not have written everything I wanted to write in that last paragraph, but the point I am trying to make and that everyone at the CA meeting was trying to make is that the drug addict has to help himself. The addict has to decide when he is ready to start facing life as a recovering addict and to cease active addiction. The first step comes way before this, however, in that the person who is abusing drugs has to admit that he has a problem. The point is that the person has to want it, the person has to have the desire for a drug-free life.

Unfortunately, there is very little we can do for the addict until he reaches this decision. We can't force people into treatment, and we can't make them get treatment for someone other than themselves. Addicts have to do this for themselves. Many people don't think they are addicts. Other people just aren't ready to give up the lifestyle. Irrespective of people's reasons for not seeking treatment, the point is that those of us who are in treatment can't really do much for those people who are not ready for treatment. This fact can be very painful.

Imagine knowing that someone is taking himself close to death every night when he is out doing cocaine and that you could get a call from the hospital at any time. Imagine knowing that someone is so powerless over some drug and unable to stop it from destroying his life. Imagine watching someone play with a drug just like you did at the beginning and then tell you he can handle it. Imagine watching people lose their self-esteem and dignity over some fucking white powder.

Man, all you can do is want to help, but you just can't. Of course, you can be there to drive the person to the hospital when he overdoses, but you can't tell him not to get into that position. Active addicts don't hear anyone but themselves; therefore, your words of advice and concern are fucking useless. What a slap in the face. What a knife in the gut. You want to help but can't. And so, even if you are doing well in recovery, you are still powerless. Even when you want to help someone else with their problem, the addiction has rendered you powerless to help someone else who is using, who is also powerless as well. Pretty fucking debilitating, huh?

AUGUST 3, 1988

There is a movie out now about addicts in the fellowship. The movie is called *Clean & Sober*. I haven't seen the movie yet—just previews. It all looks pretty familiar to me, but I get the impression that it will be greatly sensationalized. I don't really care about this movie. I don't care if it educates the public or not, and I don't really care if it does injustice to my addiction and the fellowship.

If there is one thing I want from the movie, it is that it had better not have a happy ending. The only message the movie should get across to everyone else in the world is that drug addiction is a permanent condition. There is no cure for the drug addict. I will be a drug addict for the rest of my life, and nothing will ever change that—no matter how long I stay clean and no matter what treatment I get.

What I mean by my statement concerning happy endings is that the drug addict doesn't have a happy ending to his addiction. Each of us faces our addiction every single day of our lives. If there are any endings to addiction, they are sad ones where people have died from overdoses. The point I am making is that each day can have a happy ending to it, but you can only go one day at a time. This notion of a happy ending is nonexistent.

If you wake up in the morning like me and say to yourself, "Don't pick up [drugs]—and get to a meeting," then things get considerably easier after that. If you stay drug free for the day and if you get to a meeting, then your day has had a happy ending. The only thing is that you have to go through the same shit the next day. Your happy endings can only come one day at a time. Each day that you don't use is a wonderful day, but it doesn't end there and it never will. Drug addiction is a permanent condition you must face every day. Each clean day that you have is one day more than you had before.

And so this is the true story of addiction. This is the only message that I hope *Clean & Sober* conveys to its viewers. An addict's happy endings come one day at a time and no faster than that. It is with this fact that the addict must learn to live. I've been doing it for almost four months now and it's not too bad. There is happiness in life for me; but [the struggle for] it never ends, and it never is accomplished. I fight for it day by day and like doing it. I wouldn't have it any other way.

AUGUST 14, 1988

Dear Christopher,

I wanted to tell you this while we were walking in Old Town, but somehow I just couldn't tell you at that time. I am very sorry for my behavior on Saturday. I should have altered my schedule in order to better accommodate both you and Nancy. I hope you will forgive me for being an asshole. Sometimes I think that being an asshole comes pretty naturally to me. I'm sorry.

There is no denying the fact that I am pretty self-absorbed. I am even more so these days than usual because I am not too happy with myself right now. I am constantly thinking of better ways to improve myself so I may like myself one day. Therefore, if some of my behaviors piss you off, I would greatly appreciate your letting me know. I love you dearly and would do anything for you. Sometimes I just get so wrapped up in the things I want to do, I forget about doing what others may want or what is right to do.

It really bothers me knowing you feel as though you intrude into my life when you come here to visit. I can understand how I did that during those months of cocaine use, but I can't understand how I give you that impression now. I guess I should just be a little more accommodating to my guests and a little less egocentric. I'm trying really hard to change, Christopher. Therefore, please be patient with me.

I couldn't help but remember your last visit when you and Nancy came down for my birthday. All of those horrible thoughts about that weekend when you and Nancy were here just came back to me, and I just couldn't get rid of them no matter how hard I tried. I feel as though I really hurt the family that day, and I won't let myself forget about it. I'm crying about it as I sit here and write. I realize that the incident is in the past and that you all may have forgotten about it, but I just can't seem to do so. It does matter to me that you and Nancy, as well as everyone else in our family, forgive me; but that forgiveness is not going to get rid of the pain I feel for that day. The pain I feel for my twenty-fifth birthday is something I will have to work out.

And so I find myself wanting you back here at my house so we could try to have a better time together. I promise that things will go better the next time that we are together. I'll see you on Friday at Mom and Dad's. Please remember to bring the bicycle rack for me. I love you very much!

Katy

AUGUST 16, 1988

I just feel weird right now. I just got back from a meeting downtown on K Street where something pretty bothersome occurred to me. I have had really strong cravings for cocaine during the past two weeks, and until today I wasn't sure why I was having them. So I spent the entire meeting deciding between two theories I conjured up to explain the craving for cocaine.

It has been 111 days since I did my last line of cocaine. I can remember vividly the strength of my cravings during the first month of clean time. I used to get so uptight because they were so strong. My cravings for coke basically stopped after that first month. Now it is almost four months into recovery and I find I am craving the drug once again. Craving cocaine is debilitating. All it takes is a craving for one single line to throw you back over the edge into active addiction. Decide to do one line and you get the entire lifestyle back—with all of the horror. It is this fact that makes abstinence very difficult during those times when you crave cocaine.

So, I have been spending the past few hours trying to determine the reasons for this craving. I have developed two theories. The first theory has to do with the meetings. I really haven't been attending many meetings during the past two weeks. I have blown off two consecutive Sunday meetings at the hospital and have attended my group counseling one time in the past three weeks. I will miss group again this week because of my trip up home with Sarah.

You know, they must say "Keep coming back" in the meetings for something. There must be a reason beind those words. There has been no real excuse for my not attending. I have been busy lately, but I still have time to attend meetings. I have just been doing other stuff with friends, instead.

I didn't crave cocaine today, and part of me wonders if it was because I knew I was going to attend a meeting this evening. One thing is for sure: The meetings are supposed to help the addict with problems like this. And to tell you the truth, it is only by attending a meeting that I can get rid of the desire to do cocaine. If this theory is an adequate explanation for the recent cravings I have been experiencing, then I think a very simple solution can be reached to ward off these cravings. Get to more meetings, Katy.

Somehow, I just don't think that the explanation for my recent cocaine cravings is that simple. Theory two is a doozy! I really wish it was totally wrong, but I have a feeling it is the proper explanation for my cravings.

I'm under a lot of pressure right now. The pressure I am under is greater than it was during the first two months of my recovery. I can only see this pressure escalating in the near future. I remember what happened to me last winter when I was under too much pressure. I did a lot of cocaine. I did cocaine every time I felt the pressure escalate and every time I wanted to escape from it all. I was constantly escaping the pressure in my life by using cocaine during the last eight months of my addiction.

Now, I just try to imagine what my life is going to be like this fall, and all I can see is that big old pressure cooker I despise. This is the first time in my student career where I will be working full-time at a real job and attending school full-time as a doctoral candidate. I'm not sure how well I will handle this schedule. I also have to attend meetings, keep in shape, and try to have some fun. I'm feeling like wonder woman again right now, and that scares me because I know I fuck up when I assume the role of wonder woman. So what do I do to prohibit myself from falling into that pressure cooker?

I can't do coke. I can't rely on cocaine anymore to take me away from that pressure and the responsibilities that will follow. I'm an addict now, and drugs are a no-no. What other recourse do I have to handle this all? I could go to more meetings, but I will have less time to do so in the fall because of the schedule I plan to entertain. Great! This means I will attend fewer meetings than I am currently attending.

Thus, theories one and two come together. What will I do when the pressure becomes too much and I want to get rid of it? How will I handle the pressure? I am likely to think I can only escape with cocaine; therefore, I probably will crave the drug more often. The problem is that only the meetings can help me handle the cravings and I will not have much time to get to them. Right now it seems as though I will inevitably turn to cocaine. You know, a lot of times when I write about a problem on this computer, I usually figure the answer out myself. Well right now I am at a loss for a solution to this growing problem. I guess it is time to seek some help in answering this problem. The only solution I can come up with right now is a dysfunctional one. I need to turn this problem over to someone who can help.

AUGUST 29, 1988

What a month! I haven't been keeping my journal. Dean Waldeman says that this is because I am getting better and don't need to write in it as much anymore. I agree, but would still like to write in it at least three times a week. I need to keep up with it because right now I could write about so many things, but would never have the time to write about them all.

What's first? You know, I'm having a lot of problems with my group right now. Their idea of how I should handle my disease is different from my idea. Frankly, I feel as though it really doesn't matter how they think I should handle my addiction. On the other hand, I feel as though they have helped me quite a bit and I value the advice they give me. I also think it is useless debating how one person should handle his or her addiction, and my group is bent on this notion of trying to dictate to me the proper way of handling mine. I believe it is the person's disease, and that person should handle it the best way he or she sees fit. In addition to that, each person is different; therefore, things work differently for different persons.

There is no specific goal that all of us [addicts] try to reach. And even if there were a specific goal for which we strived, we would do it at our own pace and through our own means or our own interpretation of the fellowship. The only thing that we all share in common is the desire for a drug-free life. Being drug free is something that happens one day at a time. You wake up in the morning and say to yourself, "Don't pick up any drugs and don't have a drink today"—and soon you find that things get easier after that. You have a "where and when" schedule for AA, CA, or NA meetings, and you try to get to one if you want or need to do so. Some people need to go to a meeting every night, and others don't.

I have very little in common with my group members. In fact, the only thing I do have in common with them is drug addiction. Oh sure, we share similar horror stories and we all fucked our lives up, but that's where the similarities among us end. I don't need to attend meetings every fucking night of the week like some of them do, and I am doing fine without a sponsor. I haven't had any cocaine in close to five months and I seldom drink. My life is coming back together and—for the first time in over a year—I am happy.

So what does it matter if I only attend one or two meetings a week? The meetings I do attend are very helpful. If I'm hurting one day, I make sure I find some help by calling a friend or going to a meeting. How much does it matter that I place my addiction third on my list of priorities, behind school and work? I know my addiction demands attention, but I just can't take time out from school or work to deal with it as much as some people think I should. The bottom line is this: If I concentrate on my addiction so fucking much, I'll neglect the other more important things in my life that keep me going. This will make me unhappy, and if I am unhappy, I'll definitely use drugs again.

Sometimes it seems as if there is no solution to this predicament in which I'm involved. I know there is no cure for addiction, but I know what progress is. I never want to do cocaine again. There was a time in my life when I said I would always want to do coke, but things have changed. I also have a different lifestyle now, in which drugs can play no part. I like this new lifestyle more than any other one I've ever had. I also want to do research and work with addiction—and certainly can't do that while doing drugs.

The reasons could continue, but the theme remains the same: I want a drug-free life and I have had one for nearly five months now. When I need help, I go get it. I know what I can and cannot handle now, and I know cocaine is not a solution to any problems I may encounter. I think of the serenity prayer:

> God, please grant me the peace to accept the things that I cannot change, the courage to change the things that I can, and the wisdom to know the difference.

What's wrong with that?

AUGUST 31, 1988

You know, sometimes I just fucking wonder why I have these goddamn dreams. My day went as expected yesterday. In fact, it turned out to be a bit better than I had anticipated. Everything was going great until I went to bed last night at 12:30 a.m. I woke up at 4 a.m. from a bad dream, fell back asleep at 4:30 a.m., and woke up this morning thinking about the same fucking dream. I really don't feel as if I slept at all last night. The only thing I think I did was dream about cocaine. I'm really getting tired of this. Dreams like this wreck my whole fucking day. Listen to me. I sound very angry, don't I?

The dream is vivid in my mind right now. My mind is totally consumed with thoughts about it. He overdosed in my dream. I remember a bunch of us sitting around talking about how much cocaine he was doing. I remember police in the background. I remember my friends doing cocaine. I remember everyone's faces in the dream, but somehow I can't place their names. My mother was there keeping her eye on me and lecturing me to stay away from cocaine. Everyone had their eyes on me, yet I was clean. Why were they watching me?

All I could think about was Ricardo. He had just called me to party with him, and I turned him down. Somehow I knew he had contacted a few other people to party as well and everyone said no. The police were even looking for him and were keeping their eyes on me in hopes of busting him. I could see him doing the cocaine. I saw every line he did. He was in his bedroom with a nightstand beside his bed, doing tons of coke. I watched it go up his nose. I watched him cut lines. I kept looking at the bag he had in front of him and found I just wanted to take it away from him. But he just kept doing lines and I tried to yell to him to stop, but he couldn't hear me because I was yelling at him through my dream. He continued to party.

I tried to break through my dream to rescue him—but just as I was on the verge of exiting my dream and entering his room, he overdosed. I stopped in my path to look at him. He looked lifeless, dead. And so I just stayed in my dream and looked at him.

The cops broke into his room and rushed him to the hospital. I continued to watch him from my dream and saw him lying on a gurney with a ton of IVs in his arms and hands. I tried to talk to the nurses from inside my dream, but they couldn't hear me. They didn't respond to my questions. Why weren't they listening to me? Why wouldn't anyone give me any answers? I just wanted to know how he was doing.

And so I went back to the room in which I had been sitting, and Rick came to me and said that Ricardo overdosed. And I told Rick that I knew he had. Rick asked me how I knew, and I said that I had just witnessed the entire scenario in a dream. And we both looked at each other in total amazement.

The police caught wind of my dream and came to me with questions. They kept insisting that I give them more information, and I proceeded to give them all that I could. They pursued further questioning and I tried to oblige them. But I was becoming more and more upset as the questions continued. I asked them to leave me alone and they wouldn't do so. They kept asking and asking and asking. I asked my friends around me to tell them to stop, but not even my friends listened to me. Why were these people treating me like this? What did I do to deserve this?

And so I woke up and looked at the clock to see that it was 4 a.m. I went to the bathroom and then lay back down. The dream continued as soon as I fell asleep. It got worse. This time, there was a familiar female doing lots of drugs in a house. I know this female but I just can't seem to place her face or recall her name. I'm positive that I know this woman.

The woman kept inviting men up to a room in this drug house for sex. She had just invited a famous rock star up to her room, but I can't remember his face or name either. It's right on the tip of my tongue, but I just can't seem to remember. Just when this guy thought he was going to score with this chick, she went over to a closet and pulled out a can from a large stack of cans. The closet was packed with cans of this type. She opened the can and poured out ounces of cocaine. The cocaine looked good. It was dirty and rocky—just like I had it the last time I did it. They began doing lines for foreplay, and soon they were doing them constantly. Their desire for sex soon vanished and they continued to party.

He was cutting lines for both of them. He cut himself a few large ones and did them, and then she told him to cut her only a few small lines. Instead, he cut her so much cocaine that it probably would have covered a dinner plate. She was about to stick her face in it and I tried to yell to her from my dream not to do it, but she stuck her face in it anyway and did it all. About three seconds later, she started having seizures and he just sat there and watched her.

She was sweating profusely and was gasping for air. She put her hands on her heart and tried to utter, "It hurts so bad." She was rolling all over the room. Her seizures took her from one side of the room to the other. She was totally out of control. I yelled at him from my dream to help her, but he didn't do a thing. I told him exactly how to help her, but he just sat there. All he had to do was get her some water and comfort her. He just had to hold her in case she stopped breathing, but he couldn't even wipe the sweat from her brow. Why was he doing this to her? Why didn't he listen to my instructions? Why didn't he help her?

She died.

Interpretation: Part 1. I have an anxiety complex about people watching me to see if I'm doing cocaine or not. This is a product of my addiction. I can remember, while I was using, I was constantly concerned about hiding my use from others. It got to the point at work where, if I came to work in a good mood, they thought I was high; if I ran at the mouth and sniffed my nose too much, they thought I was using on the job; and when I came to work in a bad mood, they figured I had been up all night partying. I just couldn't win. In addition to these things, I also worry what people will say if they find out I have missed a meeting or other type of treatment. They probably think I am going back to using drugs.

My interpretation of part one is that I am tired of people watching me. They should be concerned about people like Ricardo. Also, a part of me actually wants to see something bad happen to him because I believe that my current condition is partially his fault. He enhanced my drug addiction by providing it to me all of the time. I know I made my own choices and decisions, but he greatly influenced those choices and decisions. I regret the friendship even though I may speak kindly about him.

Part 2. This part of the dream was a reenactment of the three times I overdosed while with Ricardo. Each time I overdosed, he just sat there and watched. He didn't do a thing. He didn't even stop me from doing cocaine. He just kept putting more in my face. Fuck him! Didn't he care that I was about to die? Didn't he see what was happening to me? Didn't my life mean anything to him? This part of the dream is where I have finally started dealing with those overdoses. I have never tried to deal with them before, but I guess I should start doing so now. I guess the girl in the dream was me and the rock star was Ricardo. I never intended to sleep with him, but I guess I would have done so at some point to get the drug. Sick story, huh?

September 9, 1988

Last night I had a strange one, but it wasn't as devastating as the one I described above. Maybe last night's dream was a response to all of the financial pressure I am under right now. You know, someone once asked me how many times I wake up while I am sleeping, implying that this was an indicator of stress. I replied, usually two times. This was the case last night. I think the stress in my life is mounting at a rate too fast for me to handle. Consequently, I am having dreams about using. Last night's dream was simply a case in point.

I was with Sarah's brother Vincent last night in my dream. I can remember Vincent not looking too well. He just wasn't as good looking as he was the last time I saw him. He was very thin, almost frail. His face was wrinkled, and his hair wasn't combed. He was sloppily dressed and his clothes were dirty. Somehow, Vincent's appearance shocked and concerned me, but it really didn't matter. I felt very strongly about him. His appearance didn't hinder my feelings for him. I can remember being very attracted to him last night in my dream and wanting to be with no one else but him.

Things didn't turn out the way I had planned. I planned for the two of us to have a nice evening together, but somehow we ended up at Ricardo's house and spent the evening with him and a few others. I remember there was a lot of traffic at Ricardo's place because of his drug sales. People were constantly knocking at his door and coming in and out of his apartment. There was this one guy, in particular, who kept knocking at Ricardo's door. Ricardo let him in the first time and took him into the back room. I assumed he sold him some cocaine because the guy flew out of the apartment on his merry way.

About an hour later, the same guy came back again, knocked on the door, and demanded to see Ricardo. Ricardo did not want to let him in and told him to go away. The guy begged Ricardo to let him in, and eventually Ricardo did. Ricardo sold this guy some more cocaine and sent him on his merry way. The guy came back a few minutes later begging for more cocaine. This guy was becoming a nuisance. Ricardo refused to let the guy in this time, and he proceeded to threaten Ricardo.

The guy became very loud. He was screaming at the top of his lungs, "Let me in or else"—and he banged so loudly on the door, the neighbors began to telephone Ricardo to complain about the noise. I kept saying to Vincent, "Let's get out of here before someone calls the cops." But Vincent just sat there without saying a word. I said to Vincent, "Let's leave right away." I begged him to leave Ricardo's with me, but he wouldn't do so. I knew it would only be a matter of time before the cops busted in, so I wanted to leave. This guy outside was becoming unbearable, and I knew it wouldn't be long before someone called the cops to complain about the drug activity upstairs.

All I could think about was being in that apartment with Vincent, Ricardo, this irate addict, and a pile of cocaine that I was sure was hidden somewhere in the apartment when the cops came. All I could think about was being busted for drugs, losing my job, dropping out of school, and disappointing everyone in my life. All of this would happen to me if I didn't get out of that apartment right away, but Vincent didn't want to leave and so we stayed.

The cops came, but not before that irate addict broke down the door to beat the shit out of Ricardo and take his drugs. I watched this addict smash his fist into Ricardo's face and stomach time and time again. He broke Ricardo's skin and the blood went everywhere. Ricardo fell unconscious to the floor and lay in his puddle of blood. The addict pulled a knife on Vincent and me and told us to stay away from him as he proceeded to get this huge bag of cocaine from Ricardo's bedroom.

The addict stopped in the room in which Vincent and I were sitting and stuck his face right into that big bag and just inhaled. He did this for about a minute and then stopped. He got up to leave the apartment and then began to have seizures. He flew around the room until he collapsed from respiratory failure and fell to the floor. The cocaine was now all over the room with two people flat out on the floor. The police came in at this point.

Vincent and I were busted. We were arrested, yet we were innocent. And as I was walking to the police car with my hands cuffed behind my back, all of these familiar scenes came back to me. I saw myself at school with friends. I saw myself at Christopher and Nancy's wedding, and I saw myself with Sarah at work. And all I could think was that my life was over. I was innocent yet still charged. And this is the story of my life in recovery: clean from cocaine, but still haunted by its memories.

PART TWO

September 15 through December 16, 1988

Friends, family, and work became less important during the next three months. It was all I could do to get through the day without using. The cravings for and dreams about cocaine continued, which both angered and frightened me. It became more difficult to make it through a day without using cocaine.

I knew I was very close to relapse, but spent many days thinking and fantasizing about cocaine anyway. I resented other people around me who could still do it, and I resented myself for becoming an addict and doing all of the horrible things I did while using. But what I resented most was sobriety. I resented sobriety, but I knew I had to be sober. It was difficult.

Somehow, I managed to stay clean, and celebrated six months of sobriety. But it was anticlimactic. At the time, I didn't think six months of abstinence from cocaine was much of an accomplishment. Instead, the celebration was a reminder that for me, sobriety would be hard and permanent: I was going to have to keep staying sober for the rest of my life, day after day after week after month. So I went in and out of the black hole. I desperately wanted to close the door on my past and became frustrated that I could not. By the end of the year, I wanted to give up the fight to stay clean. I just wanted to get high.

SEPTEMBER 15, 1988

A lot of things have been happening lately, some of which I am concerned about and others I am not. I have been dealing with the issue of leaving group for quite some time now and I think this Saturday will be my last time there. In addition to handling the group decision, I also have to decide whether to take this job or not. I had my mind made up for the past two months about it, but things have changed. I thought the job would have a bigger salary than it does. The proposed salary is a $5,000 drop. The only other thing on my mind right now is my schoolwork. I need to find a way to deal with my new schedule and lifestyle.

The first problem I am going to deal with is the job. I am going to take Sarah's advice right now and make a list of pros and cons about taking it. Here's the list:

Pros

1. Good research experience
2. Fun people to work with
3. Set schedule with real paychecks about $1,250/month
4. Gives organization to my life
5. Good educational experience
6. Feel as though I am doing important work
7. Gets me out of restaurant business and somewhat out of student lifestyle
8. Insurance coverage
9. Makes me feel good about myself

Cons

1. The commute to work is killing me in terms of time and money
2. Thought I would be paid $29,500 and am only getting $24,500—greatly tightens my budget
3. Have to pay my own tuition
4. Makes my schedule much more regimented
5. Can't work at school

Issues Outside of Work

1. Learning to handle my schedule
2. Getting to meetings
3. Financial security?

September 20, 1988

Dream. So now my cocaine dreams include my family members. What next? When I write and think about this dream, only one word comes to mind: powerlessness. You'll get the picture as I begin to describe it to you.

My grandmother lives in a big green house in a small town in Pennsylvania. The house is very old. It is the one in which she spent her entire life and she is 70 years old. The house needs work done on the outside and my father says that her plumbing is nearly shot, but the place is immaculate inside. Houses like this one just aren't built anymore. Each room in the house is huge. The house has two living rooms, a dining room, kitchen, three bedrooms, a foyer, a basement, an attic, a balcony, and a huge bathroom with a cast-iron bathtub. Needless to say, many items in the house are antique and all are perfectly kept.

The house sits on a street that is five houses away from the church that my grandmother and my whole family attended throughout our lives. My grandma's town is about 12 miles outside of my hometown and is very small. It consists mainly of farms, but there is a small residential community there as well. There are very few new structures in Grandma's town. The most contemporary things there are a trailer park and a Minit Mart. The town has two churches, two bars, a bank, a schoolhouse, and a fire hall. That's about all that my grandma's town has to offer its residents except for a few parks.

My grandmother is well known there, but then again everybody is well known there. Everybody knows everybody in Grandma's town, and the only time strangers come to town is when there is a horse show or polo game up behind the cemetery that lies behind my grandmother's house. Not even many tourists for the Amish country come out this far to see the backward culture.

My grandmother's house is the only green house in her town and is, therefore, a well-known house. I have always loved this house. It is a perfect country home that sits in between a church five doors down the street and a one-room schoolhouse three doors up the street. I always loved going out to visit my grandmother because she had so much land on which we could play and she lived about 100 yards from a playground with a seesaw, basketball court, and a baseball field. It was even exciting to go out to her house on Sundays—despite having to go to church—because we usually got to go see a polo game and have homemade ice cream. Going to the country meant leaving our cramped city row house for peace and quiet in the country where freedom seemed almost endless. It was just so peaceful out there at Grandma's house.

In my dream last night, my grandmother was sitting on her stairway that ran from the foyer and wound its way up to the next floor, and she was crying. My grandmother was crying, crying her heart out. I have never seen my grandmother cry before; in fact, I have never seen her express much sadness at all. My mother was sitting with her and was trying to comfort her. I was watching both of them and was trying to find out the reason my grandmother was crying.

And so I asked my father what was happening and he told me my grandmother had lost her house. He told me these drug dealers had bought my grandmother's house from her landlord and planned to move in next week. And I just stood there listening to what my father said and found that I just couldn't believe any of it. I said, "Come on, Dad, drug dealers out here? Why would they want to take Grandma's house, and why would they want to live way out here?" My father proceeded to show me it was true. My grandmother had lost her house to a couple of sleazy, slimy drug dealers.

I just couldn't understand how it could have happened. How could they have taken her house? Why were they doing this to her? The woman never did anything illegal in her life and she never harmed a soul. It just wasn't fair. Why was this happening to her? And so I ran around the house looking for answers to this predicament, but was unsuccessful in finding any. Then I decided to call the real estate agent to try to get the house back. He was so arrogant with me on the phone. He told me there was nothing I could do. He said, "Your grandmother's house is no longer hers. She must be completely out of the house in a week." And so I said to him, "How could you let this happen? You have been her agent for years now. You have seen this family grow in this house and you know how much it means to her and to all of us—so how could you let this happen?" He hung up the phone.

And so, realizing that what my father said was actually true—that my grandmother had lost her house to a couple of drug dealers—I walked over to her and sat down beside her and began to cry myself. I tried to comfort her, but she was just too devastated to absorb any of my compassion. So I looked at her and noticed just how beautiful she was. I loved her so much. She had done so much for me, and now I couldn't do anything for her. She had just lost everything she had worked so hard for. Somehow I knew deep down inside that losing the house meant more than just losing a house. It meant losing her life. That house was her foundation, and it stood firmly because she had breathed life into it. But now it was gone.

The movers came to take her things away. She stood by solemnly staring as she watched her life disappear. We all stood there watching these people come in her front door and take her things outside into some truck. And it was at this time that I truly began to notice how beautiful the house really was. As the rugs were lifted, I could see the beautiful hardwood floors underneath. I watched the movers take her wood furniture out of that beautiful house. I watched them disconnect her telephone and turn off her pipes. In other words, I saw them take the life out of that house.

We experienced more this day than just my grandmother losing her house. What we witnessed this day was the cessation of a major artery of our family lifeline. A part of our lives taken away from us because of drugs. And there wasn't a thing in the world that we could do about it. We just stood by and watched that artery die.

Somehow I knew this was all my fault. I was responsible for my grandmother's losing her house. Why? Many reasons come to mind. Much of my money went to these drug dealers while I was using cocaine. I supported their business. I gave them the money to do this to my grandmother. And another thing: I was sure someone was punishing me for developing a cocaine addiction—by harming my grandmother. Thirdly, drugs never would have been a part of my family's world if it hadn't been for me.

I wanted to apologize to my grandmother, but she doesn't know I am an addict. She is the only close family member who doesn't know about my experience with cocaine. My family and I have decided to keep it this way because she may not understand and because she may be extremely hurt. I wanted to apologize to her for what had just happened, but that would mean telling her I am an addict. I couldn't do that to her. Bullshit! I couldn't do that to myself. So fucking selfish I am. And so, while everyone stood around crying and watching the movers do their work, I just stood there thinking that I was responsible for this entire situation and there was nothing I could do to make it go away. I'm sure my grandmother wanted to die right now, but little did she know I wanted to die as well.

SEPTEMBER 21, 1988

It was five months yesterday that I gave up cocaine. I have been clean for five whole months. Sometimes I think these five months passed quickly, but most of the time I feel they have dragged by rather slowly. I sure feel differently today than I did five months ago. One thing has remained the same, however: The memories are still very clear in my mind. I am still haunted by cocaine memories. Just today, I found myself thinking quite a bit about the drug and subsequently suffered a flashback to my drug-infested past. It's beyond my understanding why these memories are still so vivid in my mind. It's not just the memories that constantly reappear in my everyday life, but also the feelings and emotions those memories created. And so, all I can bring myself to do is to write about it all in my journal.

I thought endlessly today about what it would take to finance a drug habit. If I were still doing cocaine, I'm sure it would take about $700 a week to satisfy my habit. I could sustain my habit with about a half ounce [14 grams] a week. This amount would cost me about $700 a week, $1,400 every two weeks, and close to $3,000 a month. Some kind of expense for a graduate student, huh?

That's not even the worst of it. I would constantly have to purchase coke in large quantities—probably an ounce at a time. This would present me with several problems. The first problem would be finding a dealer who could supply me with this amount. Second, [I'd have to] find a dealer who wouldn't give me a hassle about the amount of cocaine that I was doing. This would inevitably mean dealing with a stranger and probably driving downtown to get it. Knowing this, I face a third problem in keeping away from the police. Deals as big as I would want to make aren't as easy as are smaller deals. Cocaine is more readily available in small amounts than in amounts as large as an ounce.

Other problems I would likely encounter in financing a drug habit of this proportion would be hiding my addiction from others, sharing my cocaine with my "cocaine friends," contemplating the possibility of dealing (after all, where would I get $3,000 a month?), keeping up my job productivity, finishing my Ph.D., and keeping in shape so I am in good health. I can't even begin to list out the vast amount of problems I would face in dealing with my family, nonusing friends, colleagues, employers, and professors.

Look what I have just done. I have talked myself out of using by writing about it. This computer is definitely my Higher Power. When I thought about using today, all I could think about were all of the problems I would encounter in doing so. What ever happened to all those great thoughts and feelings that overcame me when I would think about doing cocaine or when I was doing cocaine? I can tell you what happened: I became an addict; and when I became an addict, cocaine changed from being something good, fun, exciting, and fashionable to something horrible, dreadful, frightening, and ugly.

Very seldom do I crave the drug now. I used to crave it a few months ago, but the cravings are greatly diminishing. I never fantasize about being able to do it again. All of the fantasies and dreams I like to imagine in my head at times have been redefined to not include cocaine any more. I am not saying that I never desire the drug anymore. All that I am saying is, I am learning to live without it. I am learning to live as an addict. You know, it's not too fucking bad either!

SEPTEMBER 23, 1988

Dream. Last night I did a few lines in my dreams. I told everyone that, if they put me in that situation, I was going to relapse—and they did it anyway. So it's not my fault that I did cocaine. At least I didn't do the whole fucking ounce. I mean, I only did a few lines—so what's the big deal? Oh, I know. You all think I am going to start doing it on a regular basis now. Well, that's your belief, not mine. I have been abstinent now for five months. Don't you think I have built up the strength to be able to control my consumption of the drug? Listen, anyone who can stay away from the drug for five months clearly can control her desire to use drugs. So why do you think I'll fall back into the pattern of excessive abuse?

Why can't I just do little bits of it here and there? Haven't I proven myself? I won't do more than a quarter gram—$25—a day. I make good money now, so I can afford it. Look, I have worked out my finances so I can spend $400 a month on the drug and still pay my bills. Why save my money? I have the rest of my life to save money. And besides, do you think that my salary will always stay at $30,000 a year? I want to have fun while I'm young. I know I got a little out of hand last time and spent every dime I had, but things are different now. I have money and I have been clean for five months. I have learned how to party now. I know I can't do more than a half gram a day and that I can't stay up all night doing it. I just don't understand why I can't do cocaine? Please let me do it. I promise not to fuck up again. I promise. I promise not to hurt others. I promise to do my work. I promise, I promise, I promise!

Get the fuck off my back!

Chalk another one up for the powerlessness dreams. I'm glad I woke up clean and sober. Guess I was pretty lucky.

SEPTEMBER 27, 1988

The dreams still annoy me. I will no longer question why I keep having them. I have come to accept the fact that they are a permanent scar of my addiction. But I am still afraid to have them. I relapse in most dreams, and this is the biggest fear in my life right now. The only other fear that even comes close is the thought of my parents dying. I'm not big into dream interpretation, and I really don't have to be to understand the dreams I am having. Obviously I have guilt about my addiction and how my addiction has affected my family members. Obviously I am petrified of relapsing, and obviously I have a lot of anxiety about keeping my addiction from my grandmother.

This is all so clear in my mind. Addiction is so clear in my mind every fucking day of my life. I can never seem to forget it. I can never go through a day without thinking about and without talking to someone about it. It's like staying clean is a 24-hour job with no fucking sick or vacation time. Bum deal! Who do I talk to, to change this? Who makes my life better? When will this all go away? Powerless again and angry at being so. Remember the words of that famous Jewish philosopher, girl: Life's a bitch and then you die. Oh boy!

SEPTEMBER 28, 1988

I had one interesting day today. Today was one of those days where it seemed as though everything was tied to cocaine and drug addiction. Let me explain these events one by one in the following text.

Graphics Conference. I have spent these past three days at a computer-graphics training session for social science professionals. Today, one of the instructors was discussing levels of graphics software and I found myself drawing an analogy between her hierarchical stratification of computer-graphics software and the experience of cocaine.

At one point in her lecture, she gave the following demonstration: "There is a bunch of software that can satisfy your basic needs, and it is at this level." Her hand was about chest level. "Once you become familiar with this software, you may find your needs increase and you have to move on to a more advanced, middle-range group of software." And she moved that same hand up to her chin. "Later on, your needs escalate to a point where you need the top-of-the-line software in the field to satisfy your office's needs." And she placed that hand of hers over her head.

Now I thought to myself, "What a fucking analogy to cocaine!" When you begin using cocaine, you start out wanting to do some and only needing to do a little because you have no tolerance to the drug. So, you start at a very low level with the drug—and if you made the computer-graphics analogy, your hand would be at chest level now. As time passes, your needs for the drug increase because your tolerance builds. You find you need sizable amounts to maintain the same high you first experienced a few months ago. And so you increase your use. Your hand has now moved from your chest up to your chin. Eventually, your needs for the drug increase so much where it seems as though you can't find enough of it to satisfy your craving. Your tolerance is sky high, and the only solution you can think of to satisfy your need for the drug is to find more of it. If you look now, you will see that your hand is over your head. Just like the lady who said that as your need for computer graphics increases you will have to keep moving on to a higher level of software, so you will find that you'll have to do the same thing with cocaine. Funny how in each scenario the hand is above the head. Think that means you are in over your head? I do.

And so I sat back in my chair and thought that this is some kind of society in which we live. At every juncture in our lives, at every turn, every point, we encounter some kind of stratification system that features a hierarchical structure in which there is an inevitable upward mobility. It is upward mobility that is desired; therefore, even though downward mobility may exist, it is not valued. Downward mobility is simply not prestigious.

Cocaine fits well into this hierarchical structure of a capitalist society. I call cocaine a capitalist drug. How so? Oh, please let me list the ways:

1. According to Marx, it is a drug of the bourgeoisie and not the proletariat because of its market value. It is a drug that only the "haves" can afford and the "have-nots" cannot afford. Basically stated, it is a prestigious drug because it is so expensive, fashionable, relatively clean, and thought to be only psychologically addicting. Bull shit to this all. I'm sure that Marx would also have a great deal to say about third world countries producing this drug for capitalist gain in the U.S.

2. According to Merton's theory of anomie, those who value the goals of life [material goals] and accept them as their own will be called innovators if they substitute their own means for socially approved means in obtaining those goals. In other words, this is the drug dealer who sells coke because he wants that nice Mercedes Benz he could not otherwise afford. Some kind of goals our society has, huh?

3. Howard Becker on labeling theory and self-fulfilling prophecy: People are given the label as drug addict because of an encounter with an official source that has resulted in a formal sanction for that deviant act. The person buys this label as addict and then falls into a lifestyle where he lives as one. I knew I was an addict for quite some time before I actually admitted it. Other people at the meetings have said that they knew they were addicts and just accepted it as a way of life, never thinking they could do anything about it or ever become anything more than an addict.

4. Max Weber on bureaucracy: The overwhelming amount of paper work that large organizations impose upon their employees leads to alienation of the worker from his/her work and subsequently life. The bureaucracy demands speed, efficiency, excellence in everyday operations. Workers become entangled in this bureaucratic machine and soon find themselves alienated from their work and from each other. Perfect picture for cocaine addiction. The drug initially enabled me to do my work with speed, efficiency, and excellence, but shortly thereafter led me down a path of destruction where I was not only isolated from my work but also from my friends, family, and colleagues.

Look, people, I could go on forever about the stratification inherent in all aspects of capitalist life, but the point I am trying to make is that we live in a society where cocaine use seems to fit in well. Indirectly, we welcome it into our neighborhoods by allowing its sale to reap profits for the underpriviledged, and by teaching our children that the best things in life are more likely to be seen than felt, and that those things can be bought with money and not achieved with education. We then cast out members of our society by labeling them as criminals or addicts without providing adequate support systems for them, and we later expect them to work in large, impersonal agencies where they are more likely to experience job burnout than personal satisfaction.

So don't even try to tell me we don't reinforce drug use here in the States. This "say no to drugs" stuff is all well and good, but it goes much further than that, Nancy [Reagan]. Just like I have to deal with addiction every day in my life, the American public has to deal with the reality of drugs. Don't you think it's time to get serious about this thing?

Graphics Conference: I met an interesting woman today at the conference, who is working with the city's police department on some major drug operation to clean up the city. She has some data to analyze and graphically present this October, and she asked me to help her with it. I am ecstatic about working with her on this project because it is the closest I will get to doing work with the drug problem. I want to do a lot of work with the drug problem, but I find I have to do it confidentially and as a nonaddict. This severely limits the type and amount of work I can do.

Sometimes I really get frustrated with keeping my addiction anonymous, but most times I am glad I am. I couldn't imagine telling everyone at the office I am an addict. All I need is for them to be suspicious when I have a runny nose or when I come into work late or call in sick. They have this great image of me right now and I don't want to spoil it. On the other hand, there is one person at the office that knows about my addiction, and she has discussed with me the possibility of conducting drug education programs for youth in the city. We both felt I was qualified to do the work, but decided against it because it would mean exposing my addiction to others. To make a long story short, I really am looking forward to doing work in the area of drug education; however, the work that I want to do now will have to wait. I can help this woman out with her study, and I can send this journal out anonymously for publication, but I can't do anything that will run the risk of exposing my addiction to others. I guess that I have got to learn to be patient.

SEPTEMBER 29, 1988

That day at the computer-graphics conference was truly amazing. I thought I really had my shit together this week, but then I fell apart again tonight while I was going to dinner with Sarah and her daughter. All I did was go to a money machine and find that I had a negative balance for about the tenth time in the past three months, and I soon found myself in tears once again.

You know, I was so accustomed to living a certain lifestyle. Things were so good for me in 1985, 1986, and 1987. I lived very comfortably during those years. I had money to do just about anything I wanted to do except travel to Europe. Compared to what I had grown up with and how I lived during my undergraduate years, life here was luxurious for me. I no longer had to worry about where the money was coming from for tuition or even for dinner. I could afford to take other people out for dinner now. I could spend my money on other people like my nephews and my family and friends. I was living the good life.

I deserved all of it as well. I truly believed I had paid my dues and it was now my turn to live well for all of the hard work I had done. And so I lived very well for three years. I shopped at Ann Taylor, I bought a computer and a new car, I went for sushi whenever I desired, and I took vacations to the beach all the time, I spent, I spent, and I spent.

Something soon thereafter happened to change all of that. I developed a cocaine habit. And when I developed a cocaine habit, my lifestyle drastically changed. To make a long story short, I am in a real financial bind today. I owe money here and there and everywhere. I am so financially insecure that I stay away from the mailbox, refuse to ask for a balance at the bank, and seldom open credit-card statements because I am afraid of what I'll find. It really seems as though my world is falling apart financially right now, and I'm finding it quite debilitating.

I am falling apart because I used to have the money for everything before I blew it on cocaine. I never used to bounce checks before I was an addict. I never had so many debts until now. And even though I have been clean for five months and have a new well-paying job, I still find myself financially strapped. It's just so fucking hard to swallow it all because it used to be okay. I used to be okay and now I'm not. I'm a financially broke recovering addict. I had it all, and much of it was in the bank—but it sure isn't there anymore. I blew it all on cocaine and now I am still paying the price.

I just want it all to be over, but I can't seem to get over the permanence of this addiction shit. What in the fuck do I have to do to be normal again? How can I get that lifestyle back? I know what you're going to tell me: "Don't pick up, and get to a meeting." But that shit is not going to pay that bill tomorrow, and it is not going to stop that check from bouncing. I have to reorganize my lifestyle, and it kills me knowing I have to do this. My pride is so fucking strong sometimes. I felt it slip away from me during those first 60 days of recovery, and then I felt as though I was getting some of it back. Now it's slipping away again, and I just don't know how to deal with it.

And so I called my brother to get some advice because he has been in the same financial situation but not because of drugs. He told me to keep doing what I was doing. He told me to keep paying what I could on the bills and to start curtailing my expenditures. This includes not going out to dinner or to clubs, not going shopping, and not taking trips. It also means taking lunch to work and making dinner at home. What he told me to do was to cut out all of the luxuries I had become accustomed to and to get back to living with the essentials. He has had to do the same, and he hasn't really enjoyed it. He comforted me by saying I'd get used to it in time and by telling me he loved me.

I love my brother dearly and I cherish any words of advice he has to offer. I know he and the rest of my family will stand behind me, but I want to do it alone. I know I need help with handling my addiction, but I can't take any financial help for alleviating a situation for which I am totally responsible. I want that power back, but I'm finding it is one tough cookie to get my hands on. Cookie: it's like it's in the oven but is not ready to come out yet. Sounds a lot like me. My mother always told me to be patient and wait until that cookie was ready. Guess the same thing applies here to my cocaine addiction.

OCTOBER 2, 1988

Dream. This one was a betrayal dream. I was betrayed by a very close friend of mine. A friend that I have just recently come to know. A friend with whom I work. This friend's name is Sarah.

You know, I just looked at her name on this screen and I was horrified to see it there. I actually hate to admit to myself that I had a betrayal dream about her last night, but the mere fact is I did. I will keep this dream to myself and will not discuss it with anyone else. I couldn't bear the thought of having to tell her about this dream. I am uncertain of how she would take it.

The dream had something to do with work. I had been on vacation for a month and came back to the office to discover that my job was in jeopardy. When I got back to the office, I heard that Sarah had informed a city administrator about statistical advice I had given her concerning the drug problem here and the administrator took the advice and used it incorrectly. I [was the culprit,] of course, because it was easier for city officials to place the blame for this mistake on my shoulders—a mere research analyst—than a city administrator's shoulders. Sarah is the one who pointed the finger at me when she was questioned. Hence, it is Sarah that betrayed me.

I couldn't understand what had happened, and so I gathered as much information about the event as possible. What I discovered was that, a while ago, I had mentioned something to Sarah about a professor on campus who has done extensive drug research. I don't remember what I told Sarah exactly, but I do know I shared it with her only as an interesting piece of information for conversation. I don't even know what the drug research was about. All I do know is that Sarah took this piece of information and reported it to this city administrator and he used it in a press conference. The press conference was extremely important and was widely covered by the press. Many important U.S. figures were there.

This administrator used this fact about drugs without placing it in its proper perspective and reported statistical information incorrectly. Subsequently, he was attacked by other researchers and city officials, as well as government officials, for misrepresenting the truth. His credibility as a public speaker was severely damaged, and so he chose to get to the bottom of it all.

He must have spoken to Sarah about the whole fiasco, and this is when she probably pointed the finger at me. I came back from vacation to an attack against my professional skills and my personal values. I came back from vacation to find my job in jeopardy. I came back from vacation to aggravation and confusion—but most of all, to disappointment. Disappointment that my newest friend had betrayed me.

Disappointment was not the only feeling I had. Sadness had overcome me. I felt it sink down from my brain to my heart. All I could think about was, I had just been let down by another friend. I thought this friend was the truest friend in the world and actually thought the two of us shared something special. Before I left for vacation, we had discussed just how much our friendship had meant to each other and how much we would miss each other while I was away. Can you believe I came back to this mess? What did I do while I was gone? What changed in our friendship? Why did she turn her back on me?

And all I can think about is that this has happened before to me. I give so much to my friends. I put so much value on my friendships that they take precedence over many other things in my life. I thought *she* was a giving person as well. I thought she cared about me a great deal, but obviously she did not. I put my trust in her and she betrayed me, she turned her back on me. Now, my job is on the line, my credibility as a researcher has been damaged, and I have lost all faith in that friendship I once cherished very much. I feel empty once again. Why does this always happen to me?

Well, by the end of the dream, I had worked my ass off to show that city official I was right after all and my statistical methods were sound. He apologized; however, I was not interested in his apology. I also confronted my office members with the truth and proceeded to show them that they were wrong in accusing me of something that was not my fault and of questioning my credibility as a research analyst. They apologized as well; but once again, I was not interested in their apology.

I told them, "Do you think I want to work in an office that doesn't respect the work I do? Do you think I want to work in an office that does not entrust an employee with a task in which that employee is an expert. And do you think I want to work in an office where I can't even trust my co-workers with the simplest of things? No way José! I'm going back to academia where I belong. It really upsets me that you people stooped to this level to crucify me in front of city officials. My credibility will probably be permanently harmed."

I never really finished talking about this dream and I never bothered interpreting it either. If you'll notice, there are several familiar themes that exist in this dream. Some of these themes are betrayal, paranoia, anger, and sadness—themes that are very common in my recovery today. In fact, I still allow these themes to run my life at times. More importantly, however, there is this notion of having to constantly prove myself to others and correct for any wrongs I may have inflicted on others that not only exists in this dream but also dictates my life right now and probably will for the rest of my life.

It just doesn't seem fair to me that I only used the drug for about two years and now have to deal with abstinence from it for the rest of my life. Who said life was fair, anyway? I guess all this justice studying is proving detrimental to me. It's giving me an ideal picture of the world that just doesn't seem to exist.

OCTOBER 12, 1988

This entry will be short because I have to leave for a meeting in 20 minutes. I have been feeling very good lately. Wait a minute. The word "good" is not good enough to describe how I'm feeling right now. I feel great! Everything in my life is just fine. I haven't felt this good in such a long time. And although I could sit here and list out many reasons for these great feelings, only one really needs to be mentioned right now.

I like myself again. I like who I am. Yes, folks, Katy is nuts about herself. I'm just doing so incredibly well right now that I can't help but brag about it all. School is going great. Do you know what it feels like to be able to communicate with your colleagues once again? To have their respect back and to respect the work they are doing is something I thought I would never have again. And yet it's all mine. Every time I go to class I encounter these feelings. They are feelings of respect as well as concern and caring. I can't even tell you how happy I am that I belong once again.

And to think I almost lost it all because of cocaine. It was so very hard for me to go to class last year. Besides having to worry about hiding the signs of my addiction from others, doing cocaine in the bathrooms over breaks, worrying about unfinished assignments, I also had to worry about losing face with all of my colleagues. I was so arrogant to them. I criticized their work because I thought it wasn't good enough, yet my work was either nonexistent or horrible. I hated them all last year, and I hated going to class as well. I hated my professors because I thought they were jerks, when all along it was I who was the jerk.

Do you know how hard it is to hate? It's so fucking hard to hate someone or something. The feelings of discomfort that accompany hate simply render you dysfunctional. You can feel the tension come over your face when you run into someone you hate. Your skin pulls tight across your face, and your lips stay sealed. And it's almost like this force is keeping you from making eye contact with the one you hate. You can't even look around at your environment when there is someone in it you hate. Hate just takes over your thought processes, and you can't do anything but stay in your hateful disposition.

This shit hurts. You know, if hate doesn't hurt so much, then why do you always want to leave the place where the hate exists? I never wanted to go to class, I never wanted to socialize with my colleagues, and I never wanted to meet with my professors or work on my class assignments. I hated it all! Cocaine creates the hatred. Nothing else can be responsible for making you feel so much unsubstantiated hate as can cocaine. And don't think the hatred stopped there. The cocaine kept right on working. I began to hate my job, my friends, as well as myself. The only things I liked in my life were cocaine and the dope man. I cared about my family and a few other friends, but I managed to shut them out of my life so I wouldn't have to hate them. Cocaine did all of this to me.

The discomfort that comes from hatred is unbearable. Hatred does not stand by itself. Along with hatred comes a lot of other shit with which you must learn to deal. When you talk about hatred, you are not just describing one feeling, but rather many others as well. Some of these feelings include anger, deceit, solemnness, despair, frustration, ignorance, adamancy, etcetera. All of these feelings have one simple result: discomfort. Other people would call this "pain" or "uneasiness," but the point I am trying to make is that hatred is discomforting—and the pain it generates is debilitating.

You come to know very little else but hatred when you are actively using; therefore, you are in a constant state of discomfort and pain. And because you're an addict, you know no other way of dealing with that pain than using. You deal with the pain in your life by using cocaine or any other drug of your choice. And so you see a cycle involved here. You begin using drugs and you eventually begin to hate people—or even if you don't hate them, you dislike them very much. This entity you hate or dislike becomes larger and larger, encompassing more and more of your life. Soon you feel the discomfort that is involved in hating someone, and you think you can get rid of this discomfort and pain by using more drugs. And so the model looks like this:

Drugs——Dislike——Hatred——Discomfort & Pain——Drugs

You know, I never thought I would come to know what hatred was. I never thought I would ever experience it. Think about it: I have no real reason to hate anybody, but I'm not trying to say that people can have reasons for hatred. I am simply saying that some people would seem to have a reason to hate because they have "better" reasons—such as, they may have been a victim of a violent crime, they might be [a member of] an oppressed group, or they may have suffered the loss of a body part due to [someone else's] negligence. These seem to be real justifications for hatred—not the shit I used, to justify my hatred. I had no reason to hate people and things. I just did. And the thought of this really tears me up inside; but more importantly, it is the thought that I have hated myself that I find most horrifying, and it is this fact that I will have to live with for the rest of my life.

What is the message here? All I can tell you is, I have done a lot of growing in these past six months. I have seen myself grow from someone who hated both herself and others, to someone who currently loves others and likes herself. I know I still have a lot of growing to do, and I know that I have a lot of work to do to patch up every part of my life. However, I can't just sit here and not tell you how wonderful it feels not to have to hate anymore. I can't tell you how wonderful it feels not to feel the pain and discomfort of being alone in my hatred anymore. And I can't tell you how wonderful it feels to be able to love again.

So as I sit here with tears in my eyes, I can only think of how much I am grateful to the program for helping me to grow over these past six months. And I also can't even begin to fully express my gratitude for those people who have stood by me when I was a sleazy, hating drug fiend and who now help me walk down this path of recovery. I love them all, and no one in this world will ever be able to take any of them away from me ever again. But more importantly, I don't have to push any of them away myself. And it is because I am not using cocaine today that not only can I love everyone else in my life, but I can also learn to love myself again. It is a gift from God!

October 14, 1988

Tonight I had a very disturbing experience. Tonight, I journeyed into drug-infested territory by myself to pick up something at an African store. Never before have I ventured into that part of town by myself except for when I was using. And so tonight, I found myself—for the first time since giving up cocaine—in the heart of the drug world. The feelings that overcame me were tremendous and so I guess I should write about them.

Driving down that road was horrible for me in many respects. What I saw on the street just took me back to my drug-infested past and brought back all of those horrible memories once again. To top it all off, I actually had a craving for the drug while I was down in that part of town, and this proved to both frighten me and piss me off. I almost lost it down there. I came so close to picking up some cocaine, but somehow I didn't do it. I just got in my car and drove home.

As I was driving down this street to the store, I realized I was entering a part of town that was drug infested. I had to stop at a gas station to get some gas and I encountered two drugged-up young Spanish men. I simply asked them to move their car up a bit so I could get close to a pump, and they proceeded to tell me to "Take it easy, lady—you'll get your chance." I wanted to yell at them for being such fuck-ups, but I kept my mouth shut. Their music was playing so loud and they were being so arrogant to everyone else at the station—but the thing that pissed me off the most was, I could see that they were so fucked up and that they had no fucking concern about anyone else there.

I guess I used to be like that, and I guess this encounter is what changed my mood from good to bad as I was driving down that street. It was hard seeing those two men; but more importantly, it was very hard to accept the fact that I may have behaved like that while I was using. And so I found I was angry at myself again. I found myself scolding myself as I continued to drive down that street to the African store.

And as I was driving, I couldn't help but notice all of the European cars on that street—which I knew belonged to drug dealers. How do I know they were the cars of drug dealers? Everyone in this town knows what a drug dealer's car looks like. Who else would take a Mercedes and jack up its wheels in the back, put a gold license plate on it, put mags and ornate wheel covers on it, and dress it up in as much gold as possible? And if these people who would disgrace such a conservative car as the Mercedes in this fashion are not drug dealers, then they would [have to] be over 20 years of age. After all, how many 20-year-olds do you know who can afford a $50,000 car?

I didn't only see cars on this street; I also saw a lot of traffic—drug traffic. Many people standing on the corners in alcoves waiting for the sun to go down so they could sell their drugs or buy their drugs. They all looked so terrible. They were so dirty. They were all just waiting until the time was right. They were waiting for the dope men to come around so they could buy their drugs. And this is how they spend their lives. They sleep all day and drug all night. Their lives are not their own. Their lives belong to the drugs, and the only people they have to interact with are the dealers. And the dealers treat them like shit. These people are slaves to drugs, and their masters treat them like shit.

I never hung out on corners, but it frightens me to think I might have. In all honesty, I was a slave to drugs, but my master didn't treat me like shit. Sometimes I wish my dealer would have been mean to me, would have treated me badly, or would have been an asshole. My master made things so easy for me to get the drug, I didn't have to stand out on any corner in a seedy part of town at night. However, sometimes I wish he would have, because I don't think I would have developed an addiction so fast or waited so long to come around. All of this shit is neither here nor there.

What really upset me the most while I was driving down this street was the memories it brought back to me of the relationship I had with my dealer. I used to drive the man to school constantly, and his school was right down the street from this African store. I can remember being high while we were in my car on those streets. I can remember walking into that school and doing cocaine in classrooms with him and in bathrooms. I can remember picking him up from school so that we could go party, and I can remember taking him to school after two- or three-day binges with cocaine.

So you see, it is these memories that disturbed me tonight and not so much the people on the streets, the guys at the gas station, or the fancy cars on the road. I felt my anxiety get stronger and stronger as I approached his school, and everything I saw along the way just added to the anxiety I was feeling during that time.

And so the reality of it all is that I will never journey down to that African store again by myself because it is just too traumatic for me to do so. I have a hard time dealing with all of the shit in my drug-infested past—I can't even begin to deal with where it all took place. I have such bad memories of it all now. None of it brings a smile to my face. The only feelings that come over me are ones of pain. And I am choosing not to experience any more pain—by staying away from that part of town and by staying away from my dealer. These are two things I have to do to stay clean today.

OCTOBER 17, 1988

Last night I celebrated six months' clean time, but it is only this morning when I begin to realize how it really feels. I feel very good today. Despite problems with my roommates—Carolyn in particular—I am having a good day. The day is only a few hours old, but I am still having a good one thus far. And maybe all of this has something to do with six months' clean time.

If I could turn the clock back to last year at this time—October 17, 1987—I think I'd pass up the option to do so. I was an addict at the time, but I didn't know it yet. My addiction proceeded to get worse as the months passed—and by the time 1988 came, my life was really fucked up. I was miserable last year at this time, but I didn't think it had anything to do with the drugs. Therefore, after living in hell for about eight months, I finally came to realize the misery in my life was due to cocaine; and so I gave up cocaine on April 24, 1988, and have not used any of the drug since.

There is nothing in this world that would make me want to turn the clock back to last year. I don't care to remember much about 1987, although some good things did happen during that year. Those few good things are clouded by the memories of my addiction. Every time I try to remember something about 1987 and the first four months of 1988, I can remember only the misery and horror I lived in during that time. I cannot remember starting my Ph.D. I cannot remember going to Montreal for the meetings. I cannot remember Rebecca being fired from the restaurant. I cannot remember breaking up with Wayne. And I almost cannot remember running the marathon last year. Anything less important than these events I surely never will be able to remember ever again.

Even if I can remember something about the events I listed above, none of the memories are pleasant ones. Maybe they were pleasant for me at the time they occurred, but they are not pleasant now and that is what is important. All I can see when I look into my life during the past two years is cocaine and how that cocaine dominated my life.

And so I feel as though I have lost almost two years of my life. All I can remember about those years was doing coke here and there, getting in trouble here and there, fighting with this person at this time, lying to my friends and family, spending endless nights doing drugs—et cetera. The list could go on forever. Some events are even so painful to remember, I have pushed them far into my subconscious so as to not have to go through the pain of remembering them ever again. One of these events is my twenty-fifth birthday.

It would be wrong for me to end this journal entry on a bad note. I do feel good about being clean for six months, but I continue to realize day by day that beating this thing is difficult. However, it's something I have to do. I have to stay clean today. And so when my friends and family say to me the six months went by quickly, I have to disagree with them all. I have counted my clean time day after day after day. Sometimes making it through one day seemed like making it through a year, and sometimes it seemed as though the minutes I craved cocaine during these past six months were more like hours.

So, despite feeling good about being clean from cocaine for six months, I do not feel as though it is an accomplishment. That word "accomplishment" has something final about it. It implies that a given task has been achieved and is over. This is certainly not the case with addiction and never will be. There is no sense of accomplishment in staying clean. The only satisfaction you get comes from being alive and trying to get your life back together. This is what makes me happy today.

OCTOBER 18, 1988

Today I thought about what I would say if I were asked to lead a meeting. And so on the way to work today, I thought about this. I said to myself, "How would I tell my story of addiction and where would I begin?" I must have started the story ten different times and in ten different ways—and needless to say, I never really reached an ending.

I never really realized how difficult it would be to tell my story of addiction; and I think the reason for this is, I still do not know why I became a cocaine addict. Why did I do so much cocaine? Why did I almost let it ruin my life? Why did I risk death for more of it? And what is going on inside me that would force me to push myself over the edge with cocaine? You know, a few months ago in my journal I made a list of questions for which I wanted to find answers, and I never bothered finding them. Although I have discovered answers to some of those questions, many of them are still unanswered. Am I not growing?

I always expect things to happen so quickly in my life. I have to get my Ph.D. by the time I turn 26; I have to be tenured by between 30 and 32; I have to be able to ride my bike to my hometown this year and across country next year; I have to publish this article this month and start that project next month; I have to have this car by this age, and have to have kids by that age. More importantly, I feel as though I have to be progressing *x* amount during recovery. My mind tells me I should be over the cravings, rid of the anger, and financially back on my feet all within the first six months. I even expect I discover the reasons behind my cocaine use as well as mastering the 12 Step program.

All of this concerning addiction is unrealistic. I hear some people at the meetings say they never get rid of the cravings or the dreams. Others say it will take them years to get back on their feet financially and all they pray for is health and happiness in the meantime. I hear all of these things coming from the majority of the people in the program, yet I do not hear them coming from myself. I am still caught up in this mode of trying to distinguish myself from others. My attitude is that other addicts take this amount of time to do this and to do that, but Katy doesn't. It's all bullshit!

I am just like everyone else and I wish I could see that. I really don't believe that for one moment, however. I think I am special, and I keep running my life accordingly. I need to come to the realization that I can be just as special, wonderful, successful, and all that other good stuff if I just slow down a bit instead of plowing ahead at full speed. I am special, but my experience with cocaine has rendered me a normal addict.

Speed. No wonder I love stimulants. I drink tons of coffee, I did tons of cocaine, and I love anything else that gives me energy to plow ahead at full speed. There must be something inside of me that needs to do everything imaginable in *x* amount of time. I want to do so many things, and they all have to be done at a specific time in my life. No one imposes these deadlines on my life. I am responsible for setting my own limitations, expectations, and deadlines.

Look, I am really in my head right now and I can't seem to get out of it. I thought I was in a good mood, but I guess I am not. Maybe I'll cheer up at lunch. I just get so depressed at times when I sit back and think about all of this. I *realize* I have made enough progress in the past six months, but apparently I do not *think* it is enough. I need to come to terms with this because it moves absolutely nowhere; it just stays there and swelters. Goodbye!

OCTOBER 23, 1988

Once again I find that I have waited too long to write in this journal. I should have written in it every day last week and each day this weekend;

however, my lazy ass couldn't make it to the computer. I guess I can briefly recap what has happened during this time, but then I want to focus on what happened this weekend.

I had a few cocaine dreams again this past week. Oddly enough, these dreams were not relapse dreams. One dream was about Rebecca, Billy, and Jim. The dream had something to do with Billy and me being together looking for Rebecca, his mother. We knew she had gone to another country on a plane and was expected to return a week ago; however, we did not know where she was. I was keeping Billy and was taking care of him during this time. Jim was isolating himself at home and was mourning her loss. It struck me as strange that Rebecca had only been gone a week and Jim was already mourning her loss. It was not as though he had given up the search for her; it was that he was just incapable of functioning without her.

And so Billy was living with me. We were getting used to one another, but we kept our hopes up that Rebecca would soon return. It was during this dream that some very strange emotions came back over me. Feelings I hadn't felt in several months. I missed Rebecca. I found myself missing her tremendously. Both Billy and I were devastated without her at this moment in my dream. I haven't felt this way about her in such a long time. I don't even feel that way about her right now as I sit here and write about her. I guess I feel this is strange because I thought I would never miss her again. I thought my feelings toward her had drastically changed, but my dream is telling me they haven't.

We heard on the radio that the plane Rebecca was scheduled to be on had crashed and there were no surviving passengers. The plane was being trailed by the CIA because it was believed to be carrying a major shipment of cocaine to the States. The CIA shot the plane down and the plane had crashed somewhere in the Atlantic Ocean. Rebecca was on this plane. Soon after witnessing this news report, Billy and I received a phone call verifying that Rebecca had been on that plane and was dead. We both fell apart.

Billy just grabbed me and held me so tight. He wouldn't let me go. He cried and cried and cried. He just wanted to know why she had died and I found I couldn't give him an answer. I just held him and cried myself. I couldn't tell him things were going to be okay, I couldn't help him to understand what happened, and I couldn't bring his mother back. All I could do was sit there and hold him.

And so I started thinking about what life would be like with him as a son. Jim was totally devastated at this point and was therefore unable to care for Billy. Somehow, what really mattered to me was not that Billy would now be my responsibility, but that Rebecca would no longer be in our lives. Rebecca would no longer be in my life. And the only thing that came to my mind was, I had lost her because of cocaine. Why was she on that plane that was carrying cocaine? Had she slipped back into using? Had she deserted her son and her fiancé for cocaine? Had she lost her life because her addiction had escalated once again? Did any of this have to do with me?

These questions were going through my mind as I sat there and held Billy. Almost at once we both picked up our heads and looked across the room to see Rebecca sitting there. We both just looked at her in total amazement and said, "But we thought you were dead?" She replied, "Why? My plane was just delayed at LaGuardia. Why would you think I was dead?" And we told her about the news report and about the phone call and she just answered, "Now why would I be on that plane?"

OCTOBER 27, 1988

Last night I really wanted to write about how much I hated cocaine, but I was unable to do so because my day was just too busy to get to the computer. I did do a little writing by freehand on my class notebook while sitting in class, but I found I was unable to fully develop my thoughts and put them down on paper because of the classroom discussion. Since last night, I have attended a meeting and have discovered new facts about the drug world that make me hate it even more. Hopefully, I will be able to recapture the feelings about cocaine that I have experienced these past few days and will be able to write about them in the paragraphs below.

Does it make you feel good to know that you are so fucking desirable? I bet you like the fact that everyone wants you, craves you, and can't get enough of you. I have to give it to you, man. You are so fucking smart. You trick us into thinking you are something good because you make us feel so good; but as soon as we stop using you, we feel terrible. You know we have to have you to feel good—that we can't live without you. I sit here writing about you, reasoning with you, day after day after week after month only to realize that I will be writing about you for the rest of my life. Why? Because I am one of your many victims. I am your slave. You have beaten me. You are more powerful than I am. And so I have thrown up the white flag and have surrendered to you. You are the most powerful thing I have ever known and fighting you is the hardest thing I have ever had to face in my life and will always be. I am your addict.

But let me just tell you a few things. You are nothing more than a fucking drug—just some white powder. You were once very active in my life, but you are no longer. I am fighting you day by day and I am winning. I have a program now that has helped me start this battle and assists me in waging it. And do you know what is happening to me? I am coming to know something more powerful than you, and that power is restoring me to sanity. So you're not so fucking hot after all! I know what I have to do to keep you out of my life and to win this fight that I am in with you, and I've been winning for six months now. You're just so fucking lucky that everyone else hasn't received this message yet. But they will. So you better pray that my secret doesn't spread around too much, or you'll be history.

Cocaine. It just sits on the glass and stares you in the face. You stare back harder and harder and harder until you lean over and taste it. It is so small. It weighs nothing. It just continues to sit there and you can't seem to leave it. In fact, you can't think about anything else. And you feel it in every part of your body. Your lips and gums are numb. You feel your arms and legs tingle and you feel your head buzz. You feel so good right now. You have never felt this way before. All of your pain has subsided, all of your worries are gone, all of your feelings are high, and you are just above everyone else—or at least you think you are.

OCTOBER 28, 1988

I'm getting nervous. I'm getting scared. It is because I have to move again that I find my world has been shaken up. I have to move in two months and I am not looking forward to it at all. I will move into an apartment by myself this time, and this scares me very much. I also must move back into the city—which frightens me even more. And so I decided to write about these feelings in my journal today. I guess I will share these feelings at the CA meeting tonight.

All too vividly, I can remember exactly what happened to me the last time I lived alone. All I did was party with cocaine. At the time my old roommate left and my new one moved in, I found myself deeply involved in cocaine because I was developing a strong friendship with my dealer. Our friendship continued to develop because my new roommate was never home; therefore, my dealer and I always had a place to ourselves to do cocaine. Living alone played a major role in the escalation of my addiction.

Living alone means not having to answer or deal with anyone else. I have proof of this point because as soon as I moved out of that apartment and into a town house with three other women, I stopped using cocaine. There was no way in hell those three ladies were going to tolerate my drug use. They kept insisting I give up the drug and go get help. They were on my back about it night and day. I could not take it any longer, and so I gave up cocaine three weeks after moving into that house with them.

I am afraid I will use again because I will no longer have anyone to answer to when I go home from work. Despite my complaints about my roommates, I really do care about them a lot. They were there for me when I needed the support, and they helped me through a very bad time in my life. For this I will always be grateful. But they aren't going to be there anymore; and to tell you the truth, I am not confident in how I am going to do without them. I guess I will find out soon enough.

There is a very big part of me that really does want to live by myself. Sometimes I think it would be great to do so, and other times I do not. I want nothing more than a place of my own, but I don't know if I am ready for it. More importantly, I do not know if I have what it takes to survive when living alone. And so I find I am confused, frightened, and angry right now. Writing about it all is helping me to get rid of these feelings, but I'm afraid they will only reappear tomorrow.

OCTOBER 29, 1988

The marathon is next week at this time and I think I am ready for it. I had the best run of the fall today. I actually didn't want to stop, but did so anyway. I kind of regret not going any farther than I did. Runs like today don't often come when you are training as hard as I am. Your legs and knees are usually too sore to put in any extra mileage, and your body is too fatigued to do so anyway. I should have run a few more miles when I was in the mood to do so.

You know, what I did in the last paragraph is so typical of me. I had a great run and a good day and yet I still found a way to discover something bad or negative about it. I always seem to capitalize on the negative side of things when it comes to me. I beat myself up about the most absurd things. Nothing I do ever seems to be good enough for me. I can't seem to please myself.

My group always used to tell me the same thing and yet I never listened to them. I heard them say what they did concerning this topic, but I didn't do anything about it. Their advice went through one ear and out the other, just like the advice about giving up cocaine used to do. And the constant pattern that seems to emerge through all of this is that I am never fully satisfied with anything that I do. I don't look at the things I have done and say, "Nice job, Katy." I just seem to say, "Well, you could have done it this way, Katy; and that, you should have done it that way, Katy." And then I beat myself up about it all.

When am I going to stop this? When am I going to stop dwelling on the negative when it comes to things in my life? Will I ever be satisfied with anything I do? Sometimes I think I am my own worst enemy. No one else in my life is as hard on me as I am on myself. Yet I am a likable person. Other people really do like me. Other people are happy with the things I do, pleased that I am in their lives, and proud of my accomplishments, but I can't seem to feel any of these things for myself. Therefore, it really doesn't matter what other people feel towards me if I can't feel it for myself. I do care about making others feel good, but I should care about making myself feel good first. I just can't seem to do it, and it really gets to me sometimes.

Well, I'll go to a meeting in about an hour and I hope I find some advice there about this predicament. Those rooms of the fellowship have greatly helped me. Those rooms are there to help me get my life back together and to find peace in my life. Man, am I ever going to ask them for their help tonight! Good thing I listen to the simple phrase, "Keep coming back. It works!"

OCTOBER 30, 1988

Today was the day we turned our clocks back an hour. I hadn't realized this until my roommate came in the house and asked me why I was up so early. She then told me it was time to turn the clocks back. I sat on the couch for a few minutes and thought about this turning the clock back an hour. I soon became very anxious about the idea of turning the clock back any time longer than that. And so I guess I will write about these thoughts and feelings in the journal entry for today.

Imagine turning the clock back an hour and finding you couldn't stop it at that hour. That the clock kept going farther and farther back in time and stopped at April 24, 1988. The thought of this really shakes me up. I know we turned the clock back a simple hour today, and I know I had a good day today because I said no to drugs, but the mere thought of having to go back in time really fucks me up. It doesn't matter what length of time we are talking about. The only thing that matters is we had to go back in time.

It's hard enough sometimes making it through a 24-hour day without using any cocaine, let alone a 25-hour day. It may seem insignificant to you, but one extra hour in a day for a recovering addict is a major deal. Remember, it only takes a second to get a craving for a drug and even less time than that to put a line up your nose. I didn't dwell on this idea today and I didn't turn it into a crisis, but that's because I am working the program well and I have six months under my belt. I can only imagine what it would have felt like if I would have had to turn the clock back an hour on April 24th. Yuck! Or, if I would have had to turn the clock back an hour while I was using, because that would have given me another hour to do blow and that hour might have proven fatal. Or, if I would have had to turn the clock back an hour at one of the hundreds of times I have craved cocaine since giving it up on April 24, 1988. It's just hard sometimes making it through a 24-hour day without using—you just don't need another hour to think about it.

I guess I could look at the extra hour optimistically. I had extra time to sleep today, extra time to run, and extra time to relax. I was not rushed one single bit today, but rather took my time in doing everything I did. I am thankful for the extra hour and actually wish that we could do this more than once a year.

The reality is, then, that the extra hour today worked for me. It was an extra added bonus to my weekend. You must realize, however, that some addicts may have had problems with the hour like I mentioned above. An extra hour to an addict can mean many negative things and can prove harmful. I hope every addict in the world made it through that extra hour today, but I'm sure someone probably relapsed. My prayers go out to those addicts who couldn't handle that extra hour in today's day, and I hope they find their way back to the rooms of the fellowship. I am happy for myself, however; my extra hour turned out to be sensational. Thanks go out to my Higher Power.

NOVEMBER 7, 1988

Today is the day after the marathon—and boy, do I feel terrible. I am very tired and sore. Basically, I am miserable. I did not really enjoy running the race at all this year. As a matter of fact, all I could think about while running the race was how I was going to finish it. I did not daydream one bit and I usually do this while I am running. In fact, I never daydream while running races and I find this extremely odd. Maybe it is because I am so psyched up about the race that I am too nervous to daydream. I don't really know.

I do know I will never run a marathon again. I am in too much pain today to be able to go through it all again. Usually the payoff is high for running a marathon. The satisfaction I felt from running the race the past two years was greater than the pain I experienced in doing so. Things were different this year. The pain I felt was greater than the joy. It is because of this that I care not to run another marathon. I have completed three marathons during the past three years, and now I am ready to hang up my marathon shoes. I will continue to run, but will never train for a marathon again.

I guess I really want to talk about something else in today's journal entry. During the past three days, I have witnessed four people partying with cocaine in their cars while driving. My reaction to these events was disturbing. I got really tense after seeing these people partying in their cars and proceeded to enter into a lousy mood. I did not have feelings of envy for these people. I felt sad for them. I was sad that one day they will end up like me—an addict. And so I could only feel despair for those four people because I don't want them to have to go through what I have gone through each day of my life for the past few months.

The two people I saw Friday night were a black male and female and were obviously involved in a relationship. As the guy was driving, I saw the girl hold the vial of cocaine up to the guy's nose at the red light and I saw him take his hit. I couldn't help but turn my head away from the two of them at this point. I just didn't want to see what was going on with them in that car. It just brought back too many bad memories for me—memories I have no desire to experience.

I proceeded to drive home and soon found my thoughts were totally consumed with what I had just witnessed. I was on the verge of getting angry at both of them because I realized how their foolish actions in that car could have harmed me and several others. I can remember all too clearly driving very carelessly while doing cocaine in my car. All I could think about was that these two were doing the same thing. I could just tell they had this blatant disregard for anyone else on the road—and that scared me.

In the last paragraph I mentioned I was on the verge of getting angry at these two people. I did get angry at the two of them, but it was a controlled anger. If this is at all possible, I was both angry and happy. I was angry at these two irresponsible young fools who didn't know what they were doing, yet I was happy at the same time knowing I no longer had to go through that. The fear, paranoia, and insanity of doing cocaine in your car or doing cocaine anywhere are things I am glad to have out of my life. I will never forget the fear, paranoia, and insanity that dominated my life for almost two years until six months ago. I carry those painful memories with me each day. But I am here to say that I am thankful they are no longer a part of my life. I am glad I don't have to live like an addict anymore—just a recovering addict.

I owe it all to the program. I never would have been able to stay clean for six months without the help of NA and CA. Without these two programs, I never would have learned how to deal with recovery and I never would have been able to get my life back together. The program has even helped me deal with instances like these. If I were not six months into this program and doing as well as I am, I never would have been able to handle seeing those two people partying in that car. So it is for these things that I am thankful to both NA and CA.

I do not want to drag this out, but I just want to mention that I saw another couple doing the same thing on my way to work this past Monday. It just feels good to be able to look at these people and know I don't have to be there anymore. It feels good not wanting to be in that car with them. It just feels good to be clean.

NOVEMBER 10, 1988

I had the "big date" with Kevin last night and so I thought I should write about it. I really don't know what to say or where to start. The date was okay; everything was fine. I don't want to describe him and I don't want to take his inventory. I just want to talk about the way I feel about him. To be continued.

NOVEMBER 17, 1988

Once again I have pulled the old dope-fiend routine and have neglected my journal writings. I don't really know what comes over me to prevent me from writing in this journal. I remember when I was writing in my journal this past summer. My writing was so good then. I was so disciplined in writing every day. With fall came a lot of stuff that has prevented me from keeping this journal every day. But that is not even the worst of it.

When I write in my journal now, I never seem to have enough time to fully develop my thoughts or to let my imagination flow. Part of this is due to the fact that I am keeping my journal at my office now and not at home. I am interrupted more frequently down here and am always worried about someone seeing me write in this thing. I wish I would just keep my journal at home, but I am never at home because of school and meetings.

You know, writing in this journal is like working the program for me. Not writing in the journal has the same effects on me as missing meetings. I do much better when I attend meetings and when I write in this journal. There have been so many days where it has saved me from relapsing or having an emotional breakdown. I can come to the journal and write down everything that is going on in my life and be honest about it all. I don't have to hide anything from anyone in this journal. I can let my hair down and talk about what I want to talk about. In other words, I can be me. I can be Katy in this journal.

This is what the program does for me as well. I am Katy when I go to meetings. I don't have to be a sociologist, a runner, a computer expert, a research analyst, a snob, or anything else. I can just be Katy at the meetings. The people who attend the meetings feel the same way I do. All anyone talks about is how much they love the program because it allows them to dump all their shit and to be themselves. We are all very grateful for the program, and many of us would never trade what we have in the program now for anything else in life. Not even an endless supply of cocaine!

And so I consider myself pretty lucky. I have my journal and the meetings to help me with recovery. I can dump my troubles off at two places. I have two resource centers for help. And if for some unknown reason I can't make it to a meeting, I know I can write in my journal. I always have one or the other if not both. I can't tell you how good it feels to have these support systems at my disposal. I feel very secure knowing that I have both the program and a journal in my life to help me with recovery. I never would be able to make it through recovery without either of them. In fact, I would have no recovery if it weren't for my journal and the program. Thank You!

NOVEMBER 21, 1988

My heart is not into the entry I started above. I'm not exactly sure where I want to go with it and so I stopped writing. Today I feel pretty good. I guess that a lot of these feelings are a result of last night's meeting at the hospital. Charlie led the meeting. I always get a lot out of what he shares. His story is so powerful and is filled with a lot of other problems besides addiction.

Anyway, I wanted to share last night but didn't get a chance to do so. The topic was "Why We Work the Process" (meaning the process of recovery in the 12 Step program). Many people had a lot of good stuff to share. I probably got something from everyone in that room. On the other hand, I found that no one actually hit the nail on the head when they described why they work the process. And so I guess I want to write my explanation right now.

Working the process is very simple for me. I work the process of recovery for basically one reason and one reason only: I do not want to relapse. I know there are other reasons why I work the process, but all of those reasons are secondary to the primary purpose of preventing relapse. I do work the program so I can grow to be a better person, and I do work the program so I can function well in my life, and I even work the program for other people in my life. The bottom line to all of this, however, is that I work it to prevent me from relapsing.

The fear of relapse is very great for me. Each morning I wake up and say, "Don't pick up, and try to get to a meeting." I remind myself just how much I actually do fear relapse. All I can do is cringe when I think about what relapse would mean for me. I can't even write about all of the pain I would experience in doing so and the great impact it would have on my life and others' lives. And to think that all of this fear actually comes down to one small line of cocaine. You know, that's all it would take. One single, fucking line!

It's so easy to have this incredible fear of relapse and cocaine if you just think about how easy it would be for me to do another line. I could be confronted with cocaine at a number of places and find I did it when it was put in front of my face. I could find myself pissed off at someone so much where I would actually pick up the phone to call the dope man. I could be feeling such great despair and loneliness that my only cure of happiness would be my sick notion that cocaine could alleviate that pain.

It wouldn't only take a bad day to make me relapse. I could relapse at any time. Things could be going perfectly well for me and still I might feel inclined to relapse. One day I might think I deserve a treat after *x* amount of clean time. Another day I might feel I can handle social use again. And one day I might just feel like doing cocaine today and that no one is going to stop me from doing some.

But that would be the bottom line. I could find a million excuses to do cocaine, but there is only one reason I would do so: I simply wanted to get high. And I guess it is this fact that scares me so much. All it would take is the desire to use again to cause me to relapse and force me down that desperate path of self-destruction. Relapse could come at any time in my life. It wouldn't have to wait for a crisis in my life, for a bad mood, or for a negative confrontation with someone else. All it would take is a craving that I simply couldn't control to cause me to relapse. All that it would take is the desire to get high again to bring back that misery to my life that I have been trying to forget.

I don't have to spell it out any more clearly than that. Relapse is a big fear for me. I fear it more than death because I know it will bring me death anyway. And so this is why I work the process—because, without the process, I would relapse. I cannot stay free of drugs, clean from cocaine without the help of the CA, NA, or AA program. I tried it before and failed. I have never been able to do this alone and I never will be able to do so. I have to stay in the middle of this fellowship if I want to stay clean. I can't do it on my own. I am powerless over cocaine, and my life is unmanageable if it plays an active part.

NOVEMBER 22, 1988

Boy, was I pissed off last night! I feel better today, but I was angry as hell last night. Joni's alcoholic father stopped by for a surprise visit, and he made me utterly miserable. No one else was home. I was all alone with this alcoholic and he was drinking. It really bothered me last night and I'm not sure why.

The entire room smelled like alcohol. He was drinking Michelob Dark and the shit stank. He was so drunk. He kept his coat on because he was so cold. This is typical of an alcoholic. In addition to that, he kept complaining about how cold it was in the house and so I turned up the heat hoping he would shut up. No luck! He found something else to complain about soon thereafter.

He was waiting for Joni to come home so he could see her. Little did he know that she was at her new boyfriend's house and probably wouldn't come home anyway. He must have asked me five times if I knew where his daughter was, and I kept telling him that I didn't know. This is just like a fucking alcoholic—goddamn memory loss. I'd tell him I didn't know where she was one minute, and ten minutes later he would ask again. What a royal pain in the ass! I did know where Joni was, but I just felt as though I couldn't tell her father.

Now, this dilemma proceeded to bother me as time passed. Each time he asked me about her, I came just that much closer to telling him where she actually was. After a while, I thought to myself that I could care less if I hurt Joni by telling her father she was staying with her new boyfriend. However, I just couldn't do this. It had nothing to do with the fact that I was concerned about preserving Joni's integrity. All it had to do with was that I refused to accommodate this active alcoholic. There was nothing inside of me that wanted to "enable" this alcoholic.

Eventually, I left the room and went upstairs to study. I could stand being in that room with him no longer. I locked my door and got undressed because I was a bit nervous that he was one flight below and was spending the night. I fell asleep soon thereafter and had a relatively good night's sleep. He was still there this morning when I awoke, but I didn't have to interact with him at all.

Resentment. I guess the reason for my annoyance with him was because I resented him drinking in my house and in front of me. He is a fucking alcoholic; he should not be drinking and should be in recovery. The fact is that he *is* drinking and he *isn't* in recovery and there is absolutely nothing I can do about it. The other fact is that *I am* in recovery and *I don't* drink any more. He asked me why I don't drink any more and I just told him I didn't care to. Can you imagine what he would have said to me if I had told him I was in the fellowship and was drug and alcohol free? He probably would have given me some kind of shit that would have made me feel bad, and so I didn't say a word about being in recovery.

I'm kinda pissed at myself right now because I feel as though I let him get the best of me. Not for one minute last night did I wish I could have sat there and drunk with him. On the contrary, mere thoughts of it nauseated me. I did wake up wanting to use today, and I'm not sure how much that has to do with interacting with Joni's father last night. Right now, I find I am missing cocaine a great deal. I actually thought about all of its good points on the way to work today and forgot all of the bad things that it did to me. I still think it is neat to do cocaine, and I want to get rid of this stupid idea.

NOVEMBER 23, 1988

I have been thinking about cocaine and relapse a great deal lately. I have been fantasizing about doing the drug again. I picture myself in all different types of situations with the same people with whom I used to party doing lots of cocaine. I guess I could write about today's fantasy on the Metro.

On the way to work today, I dreamed I was in Colombia, South America, and was at a cocaine factory. I was in the plant supervisor's office talking about the cocaine business. Our discussion was very businesslike. We talked about the cocaine production process and about profit margins from sales of the drug. I was utterly fascinated by the inexpensive cost of cocaine production. I told the supervisor that cocaine in the States cost about $100 a gram and he said he already knew that. You can imagine my amazement with the whole business when he told me it only costs his plant less than a quarter to produce a gram of cocaine.

We eventually left his office as the dream passed. Soon we were walking through the plant where I witnessed many factory workers producing the drug. The supervisor explained the entire purification process to me, and all I could think about was that this was a familiar scene. I drew an analogy between this tour and some of the tours I used to take in elementary school to the dairy plant and stockyards. And there was nothing different between the tours except for the item being produced. I suddenly realized this had major implications—that cocaine production had become a major business in Colombia. A business that looked just like any other business in the world. A factory that looked just like any other factory in the world.

People come to work at this plant every day in order to make a living. Some employees work the 7–3 shift while others work the 3–11 or 11–7 shift. At the end of their day, these people go home from work to their families and do what families do. I am sure some of these people are addicts, but I get the feeling that most are average workers just trying to make a living. And this is where they come to make their living, irrespective of their life situations.

Eventually, I accepted this phenomenon as a fact of life and proceeded to follow the supervisor back up into his office. I told him I greatly appreciated his tour, that it was probably one of the most fascinating and educational experiences I have ever had. I thanked him for the tour a few times, and he said it was his pleasure. He said he enjoyed giving a beautiful, intelligent, young American female a tour of his plant. I was just about to get up out of my chair to leave his office when he told me to stay seated. He went over to this big closet and opened the door. There was this huge metal drum in his closet and he proceeded to open it. He told me to come stand beside him, and so I got up out of my chair and walked over to him.

He opened this metal drum to reveal its contents and told me to look inside. I looked down and immediately gasped for air. I put my hand over my mouth to hide my shock. I couldn't believe my eyes, but the entire drum was filled with cocaine. I was absolutely stunned looking into that metal drum. He asked what was wrong, and I replied, "I have never seen this much cocaine in my entire life. It absolutely fascinates me. It must be worth millions." He just laughed at me and replied that it was nothing. He said this amount can be produced in one hour of one working day. I took my eyes off the cocaine and looked at him in question, and he reiterated the point.

I looked back down at the cocaine and soon found that all I could say was, "WOW!" It looked so good to me. It was pure white powder. Suddenly feelings of being high came over me. I could feel the cocaine in my body and soon found I was light on my feet just looking at it. He asked me if I would like to have some cocaine as a souvenir of my visit. He told me he would like to offer me a gift as a token of his kindness. I just looked at him and said, "Are you serious?" He said he was very serious, and he handed me this scoop and a big plastic bag. He told me to scoop out some cocaine and put it in the bag. So, I proceeded to do so. I didn't even think twice about it. I put the scoop down into the cocaine and pulled out a sizable amount and poured it into the bag. He helped me hold the bag open. The bag was about a foot wide and a foot and a half long. The cocaine covered the bottom of the bag.

I was just about to pull the bag away from his hands when he replied, "Is that all you are going to take? Take as much as you want." And so I put the scoop down into the drum three more times and soon I had almost half of my bag filled. I told him I thought this was enough. He said, "Just take one more scoop and then I'll let you go home." I placed the scoop back down into the cocaine and poured it into the bag. We closed the bag and walked over to get my coat. As I was putting on my coat, he told me that there was only one stipulation with his gift. He told me I could only do the cocaine he gave me in Colombia and could not take it out of his country. He was very serious about this request and soon asked me if I still wanted it.

Dilemma. I took a moment to think about his proposition. Then I looked down at the bag of cocaine again—and all I could see was, it looked so fucking good. All of the good feelings of being high came back to me. I was totally consumed with all of this cocaine that I had in my hands. And to think it was free. As I was thinking about this, he interrupted me once again to remind me of my dilemma. And I just stood there in total confusion as I tried to sort things out.

Soon I figured out what the real decision was. It was a decision about life, and I had two paths I could take. The first path was to take the cocaine and stay in Colombia, and the other path was to give the cocaine back to him and be on my merry way home to the U.S. There was absolutely no middle ground here—no other alternatives from which to choose. I had to choose between these two alternatives, these two paths of life.

Behind this decision was a whole host of other factors that proved to clog my mind and inhibit me from making my choice. Most of these factors had to do with the reality of the end product to both of these decisions. No one had to show me what the end product would be if I decided to stay in Colombia to do the cocaine or if I decided to give it all back to him and go home. I knew exactly what both of these decisions would bring me. I did not have to guess at what the end product would be. The end product to this dilemma only presented me with another choice: the choice between life and death.

All bullshit aside, this is basically how I saw things:

1. I could give him the cocaine back and go back to the U.S. where I would live a long, happy, successful life with my family and friends while in recovery.
2. I could take the cocaine and become a junkie again. If I did this, it would mean I would have to live the rest of my life in Colombia away from the people I loved, the things I wanted to do, and the places I wanted to go. Taking that bag of cocaine would mean I couldn't or wouldn't be doing anything other than cocaine for the rest of my life and that my life would probably end abruptly in one way or another.

And so as I saw it, the choice between happiness or despair was in front of me. It was the choice of life or death. And I knew my mind was made up right at that moment. There was simply no doubt in my mind. I did what I had to do. I did what I wanted to do. I turned to him and handed him the bag of cocaine and said, "No, thank you. I have a life to live."

DECEMBER 5, 1988

Last week I didn't get the chance to write in my journal very much. During the week, I had several cocaine dreams I feel I should write about. The first one I had was very weird and still puzzles me to this day.

Dream. I was at my old house on Mulberry Street in my hometown. This is the house in which I was raised. After I left to go to college, my parents moved into a new house. I haven't been inside that house on Mulberry Street for years; however, I can remember everything about it very vividly. And so in this dream, I was able to recapture the atmosphere of the house and all of the feelings I had for it. I loved that house very much. I didn't know about my parents' newer home in this dream. For all I knew, my parents were still living in this old house and I was home for a weekend.

My mother knew about my addiction in this dream. In fact, she knew just about all of the details of my using. She was hip to the fact that I had a constant runny nose. I snorted all of the cocaine I did, and now I think I have done some damage to my nasal passage.

Anyway, the dream started with me in the downstairs bathroom of my old house on Mulberry Street, blowing my nose. The bathroom was located between the kitchen and the living room, and I had the door propped open. My mother was sitting in the living room and so she could hear me very well. She yelled to me and asked if I was okay, and I replied that I was. I said, "It's just another runny nose, Mom. It's a bit sore today." She asked me if there was anything she could get for me or do for me and I replied, "No, thanks. I'm just going to put some Vaseline in it to make it feel better."

Back when I was using, I used to keep Q-tips and Vaseline around constantly to soothe my nose because it would get so sore and would scab up and bleed all the time. The Vaseline always made it feel so much better. I can remember feeling so good when the scabs would go away, but then I'd just fuck my nose up again by going on another binge. Just when I thought my nose had healed, I would do cocaine again and would make it even worse. I never really gave it a chance to heal. I had some severe problems with my nose.

Back to the dream. After I was done blowing my nose, I took a Q-tip with Vaseline on it and stuck it in my left nostril. As the Q-tip went in my nose, I felt it touch my tongue. I pulled the Q-tip right back out of my nose because I didn't believe what just happened. I put the Q-tip back in my nose and it touched my tongue again. All of a sudden, I got terribly frightened. I looked in the mirror on the medicine cabinet and saw the expression on my face. I looked like a person who had just seen a ghost. I was totally petrified at this point.

All I could think about was, I had lost my entire left nasal passage. Where was the inside of my nose? Had I burned a hole right through that part of my nasal passage with the cocaine? I just couldn't think about it.

My mother asked, "Are you still in there? Is there anything wrong?" I hesitated and replied, "No." And so, while thinking about the left side of my nose, I placed the Q-tip in my right nostril and was glad to discover that this nostril was okay. It felt like a normal nostril should, and so I proceeded to coat it with the Vaseline.

As I was taking the Q-tip out of my right nostril, this sharp pain went right up to my head and I jerked my head back. I pulled the Q-tip out of my nose in order to hold my head when all of a sudden my right nostril began to drain. Stuff came pouring out of my right nostril and onto the bathroom floor. I quickly put my head over this little trash can and let my nose drain into it. It just kept draining. I yelled, "Mom, come in here. My nose is draining and I can't stop it." She came running into the bathroom to see what was happening. She said, "Oh my God, Katy." She put her right arm around my back and her left arm and hand on my head. And we just stood there watching my nose drain.

The trash can was filling up with the mucus that was coming out of my nose. Soon the mucus changed colors. It went from a clear color to a brown color and then to a red-brown color. My mother and I just kept standing there waiting for the drainage to stop, but it never did. My nose just kept draining and draining.

It was about at this moment in the dream when I woke up. I immediately went over to the mirror in my room to check my nose and was relieved to find it clean. I checked my sheets to see if my nose had drained in my sleep, but they were dry. I took a shower and got dressed for work. I forgot about the dream until I boarded the Metro and then I thought about it again. I tried interpreting it, and this is what I concluded.

Basically, I thought I must have relapsed. I thought this because my nose would have no reason for draining like that unless I had done cocaine again. I decided I had relapsed and must have ruptured something inside my nose to make it drain like that. The decay of the left side of my nose was another product of the relapse, in that the cocaine must have eaten right through the inside of my nose.

All of this interpretation is real. What I mean is, it has significance for me in my life of recovery today. Every single time I have a runny nose, I believe it is due to my extensive snorting of cocaine. I do believe I have permanently damaged my nasal passage and I know I should go have it checked by an ENT [ear, nose, and throat doctor]. The reality of it is that I am afraid an ENT will find something horribly wrong (like no left nasal passage), and then I will have to deal with this as a health problem for the rest of my life. This is just another part of denial for my addiction.

I am also having problems with this cold weather. My nose is draining more now than ever before, and this concerns me. I feel people are becoming suspicious of my behavior. I really don't like having to deal with this paranoia of mine, but I can't help thinking that people will find it odd that I constantly have a runny nose.

All interpretations aside, I guess the only thing that matters is that I don't relapse. If I stay clean and don't relapse, then this dream will never come true. I need to stop thinking about cocaine so much, because it is following me into my sleep and is surfacing in my dreams. These dreams upset me and put a damper on my day. I guess the bottom line is, I miss cocaine and am feeling guilty about having those feelings. My conscience is punishing me for these feelings by forcing me to dream about the negative consequences that relapse would have for me.

Sometimes I think this addiction shit is just all too much for me to handle. I wish I could bury it and forget about it. But the fact is, I have to deal with feelings like these and dreams like these for the rest of my life. And worse than that, I have to deal with every aspect of this addiction one day at a time. Shit!

December 7, 1988

I can barely do anything today other than sulk. I am so upset. I am on the verge of tears and I predict I'll be crying by the end of this entry. My life is miserable right now and I don't know what to do about it. Instead of talking about everything that is going on in my life right now to upset me, I am just going to talk about some feelings.

I have never felt so powerless in my life. I am sitting here watching everything around me collapse, and I realize that there is nothing I can do about any of it. Oh sure, I could do this or that to make things a bit better, but I can do nothing to change the way I feel right now. And to think I have to go through the rest of the day feeling like this. What a joy!

Not too long ago, I wrote about how good I felt about coming out of a bottomless hole to beat my addiction. Yet today I find myself falling back into that hole once again. It's like I'm on the fucking edge just waiting for something or someone to push me back down into that hole. Powerless. Even if I should be able to keep myself from falling back into that hole, I feel as though I can't. Part of me thinks I lack the confidence necessary to stay clean in this world. That same part just wants to say, "Fuck it all and get me an eightball."

But I know this isn't the answer, yet I still find it's what I want to do right now. Why can't I just forget about that part of my life? I just wish I could deal with everything else that is going on in my life without having to worry about treating my addiction or experiencing a relapse. The fact is that I cannot do this, and it is partly because my addiction is responsible for the situation in which I find myself today. I just want to ignore my addiction and am pissed off because I can't do so. I also want everything else in my life to go smoothly, but it's just not happening that way. And so I probably will continue to sit on this fucking pity pot until I get sick of it.

Sometimes I think I don't know what it's going to take to make me happy. I have operated with the philosophy for eight years now that I have to do all of this shit just because this is where I want to be in life. I put up with so much stuff, beat myself up, drain myself both physically and emotionally, just to be able to get somewhere in life. All of this pain and trouble I experience is supposed to have a happy ending for me, but as time passes I wonder if I'll ever reach that ending—and if I want to get there anyway. What really bothers me is, I am questioning what I want to do with my life and am second-guessing whether all this pain and trouble is worth doing what I think I want to do.

And so I am hovering above it all right now and am looking down on it. Cocaine would take me to a higher place so I could really look down on this all. Cocaine would take me to a place where I could see my life at a distance. Cocaine would just take me away from all of this. It would help me escape. The only problem is that I am not really up there at all. I am sitting right here in this chair in front of my computer at my office and am writing about how shitty I feel today. I can't escape my life today, and I have got to stop wanting to do so. This is my life and I have got to learn to live with it, to be happy with it.

Cocaine. What have you done to my life? Shit. Maybe if it wasn't cocaine it would have been something else? I really don't know the answer to this question. Life, oh miserable life. Won't you please get better for me? Why doesn't life just get better? Will cocaine make my life any better? Probably not, but it's trying to trick me into thinking that it can. Well, listen up—you're not going to trick me this time, you fucking little white powder you. So just go bother someone else, because I'm not falling for your bullshit again.

DECEMBER 8, 1988

Didn't I sound convincing there at the end of the last journal entry? I think about cocaine a lot lately. I just came back from the bathroom where I thought I could probably afford one gram of cocaine next week and should call Ricardo to get it. One gram. Just one fucking gram. Wonder what it would do to me? Why don't I make a list? I'll make a list of what it will do for me and what it will not do for me. Kinda like a pro and con list. Here goes. What one gram will do for me:

1. Get me high
2. Keep me high for a few hours
3. Pep me up

Short list, huh? How about the other list? What won't one gram of cocaine do for me?

1. Keep me high
2. Make me happy
3. Take my troubles away
4. Give me an answer to the predicament in which I find myself

How about all the other stuff that one gram of cocaine would do to me? You know, all that bad stuff that made me come screaming into the fellowship. Like, I know that doing cocaine would

1. Make my life unmanageable
2. Devastate my parents
3. Cause me to crash and experience withdrawal
4. Threaten a heart attack
5. Interfere with my running
5. Interfere with school
7. Interfere with life
8. Turn me into a monster
9. Cause me more financial worries than I already have
10. Destroy all of the good things that have happened to me during recovery
11. Eventually make me hate myself again

I'm going to stop here, but just let me tell you that this list would go on and include many more things. If we were to tally up all of the good things and bad things in doing one gram of cocaine, I'm sure we would find the bad things outnumbered the good things. For instance, I have listed about 20 possible effects that doing cocaine would have for me. After tallying these points up, I find I have listed only three good effects that cocaine would have for me and 15 bad effects it would have for me. You would probably conclude from this that the answer would be not to do cocaine. There are too many negative points to offset the positive points and so I should probably not go get the gram I am talking about, huh?

What you must realize, of course, is that the items listed above cannot be weighed equally. Therefore, we must ignore the fact that the score is 15 to three and must recalculate the score after coming up with a weighting scheme. Sounds pretty complicated, huh? Even I think it does and I'm a statistician. How can I assign weights to the factors or effects listed above? It would be a difficult task to do so, and so I am not going to do it today.

I guess I just have to be content in knowing that I don't want to do cocaine today and so I don't even have to worry about this silly old list. I have more important things to do today than to worry about one gram of cocaine. I'll think about it again tonight when I'm at the meeting in Silver Spring. Until then, ADIOS!

DECEMBER 9, 1988

I took a comprehensive test today and I feel mentally exhausted. I kinda just want to put it out of my mind right now and discuss something that Sarah said to me today. I told Sarah I really felt like getting drunk tonight because of the exam. I told her I might go to this party tonight so I could socialize with everyone. She told me not to go because she said I would be brooding all night about the fact that I could not drink and would probably be sitting on the pity pot as well. I replied, "Me, sitting on the pity pot? Why, that's not like me at all."

I guess I do sit on the pity pot a lot. I know I have been doing it a lot lately because of the holiday season. Being in this fellowship means no wine at dinner with my family, no drinks at the pub with all my friends and relatives, no drinks at Maggie and Pete's Christmas Eve party, no drinks on New Year's Eve, and no cocaine at any of the above. I'm pretty sure the only time I'll miss the cocaine is on New Year's Eve. I have done cocaine on the past few New Years and it has become pretty much of a ritual for my friends and me.

Well, times have changed. I can no longer drink or do cocaine. I guess this time of the year will be a trying time for me. Everyone in the fellowship feels this time of the year is difficult for abstinence. It's good for me to know that other people are in the same situation as I. It's nice talking to these people about it all because they help get me off that pity pot.

I just wish I could accept this new definition of a social life. It used to all be so easy. Every Friday night we picked up cocaine and went out to bars and had a blast. Wait a minute. That's not exactly true. We didn't always have a good time. That is just my selective memory acting up again. I am only remembering the good times and am forgetting the bad ones.

Listen, I am not going to sit here and write about how the good times turned into bad times. The point I want to get across—and the feeling I want to express right now—is, I have lost my social life and part of me feels very empty. My social life was good when I was at the restaurant not only because we partied with cocaine and spent an endless amount of nights at bars, parties, and restaurants, but because we all were together. My social life was spent with the people I was closest to in this town. My social life was spent with the people I love.

Things have changed so much over the past year to alter that tight network of friends to which I was so close. Two have moved out of town, two still party, one is too busy working, and the other one is consumed in a relationship. My network just isn't there for me anymore, and so my social life has fallen by the wayside. I don't really know what to do without these people. I know I can't hang around the ones that party, and I know I should make new friends. But the reality of it all is that I miss the bars, the nightclubs, the drinks, the cocaine, and all of the fun times we all shared together.

Sometimes I want it all back so badly, I can just taste it. I spend hours brooding over the fact that I can't be in the places with these people doing these things. All I can do is be depressed because I can't have any of it. Instead, I have to develop a new social life and have to meet new people. I really don't want to do this. I am not motivated in doing it at all. I am living in misery and boredom.

Please don't get me wrong. I am not upset because I can't have the cocaine. I am upset because I can't have any of the stuff that went along with it. It was my livelihood. It was my escape. It was what I looked forward to, and now it's gone. And what proves to be the worst part of it all is that no one took it away from me. I took it away from myself. And so here I sit on the pity pot. I might as well stay here because I end up kicking myself in the ass when I get up.

DECEMBER 14, 1988

I had a dream the other night that I want to write about. The dream has great significance to my life, as usual. Therefore, I'd like to tell the dream first and then offer an explanation of it.

Dream. I was riding around in a car with a tall, black policeman. We were trying to make some drug busts. We were driving through the streets of Georgetown and I noticed there were several houses that were boarded up. The streets were dirty with trash and broken glass. Even the people who were milling about on the streets were dirty.

We pulled up in front of this boarded-up house because we were told that people were selling drugs in this house. As we sat in the police car, we saw these three black men climb up the side of the house in order to gain entry. I was puzzled at why they were doing this because the windows on the house were boarded up. I turned to the police officer next to me and said, "What are they doing up there? They better be careful or they are going to fall down." And sure enough, two seconds later these men fell from the second story of this house right to the street.

We pulled up a little closer to the house and prepared ourselves for what we might find; but as we were doing so, we noticed that the guys began climbing up the house again. As we drove away, I found I just kept asking myself, "Why would these guys continue to climb up the house when they know they will probably fall down again and hurt themselves? Why are these guys trying to get inside a house they can't get into anyway?"

And so we just kept driving along until we came across another house we suspected was involved in drug activity. We got out of the car this time and decided to go inside the house. The policeman told me to search the downstairs while he searched the upstairs. I agreed with him and proceeded to make my way through the first floor of the house. I passed through the filthy living room to the dining room and paused to look around. I noticed the dining room was empty and the living room was cluttered with broken furniture and lots of newspapers.

Then I heard a harsh voice say, "What in the fuck are you doing here?" I lifted my head to see this thin black female standing in front of me with a gun in her hand. I told her I was looking for her, and she wanted an explanation. I stood there in silence, unable to offer her an explanation for my presence in that house. And she replied, "Oh, I know who you are. You're some fucking cop, man. You came in here to bust me." I just shook my head affirmatively and shrugged my shoulders.

She lifted up her gun and pointed it at my face and said, "You know what we do to cops in houses like this? We shoot them." I replied, "Please put the gun down"—and she just laughed at me. She was just about to pull the trigger when I heard a voice from behind me say forcefully, "Put the gun down, Miss, or I'll shoot." I turned my head to see the police officer standing in the doorway with his gun drawn. He added, "Give us the gun, Miss." I looked back to the lady and I saw her drop the gun to the floor.

The police officer walked over to the gun and picked it up. He left the room through the door in which we entered. I walked over to the lady and took her by the hand and said, "Come with me." And hand in hand we walked over to a wall that had broken windows in the bottom portion of it. I got down on my knees so I could climb out of the house and was still holding her hand. I cut myself on a piece of glass while doing this. I felt her resistance as I proceeded to climb out the window. I looked back at her and said, "Are you coming?" She replied, "Yes."

I was outside the house by now, and she was climbing through the broken window. She started complaining about all of the glass that was on the floor and kept saying she was going to get cut. Soon enough she did. The jagged edges from the glass pierced her arm and blood started to flow. She turned to me and said, "Ouch, that hurts! Let me go. I'm not going with you. I'm going to stay inside here because it's too painful outside. It just hurts too much out there." I replied, "It only hurts for a little while." But she continued to resist me, so I released my grip on her arm and allowed her to go back inside. I stood up and walked back to the car where the policeman was waiting, and we drove away.

Interpretation. I woke up at this point, took a shower, and got dressed for work. I realized on the way to work that this was another cocaine dream that had great significance to my life. I was in a police car making busts because I work on the opposite side now. I am no longer a drug user, and I don't hang out with dealers. I work with the criminal justice system and we are in the business of busting drug users and dealers. And so, being in that car with that cop was the reality of my new role in life today.

The drive through Georgetown where the houses were boarded up and the streets dirty was just my belief that this city is eroding. Georgetown is one of the most beautiful parts of town, but it had eroded in my dream because of the prevalence of drugs. I felt a great deal of sadness for this, but I can see the city decaying as the days pass and it is frightening.

The guys climbing on that boarded-up house is just an indication of what we addicts will go through to get drugs. In the dream I wondered why these guys would put themselves through all of that because the cocaine they were pursuing was not worth it. I can see this now; but if I were still using, I probably would have tried to get into that house as well. All I needed to know was that there was cocaine around, and soon I found myself doing irrational stuff just so I could get my hands on some.

The part of the dream I want to discuss the most is the last part—the part where I met the lady in that house. Thinking back to that dream, I don't remember feeling any fear walking into the house. In fact, I felt good about going in there because I sorta knew what I would encounter. In other words, I was on a mission to take whoever was inside that house out of it so they could enter recovery. I was playing the role of rescuer once again. You can tell by the way the confrontation turned out, I thought it would be very simple for me to just take this woman by the arm and take her away from her drug-infested life and right into recovery. I soon discovered in the dream, however, that this was an unrealistic expectation.

Her reluctance to come outside that house with me was her decision to stay inside. I wanted recovery for her, but she didn't want it for herself. Cutting her arm on the glass was just an indication of all of the pain we addicts have to deal with when we make the decision to get drug free. She was unwilling to undergo the pain for a better life. I was speaking from experience when I told her that the pain would only last a little while. I meant that things would soon get better for her, and I knew this because I was an addict and was in this situation before.

But the reality of it all is that she just didn't want to deal with life outside her world of drugs. She wanted to stay there, and there was nothing I could do to convince her that she should come outside with me. My fellowship teaches me that we are powerless over this disease and other people—that we can't force them into recovery when we want them to go, but rather they have to do it themselves. I was trying to pull her into recovery, and she just didn't want it. I guess I knew this in the dream because I just let go of her arm. I let her go back inside that house.

And so as I was driving away with the cop I thought to myself that she'll come out of the house when she's ready and no one will be pulling her arm. She'll be taking herself out of that house. She'll want recovery for herself. This is how it has to be. I can't bring people into recovery, and I know that. I had to want it for myself when I got clean, and so do others. I just wish they could see how good life really is outside those houses. It's not easy out here and it doesn't all feel good. I often find myself wanting to go back to that house, but I know I can't because I'm an addict.

December 16, 1988

Last night I had another dream about relapse. This dream really bothers me. All of this thinking about cocaine is no good for me because I end up dreaming about it all at night—which only proves to upset me. Here I go explaining the dream.

Dream. I really want an eightball tonight. I'm talking to this woman in this unfamiliar house and am asking her to sell me an eightball. I know she'll take a check for it, and I just want to write her one and get my cocaine. All of my family members are downstairs socializing, and so I have to be very careful in trying to keep this deal from them.

She tells me to write the check and I take out my checkbook. I start writing a check for $250, but my hand moves and I end up misspelling her name. Hastily, I rip that check off my checkbook pad and throw it away. Damn! I ripped several checks when I tore that last check off my checkbook pad and now a whole bunch of them are ruined. I have to sift through the bad ones so I can get to a good one. I have to hurry up because someone might come upstairs and see what we are doing.

She says, "Hurry up, man. Why can't you just write the check?" I reply, "I'm trying, I'm trying. I just keep messing it up. I can't get it right." And so I finally get to a good check and I begin writing it and I misspell her name again. At this time, my sister-in-law Nancy comes into the room and asks, "What are you guys doing?" I reply hastily, "Nothing." Nancy replies, "OK"—and she leaves the room. I am ready to throw my entire checkbook away at this point because I am fed up with it. I tell this dealer to wait while I go get another checkbook and she replies, "We'll take care of this later."

Now I'm running around the house for the next several hours trying to find an opportunity to pay this woman so I can get an eightball. I go downstairs with my family and they are sitting around the billiard table, playing pool. I walk over to them and sit beside my mother and we begin to talk. All that is on my mind as I sit there is getting cocaine. I stay downstairs with my family primarily because the dealer is down there as well.

No one in the room knows this person is a coke dealer, and no one knows about our attempted transaction upstairs. I sit there and watch her moves and listen to her words as I wait for the slightest opportunity to try to make the deal again. I make eye contact with her, and she gives me a signal. She raises her eyes to suggest that we go back upstairs so we can make the deal. I say, "I'm going to go upstairs to work on my computer. I'll be back down in a bit." My family agrees, and I make my way upstairs.

The dealer comes upstairs and enters the living room with me. Another guy also enters the room and we begin to talk. I go over to the couch and sit down with this guy, and the dealer tells us we are going to begin an exercise. She tells us she wants to explain the process of addiction to us before she gives us our cocaine. A few other people walk into the room now. Reluctantly, after protest, I indulge her wish and agree to participate in the exercise. She has us drawing a chart, an *x-y* axis graph of the trend in cocaine addiction. We are instructed to listen to her and then draw the lines on the graph as we think they would look.

I have no problem with this exercise. I know what to do. The other people around me, however, don't know what to do. I try to tell them, but they still can't understand. The dealer stops the instruction so she can explain the process to them. I ask her if I can get my eightball now and she replies, "No, you have to wait until the exercise is finished." I start getting angry because these other dimwits are slowing me down. All I can think about is, I could have my cocaine if these stupid people would just hurry up and draw their graphs.

And this is where the dream ended. I spent the entire dream in a state of panic because I was trying to cop cocaine. I never got the drug. There is more to the dream than this. My family played a bigger part, and the ending was a bit different. The part I wanted to convey in this journal was that the theme of the dream seemed to be my intense desire to relapse. I wanted cocaine so badly and could think of nothing else while I was trying to make the transaction. I was getting very frustrated because it seemed as though something kept blocking me from making that transaction. I was pissed by the end of the dream.

I am sure that there is a message in all of this. I am just too frustrated to think about it right now.

PART THREE

January 12 through May 7, 1989

Depressed and tired of fighting the cocaine cravings, I found myself abusing my recovery by attending too few meetings, questioning my addiction, and neglecting my journal. This behavior resulted in my downing about four cocktails over the holiday season. On January 12, I wrote about my desire to resume casual drinking and concluded that I could and would. But I found it too uncomfortable to live on the edge of the 12 Step programs. So, although the journal contains no formal statement of the fact, those four drinks were the only ones. Today, I have decided to reset my sobriety date to January 12, 1989.

The first four months of 1989 were characterized by painful memories of my twenty-fifth birthday, troubling realizations, and financial and emotional problems. I felt empty and realized I had very little self-love or acceptance. I had used cocaine—and was still using people—to make me feel better about myself. My complaints about being lonely, having no boyfriend, being so overworked, and so on helped me see that I had to change internally to remain clean and sober. By the end of April 1989, I knew recovery was about much more than just not using drugs and alcohol; it was about finding a better way of life. And that meant changing.

It also meant taking steps one and two of my recovery program again—or perhaps for the first time—and applying its principles to my life. So by May 9, 1989, I finally accepted the 12 Step program into my life and rediscovered God or my "Higher Power" (12 Step terminology). I was extremely grateful for this.

January 12, 1989

This is the first entry I am making this year. It has been almost a month since I last wrote in my journal. I don't have particular feelings about this. I just know I haven't written in my journal for quite some time.

What's been happening in my life? Lots of things, I guess. I have been sitting here trying to analyze what my life is going to be like during the next term, or next few months, and all I see is work. Here is what I plan to do this term:

1. Continue working at the office 40 hours a week
2. Take an advanced stats class with Professor Richards on Wednesdays
3. Teach my own class on Thursdays—a job in which I am no expert
4. Make some money tutoring
5. Prepare for a comprehensive exam in May
6. Turn in a paper to eliminate an incomplete I took last term
7. Work on a dissertation proposal for the summer
8. Work on and present a paper at the meetings in March
9. Stay in shape
10. Lose weight

Looking back at that list, I realize I have left out treating my addiction. I will be unable to attend meetings on my usual nights during this term. I can just hear what everyone in the program would say if they saw this schedule and found that I was only going to attend two meetings a week. I'm sure they would disapprove and would take my inventory.

I guess this is what I am going to talk about during this journal entry. I know I have discussed feelings like these about the fellowship before. Sometimes I wonder if I'm not doing something right, because I keep getting back to this point. I just don't really feel that I'll ever be able to fully identify with all of the other people in the program. There are many reasons for this, and I guess I should talk about them right now.

First of all, I don't need to attend many meetings in order to stay clean. I have been going to two meetings a week for the past month and feel just fine. I have been dealing with issues in my life rather well, and I have been happy. Most importantly, I have had no cravings for the drug and have done very little thinking about it. There have been a few occasions when I have felt it necessary to attend a meeting because of some problem in my life I could not handle. I just haven't felt it necessary to attend more than two meetings a week.

I know I said this shit and talked this way back in April when I first came into the fellowship, and I know it didn't work for me at that time. So why will it work this time? Why will going to only two meetings a week work for me? Will I relapse because I am only attending two meetings a week? What will happen to me?

Nothing. I will never be able to predict if I am going to relapse, no matter how many meetings I attend. Nag, nag, nag. I started this entry yesterday, and now I have to finish it but don't feel like doing so.

The bottom line is, I am so caught up in what others will think about my attending only two meetings a week that I am losing track of what is important to me. There are no laws and rules dictating the amount of meetings one must attend to be in the fellowship. There are only suggestions coming from different people in the program. I know most of them would think I need to attend more meetings, and I know most of them would disagree with how I handle my addiction. It is up to me to decide just how much worth I allow their judgments on my recovery to affect my life. After all, when they offer their advice on how I should conduct my recovery they are essentially offering their judgment on how I should run my life.

Look, I wouldn't be so uptight about this all if it was this simple. I do other things that run contrary to the fellowship as well, and I guess that it is these things that concern me the most. I had a few drinks over the holidays and I went to happy hour last week with Sarah and had two scotches. I know what the people in the fellowship would think about this. They would think I had relapsed and was heading back to my drug of choice.

I don't agree with them. I firmly believe I can handle casual drinking without abusing it. I don't feel as though I will switch seats to my addiction and will go back to my drug of choice if I have a few drinks once in a while. The only problem anyone in the fellowship has with this is they don't believe I will be able to control my drinking and they feel it is unrealistic for me to think I will be able to do so.

Here is my dilemma: I want to be in the fellowship, but I want other things as well. I want to be able to enjoy an occasional drink with my family or friends, but I feel uncomfortable doing so while I am in the fellowship. I do not want to have to make a decision between the fellowship and drinking. That is totally unrealistic. The fellowship keeps me away from cocaine, and I need that very much. I do not need it like many others do, and it is not the main part of my life.

I guess I must make the decision. I can't ask anyone else to make the decision for me or help me make the decision. I am a big girl now. My decision is to keep doing things the way I am doing them. I am going to conduct my recovery the way I see fit. If that means I go to two meetings a week instead of five, then so be it. If I want to have an occasional drink with my friends, then so be it. I know not to get drunk and I know not to pick up any cocaine. End of story.

February 1, 1989

I promise to be a better journal writer this month. Enough said about that. Well, it has been over nine months now since I gave up cocaine. I feel really good about this. A lot of things have changed during these past nine months. I have gone through so many emotions and mood swings just dealing with recovery. I have learned so much about addiction and other things as well. I have learned how to deal with life—and believe it or not, I am learning more and more each day how to deal with Katy.

It feels good to be sitting here today. I can look back to that first day of recovery and see all of the pain I felt and how miserable my life was, but it's just not like that today. I feel good today. My life is back on track. I am happy once again. Probably the most amazing thing is, I am beginning to really like myself again. I feel confident in saying that one day I may eventually love myself.

February 16, 1989

Here it is almost two weeks since I last wrote in my journal and I am not going to comment about that. I am just going to write about things today. I shared in a meeting last night about fear. "Fear" was the topic of the meeting. Many people shared about how they feared relapse, troubling issues, and recovery. I shared about how I fear not feeling good enough.

How can I fear not feeling good enough? Simple. I used cocaine to make me feel better. Every time I wanted to feel better, I simply went to get high—and so I fear not feeling good enough. A classic example of this fear happened a few days ago. This is the incident I shared at last night's meeting. I was working on some grant for the office and was under a lot of pressure. I also had to finish a paper, for my evening class, that I had barely started. You see, I had planned to work on the paper during office hours because I thought I wouldn't have much work to do. I didn't know I would be responsible for this grant application.

And so I was just cranking on the grant. I told my secretary to hold all of my calls and to prevent anyone from disturbing me. I closed the door to my office and only went outside to get coffee or go to the bathroom. I was working my ass off. I was going full throttle. I felt good working at this pace. I kind of felt on top of the world. I felt like I was working on something very important and difficult (which it really was) and was doing it very well. So well that no one in the world could have done it better than I. I simply felt like I was on top of the world; I felt invincible. I felt good up here; however, I did not feel great.

There was just one thing missing: cocaine. While I was working like this and feeling this way, I stopped to think how much better I could feel if I was high. I knew I was feeling great, feeling invincible, but I thought I could feel even better with cocaine. I wanted some cocaine to make me feel better than I was already feeling. And so I was feeling good, but I wanted to feel better. The only way to feel better at this moment was to get some cocaine and finish my work high.

Can you see why I am scared of not feeling good enough? I actually had a craving for cocaine during a time when I already felt on top of the world, and the reason behind this craving was that I thought I could feel better than I was already feeling. Feeling the way I did without cocaine was just not good enough for me during that moment. I wanted to feel even better, and I thought cocaine would make me feel better. The reality of it all is that it wouldn't make me feel better anyway, but that is not the point I am trying to make.

What is the point I am trying to make? I simply want to know what is going to be good enough? Nothing I do is ever good enough. I just keep searching and searching, always thinking there is something better out there I have yet to achieve or receive. And it is those things for which I keep striving. So Tuesday's incident should be no surprise to me, I guess. I actually missed the goddamn drug that was responsible for fucking up a part of my life and for giving me a disease I have to deal with for the rest of my life. And it was all because I thought I didn't feel good enough. What's wrong with me? Why don't I feel good enough? Why don't the things I do ever seem to satisfy me? What am I searching to find?

I don't know. There is nothing more scary to me than realizing that anything I get in life will never be good enough for me. That no matter how hard I try, I will not be able to find what it takes to make me feel good enough. Even more frightening is the fact that I may come to not only think that cocaine will help me feel "good enough," but will actually go get some to make me feel better. It is scary to think I may actually relapse because I am simply not feeling good enough.

Sounds like I have my hands full in trying to figure this all out. I got through that day without using because I called my sponsor to talk about it. We discussed the reinforcing qualities of cocaine, which can make us feel good when we feel terrible or even better when we are already feeling good. Cocaine is a positive reinforcer for me. I will use it when I feel both lousy and great. I am classified in the "high risk" group for cocaine abuse, and it is this fact that causes me additional concern.

February 21, 1989

All of this worry about not feeling good enough and wanting to get high. Well, I had a conversation with Karen [my sponsor] and her husband this past Saturday night, and it was quite a peculiar one at that. Karen's husband Phil had a hard time believing that cocaine was the only drug I abused. They both called me a pure cocaine addict. Phil repeatedly said that he just couldn't believe I didn't supplement my cocaine use with any other drugs like Valium or alcohol. I explained my reasons to him and then he proceeded to ask me, "Well, why do you even think that you are an addict?"

Now, just let me tell you that this was the wrong thing for Phil to say to me. In fact, it was probably the worst thing he could have said to me. I have had a very hard time accepting the fact that I am an addict, but have reluctantly admitted I am one. Along comes this lifelong addict questioning the very fact I have been struggling with for the past ten months. And now I find myself questioning it as well. I am just about ready to say I am not an addict, but just *had* a problem with cocaine. This kind of thinking scares me very much.

I spent the rest of the weekend reevaluating the state of my addiction. I kept asking myself, "Am I an addict, or what?" "Do I really need to watch my drinking or was cocaine really the only drug I will abuse?" "Can I use cocaine again socially somewhere down the road, after a certain amount of clean time?" "Am I just like all of the other addicts, or is there something unique about me and my drug problem?"

You see, it is very dangerous for me to be sitting here asking myself these questions. Things are relatively simple when I believe I am a recovering addict in a 12 Step program. Things really get confusing when I question the reality of my addiction. Things are simple as a recovering addict because I know my limitations. And when I don't know my limitations, I get into a lot of trouble.

You know, they say the first step is the only step you have to do perfectly in the program. That step has to do with admitting that you are powerless over drugs and that your life had become unmanageable. I admitted this last April when I came screaming into the fellowship; but ever since then, I keep finding myself questioning why I did so. People like Phil and comments like his are no help in keeping me on track, keeping me where I am supposed to be.

Realistically, I can't blame any doubts about my addiction on him or anyone else. The bottom line is that, if I want to do cocaine again, I will do so. I will do cocaine if I want to, and the only reason I'd do it is to make myself feel better. However, if I did choose to do it again, I know my life would eventually get out of control once again and I would become miserable. Cocaine would dominate my life and dictate everything I did. Cocaine would control my life. And it is these facts that let me know who I really am: an addict. That's the common denominator, Phil. I am an addict!

February 28, 1989

I am supposed to write out a first step so my sponsor can read it and so I will come to understand why I came into the fellowship or why I am an addict. I guess these are the reasons why I am doing this long, arduous task.

I started the damn task two days ago at home. I guess I can continue it here and then merge the two documents together. Although I could probably sit here and list out many reasons why I think I am powerless over drugs, only one really comes to mind and seems to matter anyway. I just couldn't stop doing cocaine, no matter how hard I tried. Time after time I promised myself that this was going to be the last time I got high, only to find myself using a day or two later. When attempts at total abstinence failed, I would try to "control" my use by promising myself that I would do no more than a few grams a week or only one gram a day. All of it failed.

Who in the fuck was I trying to kid? I could not control the amount I used, nor could I control the frequency with which I used. And there was simply no way I could stop using cocaine all by myself, either. So blind I was to this during those months of using. If I would have just listened to the people around me, or if I would have looked in the mirror to see the horror before me, or if I would have seen the obvious signs that my life was falling apart, maybe I would have spared myself a lot of pain. I suppose it is too late for all of that now, huh?

As many other people in the fellowship have said before, I loved cocaine, but it didn't like me. I loved everything about it. I loved the way it tasted, the way it made me feel, the things it enabled me to do, and the people it involved. I looked forward to partying after a long week's work, and I deserved it. There is simply no doubt about it—I loved cocaine. But I can't pay the price anymore. I can't finish this now. It's time to go.

MARCH 3, 1989

I can't seem to stop crying. It's all coming back to me right now. Sometimes I think it's gone from my memory, but then it just keeps coming back to haunt me. I just can't seem to forget those fucking painful memories. Memories of what I did, how I looked, and where I was last year at this time just keep coming back to me. I wish they would go away forever. I don't want to have to deal with them, but I guess it is time to do so.

During the first three months of recovery, I thought I had done all of the crying I could possibly do. Well, I guess I was wrong. I'm sitting here at work with tears in my eyes and I can't even imagine making it through this day without falling apart. You see, I have pushed those memories so far back into my head and buried them deep in my soul because they were just too painful for me to handle. Last night they surfaced at the meeting and I haven't really stopped crying since. It's like they came out of nowhere. I was just sitting on the bench listening to everyone share when all of a sudden tears just started to pour out of my eyes. And so I found I was reliving that day in March 1988.

What a miserable memory. I don't want to have to deal with it. It's just too painful. Birthdays! Why do we have to have them? Everyone important in your life makes this big fucking fuss about your getting older. You get together with them all to celebrate the day you were born—and all that happens is, you find yourself getting so emotional. Why do we need birthdays to bring us together? Why do people have to gather in honor of you? Why do people have to go out of their way for you? Why do people have to love you so much? And why of all the other 10 million horrible things you could do to anyone else in this world do you have to hurt those people who love you the most?

I had to do it. I did it and now it's back to haunt me. Just when I thought I had buried it all for good, it came out of nowhere to haunt me. I am devastated right now and am actually finding it hard to function. I really fucked up a year ago, and the damage I did will never be mended in my mind. Denial of love is something I take a stance against, something I would never do, something I know hurts too much. And yet I find I did it. I hated my family that day, and I have never ever felt that way before. The worst part of it all is that I am very scared it could happen again. And this is why I am upset right now.

So many times before, I wrote about how difficult it was to hate someone. I could probably go back to those journal writings and merge them in right here at this point to describe what hatred really means to me. I don't feel like doing that, however. I just want to keep writing about how I treated my family that day and what ended up happening to me. I do plan to keep those feelings of hatred alive, though, as I write—because they play a major role in the pain I feel for that experience today.

Ricardo and I started doing cocaine early Friday evening. For some unknown reason, I thought I would be able to stop at a reasonable hour so I could clean the apartment and get some sleep. I was wrong, of course. We stayed up all night snorting cocaine, and I never got to sleep and I never got to clean. We did manage to get out to the grocery store before my family arrived; but as they pulled in the driveway, Ricardo and I were doing our last lines before we got out of the car. Ricardo proceeded to drive himself home in my car, which violated my previous plan of taking him home before my parents arrived. My first explanation to my parents, therefore, was why this "friend" was taking my car. The lying and the mess started here.

At this point, I hadn't showered in two days, so I didn't look very well. I was very pale because I had not eaten anything in a few days. Besides, the cocaine always took the color out of my face, making my eyes look horrible. I was always so certain that everyone could see how horrible I looked and would figure why I looked that way. Some paranoia, huh? You know, as I continue with this description, I find myself looking for reasons to leave my computer. This is very hard for me to do. I give up. I'll finish tomorrow [March 6, 1989].

March 13, 1989

I was home this past weekend to celebrate my birthday with my family and to attend a good friend's wedding. I had a wonderful time at the wedding and I had fun with my family, but I don't really want to talk about either of those things right now. What I want to talk about the most today is the relationship I have with my sister Kellie. I made a major discovery this weekend concerning myself and the relationship I have with Kellie, and it is this discovery that I want to discuss.

Last Thursday, I received a birthday card from Kellie in the mail. The card informed me to be at her house at noon on Saturday. This request immediately aroused my curiosity. Anyway, I went over to Kellie's house at noon on Saturday to give her the birthday gift I got her and to receive this "surprise" of hers. When I got to her house, she began explaining why she didn't have my gift yet. You see, Kellie thought it would be a neat idea to get me a kitten for my birthday. She made arrangements to have one delivered on Saturday at noon, but the plans fell through and so she had no gift to give.

I really don't feel like describing the course of events that day. Those things are not what I want to talk about. I do, however, want to talk about Kellie's appearance, lifestyle, and friends and how it all seems to characterize the relationship between the two of us. Kellie was very pale that day, and she had dark circles under her eyes. She was fatigued as usual. It seems as though she never gets enough sleep. She is thin, but her body looks good. I don't think she realizes how good her body does look because she constantly complains about losing another five pounds.

The point I am trying to make here is that every time I go home, or see her after a period of time, she looks older, sicker, and more tired than before. She just hasn't been looking well lately. Her friends look the same way. Renee came over to Kellie's when I was there on Saturday, and she looked horrible. She had the worst bags and circles at her eyes, and her clothes were falling off of her. Kellie and Renee actually looked the same, acted the same, and talked the same that day. It was so frightening for me to see my sister looking like Renee. I could hardly stand looking at either of them, and soon I found I desperately wanted to leave there to go home and run.

And so on the way back to my parents' place, I had a major revelation. It was clear to me that Kellie and Renee are using drugs. I know because I have been there before. Looking back on it all right now disgusts me knowing I may have looked just like the two of them or even worse. Irrespective of that, however, I don't know how many drugs Kellie is doing, but I do know Renee uses frequently. I guess I assume Kellie is doing the same since they are so close and spend so much time together. What came to my mind first in my car on the way back to my parents' place was, I couldn't believe that Kellie could not see what was going on with both Renee and herself. How in the hell could she blind herself to what was happening to her? Can't she see how she is living, what she looks like, and what her friends are doing?

Pausing for a minute, I do realize I was unable to see how the cocaine was affecting my appearance, attitudes, and behaviors. I guess it's really not that difficult, after all, understanding why Kellie can't see what she's doing to herself. It's hard to see what's happening to your life when you are using drugs. You have to be clean and sober—or at least take that first step—before you can really see what you look like. But I guess Kellie can't see any of that.

Kellie never has been able to see what is wrong in her life, what is making her unhappy, and why her life is not going where she wants it to go. She is constantly in some kind of trouble and can never rescue herself from any of it. All that she can do is to make a temporary shift that alters the pain for a few weeks or months. I really hate to say this but it is almost as if she can never seem to accomplish what she thinks she wants to do, but could accomplish it if she tried. The only problem with this is that it is the things she thinks she wants—but can never seem to get—that will make her happy. What Kellie wants out of life is what she cannot have, and she cannot have these things because she just can't seem to motivate herself enough to get them. And so she is constantly unhappy, by her own choice.

What Kellie fails to realize, however, is that she can get whatever she wants out of life. She really does have what it takes to do whatever she might put her mind to, and therefore would easily be able to make herself happy. She just doesn't think she can do any of it. And so she just keeps limiting herself by her own fucking lifestyle. A lifestyle that includes a job requiring long hours because it yields lots of money, social habits that not only occupy her evenings but also filter over into the next day, friendships with people who are nice but use drugs, and involvement with a man who doesn't think she is worth anything.

And so what I have come to realize this past weekend is that Kellie is never able to see the trouble she is in—or if she does see it, she doesn't seem to have what it takes to get her ass out of trouble. I can do that. I have gotten myself in a lot of trouble in my life, but I have always managed to get myself out of it. I am not saying I haven't had any help from others during turbulent times in my life; but for the most part, I have solved all of my own problems. I don't want to brag or anything, but I have also been able to achieve just about everything I have ever set out to do. Oh, there are some things I haven't been able to accomplish that I may have wanted, but I have been able to accomplish all of the things in life that are most important to me. And basically, I know I probably always will be able to accomplish them.

More important than this, however, is the fact that I am learning how to remain happy even if I am unable to do what I want or get what I want. I am discovering ways to reorganize my life when things don't go my way so I don't sit around and feel empty and bitter, but rather feel even better about myself. Kellie just can't seem to do this. She can't bounce back; she can't reorganize her life when things are going poorly. The football analogy goes something like this: When it is third and ten, Kellie drops back to punt without looking at her options; when it is third and ten for me, I may decide to punt, but I look at all possible options before I do so. I do it this way so I don't lose, so I stay happy, so I come out on top. On the other hand, Kellie doesn't do this, and that's why she hurts so much.

Believe it or not, it's why I hurt so much as well. It is not easy being Katy, and it never has been. I have always felt bad about getting everything right, or getting anything I wanted, because I know Kellie has been unable to do the same. And even when I was at rock bottom last year during my addiction, I recognized the problem in a few short months and was able to get my act back together. I have been clean ever since and feel great about it. And so it is like Sarah said to me one time, "You just can't seem to fuck up, Katy, no matter how hard you may try. You just always seem to come out on top. You'll make something positive out of this addiction stuff and you'll be a better person for it."

Now, it must seem to Kellie that I always get things right and always come out on top. Even though I know this is not entirely true, I do know it is no secret that Kellie is envious of me for these things. And I know it must be so frustrating for her to have to deal with those feelings, but what Kellie doesn't know is that I deal with those feelings as well. I have spent my entire life feeling bad about me. I feel horrible knowing I can do this or that or have done this or that and Kellie has not. In fact, I can see very easily why Kellie would resent me, because I almost resent myself.

Life goes on. We all make our choices. Kellie is doing things the way she sees fit. I just find it so natural to want to make her see things as I see them because I think that's how they really are. But Kellie sees things differently. Maybe she is not as disgusted with her life as I am. And maybe I don't have any fucking place to be disgusted with her life anyway.

All I know is, it hurts to see her unhappy all of the time. I wish she would stop using, and I wish she could motivate herself to get the things she wants out of life. Maybe the two are not connected and maybe they are. I guess I'll never know because it is Kellie's life and not mine. I love her so much. I want to be able to help her, but I can't. You know, I have been hearing for the last ten months how we can't help other people give up drugs. We have to let them do it themselves. I really hate this kind of thinking sometimes because it could mean that people just sit and wallow in their shit forever—like Kellie. Maybe she'll never see anything, and maybe she'll always be unhappy. And maybe I'll have to live with that for the rest of my life.

It's hard being here. I feel worthless right now, but I know I am not. I guess I should say the serenity prayer because it seems to fit. God, grant me the serenity to accept the things I cannot change, the courage to change the things I can, and the wisdom to know the difference. Later!

MARCH 16, 1989

I just finished writing the entry above a moment ago. It took me awhile to write it. Last night I began crying the blues again about how much money I spent on cocaine. I am sitting here at my office right now with absolutely no money in my checking account. I mean the balance is $0.00. And all I can do is think about all of the money I spent on cocaine and wish I had it all back right now.

These thoughts started last night when I was packing my things for the move. I realized at work yesterday I don't really have enough money to meet my expenses this month and will have difficulty doing so next month. So what comes back to me at moments like these are memories of spending countless dollars on cocaine for nothing but a fucking high. On my way up to Hechinger's [hardware store] last night, I calculated how much money I spent on cocaine during the year and a half that I used it. The figure came out to be more than $15,000. When I finally figured this amount out, all I could do was drop my lower jaw in amazement and shake my head. I can't believe I spent more than $15,000 on cocaine!

That is a lot of money. Man, what I could do with that money today! It would come in so handy right now. I could buy blinds and curtains for my apartment and all of the other stuff I wanted and needed. I could also pay an entire year's rent and not have to worry about it, and I could also pay off my credit cards. I could probably even make some double car payments. My life would be so much easier if I just had that money. I wouldn't have to get a second job and I wouldn't have to curtail my lifestyle. I could concentrate on my studies because everything would be taken care of financially. Man, how that money would come in handy!

Fuck! I just don't have it. I had it and I blew it. I blew it on cocaine and I fucked my life up. God, I hate myself right now. I hate what I did and I'll never forgive myself for it. I know I have to get past this, but I just can't seem to do so right now. That's almost enough money to finance a college education at my undergraduate school. And to think that I blew it on cocaine. I almost blew a college education on cocaine. Let me just wallow in this shit right now because I can't seem to get it off my mind.

All I want is for things to go smoothly, for things to be right in my life. When money is tight, it means that I can't pay this bill or that one; and I want to pay them all because I feel like a drug addict when I don't. I am a drug addict, aren't I? I feel like I am slimming by, screwing people over because I can't pay them right now. I feel so lousy and dishonest, and it is all upsetting me so much right now. I haven't slept well in a week now because I am thinking about my financial problems. I am tired, nervous, scared, and angry at the same time. When will all of this end?

$15,000+. The number seems magical to me. Like, pooof! I had it—and pooof! It's gone. Nothing I can do to get it back, I guess. No magic trick that will put it all in front of me right now. Looks as though I have to sweat this one out. Damn! Life is a bitch. Oh well, at least I have my health.

March 17, 1989

Today is St. Patrick's Day. I just received a call from a very close friend of mine who asked me how I planned to celebrate this "holiday." This friend is the type who looks for special occasions on which to drink, and it just so happens that just about every day could be considered a special occasion. He is a borderline alcoholic.

Well, I told this friend I have no special plans for the evening and will be spending the night packing for my move. I gathered from his chuckle and snide remarks he must think I live a pretty mundane life and am turning into a nerd. After all, I don't hang out in the posh nightclubs anymore, I don't drink anymore, I don't stay up all day [and night] doing cocaine anymore, and I am just not too involved in the social scene right now. I have retreated from the social scene and am spending my time working, studying, going to meetings, and taking care of other things.

Probably what bothers him the most (and what actually bothers me at times) is, I have discovered a new lifestyle that includes new friends—

friends that he doesn't care to meet. These friends are the people I have met in the program. I know how Rick perceives these people and so I can only assume that he perceives me the same way now. I think Rick—as well as some of my other old friends—think I am different from the rest of the people in the program, and I think many of them think I could handle my cocaine problem without going to meetings and without getting involved in the fellowship. But the reality is that I am not very different from the people in the program and, more importantly, I cannot control my addiction without the help of the fellowship.

You see, I think most of my closest friends don't really believe I am an addict. In fact, I know most of them deny most of the stuff I did and toss it off as just messing up. Make no mistake about it: I *am* an addict and I *need* the help of the program to stay drug free. It really bothers me sometimes that these friends cannot accept that I am an addict and cannot accept that I am involved in the program, but I can't expect them to accept any of it. They may never do so. And so I must learn to live with this situation.

Life gets better despite all of this. I was crying the blues this past week and I must admit I am on edge right now because of my finances and this move, but things are really so much better today than they were last year at this time—and that is all I need to think about. It's like my sponsor said last night:

> I went through some real shit these past few years while I was clean. Sometimes I didn't think I would make it because things were so bad; but then as I lie on my bed wallowing in my shit, I think about how things were when I was using. And I say to myself that when I wake up today, I don't throw up; when I wake up today and look at the person next to me, I know if I have fucked him or not; and when I wake up today, I know I don't have to worry about how, where, and when I am going to get high. And I simply thank God for that.

Kind of puts things into perspective, huh? It's nice having a sponsor to help you see what's happening, to give you guidance, and to let you know she has been there. It's just so fucking good to be clean—and if being clean means I live a mundane life and remove myself from the social scene, then so be it. The alternative is just too painful.

MARCH 20, 1989

The move is complete. I am totally in my new apartment—and boy, does it ever look good! I am so happy because I finally have a nice place of my own. Right now I am in that stage where I can't wait to get home to live in it, do things to it, and have people over to visit. I love this place so much and I have only been here for two days. What I want to talk about today is not so much the new apartment, but what took place this weekend with my family.

First of all, let me just say that the move went very smoothly. It was a perfect move. We experienced no problems with anything and actually had a nice time. I am even totally unpacked. If I wanted to do it all over again, I would do it the exact same way. Everyone was so wonderful, and everything went wonderfully. This is what I want to talk about right now.

The last two moves I made before this one were horrible. I was using coke both times. One time, only my parents helped Meg and me move; and by the time we finished, my parents were very fatigued. It was not a pleasant experience. The next move was even worse. However—fortunately—my parents weren't involved. I had stayed up with Ricardo partying the night before and started packing one hour before the truck came to pick up my stuff. I was higher than a kite during the move, I didn't know what was happening, I missed class again, and I kept right on partying anyway.

The reason I am going through all of this is to illustrate how important it was for me to have a perfect move with my parents this weekend. I needed that type of move to straighten me out, to make me feel like I am getting my life back together, to let me know I can function normally given a hard task, and to let my parents know my life is back together and I am a responsible person again. The move was perfectly organized, well planned, and well executed.

It kind of characterizes my life today in recovery. Ever since I gave up cocaine, I am becoming more organized and responsible. I am doing things the "right" way and and am not trying to get over on everyone.

March 24, 1989

Today is Friday, and it is the end of a long hard week here at the office. Somehow, I just know this day is not going to be easy—that is, in terms of work. Irrespective of that, I am in a better mood today than I was yesterday and am going to try my hardest to keep my mood here all day.

On the way to work this morning, on the bus, I started thinking about my friendship with Rebecca again—and soon found I was comparing it with my friendship with Sarah. I always promised myself that I would never do this because it is unfair to both of them. The real reason I shy away from making comparisons between the two friendships, however, really has little to do with my concern for their feelings. I don't make the comparison because I know it will only fuck me up somewhere down the road.

Getting back to my friendship with Rebecca, I was just remembering some of the good times that she and I had during the development of the friendship. We were so incredibly close. I have never been that close with anyone in my life. The warmth I used to feel, and still do feel, when I am around her is amazing. She just has that quality to make anyone not only love her, but also feel good about themselves. She is very warm and understanding. It's no wonder that most men fall so hard for her and end up loving her so much. She is very giving.

I guess I am fortunate to have her in my life, but a few months ago I didn't think so. I actually hated her a few months ago. I blamed her for the dissolution of the friendship and accused her of abandoning me during a crucial time in my life. And I hated Jim, as well, because I thought he had taken her away from me.

Eleven months into recovery I have decided it is time for me to stop assuming the role of the victim. She didn't do anything to me, and neither did Jim. I did it all to myself. I was the one who let myself down, because I expected her to do this, this, and that for me. I was the one who hurt myself, because I couldn't see I was depending on her to make me happy.

Well, the good news is that both Rebecca and Jim are back in my life now, which means I can always see both of them and Billy. All three of them helped me move last weekend, and I was totally amazed that they did so. They were so kind that day. They would have helped me do anything. I guess nothing has really changed between Rebecca and me except that she has someone new in her life—and therefore we can't spend as much time together. I mean I still feel close to her; but naturally I don't feel as close as I used to, because we are not together every moment of the day like we used to be. The fact is that I still do love her dearly and I know she loves me as well.

What about Sarah? There is no doubt that I love her and that she is probably my closest friend right now. Lately, however, I am finding it very hard to be with her. She has this fucking wall up around her that prevents people from getting close. And you can feel the wall, as well. Sometimes you bump right into it when you interact with her. I guess this is why I have so many headaches lately. No, it's not. I'm just kidding, of course.

Friendship with her is a lot of work. There are so many barriers between us. It is not an easy friendship like Rebecca's was. There are complications with Sarah that I didn't experience with Rebecca, or even Meg for that matter. Somehow, I get through the complications just when I think I want to give up. Just when I want to say to Sarah, "Shut the fuck up and leave me alone," I simply find I don't need to say it anymore. I have found new coping mechanisms to deal with the discomfort in my life and many of those mechanisms help me deal with problems I encounter with friends.

You see, friends are everything to me. It's like they are all I have in this big old impersonal city. I don't like being here alone without someone to love. I don't like feeling lonely. I can feel lonely when others are around me very easily. In fact, I spent last year feeling very lonely even though I was around the same people every day doing cocaine. What can possibly be any worse than feeling lonely when others are around you and feeling unloved when others claim that they love you? The only thing I can think of that's worse than these things is not loving yourself.

Maybe that's what this entry is all about. Maybe this journal entry has little to do with my friendships with Rebecca and Sarah, but has a lot to do with my inability to love myself. Maybe my loneliness is nothing more than an emotional by-product of my inability to love myself. And maybe—just maybe—I look to friends to fill the emptiness I feel inside, because I cannot fill it myself.

Doesn't sound too far off, now that I look at it. I can remember saying many times last year that I felt so empty inside when Meg left for New York or when Rebecca "ditched" me for Jim. I feel all alone here in this city because my family lives in Pennsylvania. I used to complain quite a bit about not being able to fulfill my needs for intimacy, and I can remember complaining about not having anyone to love. And I can remember fearing I would be all alone in life with no one around me to love.

And so when Meg and Rebecca "left," and when the emptiness inside me grew, I tried to suppress those feelings with cocaine. I hated life alone last year. I was unhappy constantly. The only thing that brought me joy was knowing I was going to get high. Of course, as it turned out, getting high added to the unhappiness and eventually made my life miserable. The void I felt in my life was widened when I found cocaine, but it took me 18 months to figure it out.

So now I have to deal with any voids in my life without the drug. I have to deal with feelings of emptiness and loneliness without the help of any mood-altering substances. I have been relatively successful so far; however, it has not always been fun. In fact, I'd say that most of this first year of recovery has been quite painful. Despite all of this, I am a grateful recovering addict—and I am starting to look forward to each new day, instead of regretting them.

MARCH 27, 1989

I just woke up. I just woke up after having another cocaine dream. The dream was not a nightmare, so it hasn't upset me—but it was still a cocaine dream. There is not much to the dream, but I'll discuss it anyway.

I was sitting in this room with a bunch of other people and was picking my nose. There was this one guy in the room who was trapped inside a glass cage. The cage was about seven feet high and four feet wide. The guy inside the cage was being so obnoxious. He kept saying horrible things to everyone else in the room. He kept calling people names and butting into conversation where he was not wanted. Everyone tried to ignore this guy, but eventually we had to do something about the disturbance he was causing. We finally asked the guy what it was he wanted, and he said he wanted to speak to his girlfriend Renee.

This "Renee" was the same Renee who is my sister Kellie's best friend. Renee went over to him and tried to calm him down, but he told her to "Fuck off." After only a few minutes of his talking to her, we could see this guy had no respect for his girlfriend Renee. He proceeded to order her to get him some vodka, and she did so without hesitation. In fact, she took that order just like a fucking corporal would take an order from a captain.

After Renee got the vodka, she asked the man inside the cage [her boyfriend] what she should do with it. He told her to pour it into the cage. And so Renee got up on this ladder and just started pouring the vodka down into the cage right on top of him. This absolutely amazed me and shocked everyone in the room. Renee just kept pouring the vodka on him and into the cage, and soon he was about knee deep in vodka. He was loving every minute of it. It was like he was taking a shower in vodka.

Soon we noticed he shut his mouth and ceased being a nuisance. Just a second later, however, someone in the room called this guy an alcoholic lunatic, and the guy inside the cage started going crazy. He started beating against the glass walls of his cage like he was trying to break out. He started swearing profusely and was back to calling everyone names again. The guy who called him an alcoholic lunatic apologized for doing so, but it made no difference to this guy in the glass cage. He was going to get us all.

And so we watched him pull some lever inside the cage; and all of a sudden, the vodka started rising up out of the cage. The man inside said, "I am going to drown you all." And soon the vodka poured out of the cage and onto the floor. What I couldn't understand was that the guy inside the cage was drowning himself by trying to harm us. Didn't he realize that we could just leave the room without being harmed by the vodka, and didn't he realize he was only going to kill himself?

Apparently not—because we watched this guy drown in his own vodka. I left the room with a friend of mine and was still picking my nose. This friend asked me why I was picking my nose. I told her it had started to bleed again and I was a bit concerned about its doing so. She made me tilt my head back so she could see up my nose and then she told me there was a big cyst inside my right nostril. She proceeded to take my hand to make me feel the cyst, and soon I felt just how big it actually was. I was petrified at this very moment.

I knew where the cyst had come from and I knew why it was so big, but I didn't know why it should develop now. I thought the cyst was a result of my extensive cocaine snorting; but I didn't have the cyst while I was using, and so I was puzzled as to why I had it now after being clean 11 months. Anyway, I just came to accept the fact that I had this cyst and would have to deal with it.

The dream ended at that point. After getting out of bed, I went to make some coffee and decided to write about the dream. You know, it was a very strange dream, which could be interpreted many ways. A lot of stuff in it is symbolic not only of my addiction, but of substance abuse in general. So I have decided to make an interpretation list of the things that took place in this dream. Here goes:

1. *The man in the cage*. Simply put, this guy was trapped by his own addiction and had no escape from it. This is what every addict feels until they take that first step.
2. *The man's attitude*. What can I say besides this was typical behavior for an arrogant addict. I've said it many times before: Addicts become monsters and don't really care if they hurt others by the things they say and do.
3. *When the guy in the cage decided to drown himself and everyone else*. I can't seem to make total sense of this one, but I do think it has something to do with the inevitable result that substance abuse

has for all who are involved. People who abuse mood-altering substances die, and they die by their own choice. This guy probably felt trapped by his own addiction and realized he was destined to live life inside that cage—a life full of misery. He probably committed suicide to alleviate the pain that he was feeling, and also wanted to take so many people with him because he probably blamed some of them for putting him in that cage.

4. *The cyst inside my nose*. Simply a symbol of my addiction and how I perceive it. I said in the dream that I came to accept having the cyst and would have to deal with it. All I have to do to interpret this one is to substitute the word "addiction" for "cyst" in the previous sentence.

Oh, life as a recovering addict. Such a pleasure—I am grateful for it each day. You know, I wrote that last sentence with a great deal of sarcasm and arrogance; but by the time I was finished writing it, I realized I didn't feel that way at all. I remembered I am very grateful for being a recovering addict, instead of a using addict. I am grateful for recovery because it is sure better than the alternative.

LATER THAT DAY (EASTER SUNDAY)

It's soon time to go to Sarah's housewarming party. Right now I just want to talk about something that really bothers me, pertaining to the party. I hope to vent my frustration and anger here in this journal entry so I don't have to take an attitude over to the party.

Rick was in charge of picking up the gift that he, Leslie, and I were going to get Sarah for her new apartment. The gift was going to be a Braun coffee maker. I called Rick yesterday to tell him to pick it up at Woodie's, and he called me back today and said he was unable to get it. It bothers me quite a bit that I will not have a gift to take over to Sarah's this evening, but it is Rick who bothers me more than the gift.

You see, Rick didn't get the gift because he didn't get out of bed until 4 p.m. yesterday because he had a serious hangover. He gives up drinking for Lent every year, and so Good Friday is his day to break a 40-day period of abstinence. Too fucking drunk to get out of bed to go get a gift. Too fucking drunk to meet his responsibilities. And too fucking drunk to give a damn anyway. Man, am I pissed at him right now.

Look, I know there is nothing I can do about Rick, and I know I am powerless over his drinking—but it just never ceases to amaze me how much of a fuck-up he is when he is actually quite intelligent and could be doing some real, good work. He lives life from drink to drink while he is here in the States. Life is one big party to him. He wants to be with all of the right people, at all the right places, doing all the right things—on a fucking waiter's salary. This is a guy who has a B.S. in economics from a local university. He is wasting his talents in that restaurant. He is doing nothing constructive with his life. He is just a party mate.

And so I am pissed at him for being such a fuck-up, but I realize that it is his life to live the way that he wants. I am just glad it doesn't matter much to me anymore whether I am with all of the right people, at all the right places, doing all the right things. I am just glad I am not wasting away in a bottle or in front of a mirror with white shit on it anymore. I am glad I am on the straight and narrow.

Oh, I guess I should probably say the serenity prayer right now. Here goes: God, grant me the serenity to accept the things I cannot change, the courage to change the things I can, and the wisdom to know the difference. I feel a bit better already. Thanks, Big Guy!

Something else happened to me today when I was playing basketball. I went down to this basketball court that Wayne and I used to go to when we lived at the house in Maryland. As I was playing basketball by myself, I started thinking about my relationship with him. I actually missed him today. In fact, I actually regretted breaking up with him. Many things could have sparked these feelings; but the point is, I missed him today and it is not the first time I have done so.

There was nothing wrong with him. He was everything I wanted in a man. Yet I had to push him away. I told him we were not suited for one another because of our personalities. I thought he was too passive and submissive. I thought he was a wimp because he would do anything for me. I didn't respect him because I thought he wasn't a real man. And so I broke up with him. I broke up with him so I could be single and free to do what I pleased. I broke up with him to get rid of the ball and chain he put around my leg.

And when I broke up with him, I ended up spending a lot of time with Rebecca, engaging in a series of meaningless one-night stands with several other men, and becoming a drug addict. And just when I thought my dealer and I had this special relationship that made me feel so good inside, I realized what I was feeling was not my love for him but a love for cocaine.

Well, this all came back to me today on the basketball court. So I just kept playing by myself because that is where I am today. I am alone and by myself. My family is in Pennsylvania, I have no boyfriend, and my closest friend is really not close enough to comfort me. I have chosen to be here, and for the most part I like it. But I can't deny that I miss being intimate with someone. Today, that someone was Wayne. I kept thinking as I was dribbling the basketball that I could be playing with him today, that I could run over and tackle him and start kissing him, that I could fall asleep later in his arms, and that we might make love when we got home. Well, I don't have any of that today and I haven't had any of it for a long time now. I want it so badly. I want to be intimate with someone again, and I want to be loved again. Somehow, it just doesn't seem to be in my near future. And so I probably will have many more days like today.

It's okay, though. I'll make it because I am stronger now. I can think properly and can take care of myself again. It's actually much better now, because I like myself more this year than I have in three years. Guess I'll just have to dream about that missing man tonight. Then again, I guess I'll forget about this when I am at the party with some other friends. So long!

March 28, 1989

I had no time to write today because I had to do something else every moment. William, my boss, was in to talk to me about my work. He said I am making too many mistakes and that I need to clean up my act. He also told me the director, the other boss, has lost faith in me as an analyst. I guess I should do something about this. I guess I want to forget about it right now.

March 29, 1989

Work around here is really dragging me down. I don't see an end to this misery soon; and worse than that, I can't imagine my attitude ever changing for the better. And so I am torn between writing about all of my feelings in this entry or just trying to forget about it all for the day. So many other good things happen outside this office for me. In fact, the days outside this office keep getting better for me. However, because things are so terrible here at the office, I have been having horrible nights at home because I am worried about the work I do here and how that will affect my job.

I haven't slept much this week. Each night, I have had dreams about the office. Most of the dreams have been nightmares, and certainly none of them were pleasant dreams. These dreams aren't cocaine dreams—at least I don't think they are. They are all bad dreams.

You know, it seems as if I never have any good dreams anymore. I can remember a time in my life when I used to dream about good things, and now I never do. All of the dreams I have now are horrible nightmares or are unpleasant. I just want to know—what happened to the good dreams? I haven't had any good ones for about two years now. What has happened?

Sleep is so important to me. I have such busy, active, and tiring days, I really need eight solid hours of uninterrupted sleep; but I just never seem to get it. It all starts when I lie down to go to sleep at night. I am lying on my back and am ready to fall asleep, when troubling thoughts of the day enter my mind. If I am not thinking about the day's crises at this point, then I am thinking about tomorrow's problems or other life problems. And so I always fall asleep with troubling things on my mind.

Even before the move to the new apartment, nowadays it takes me longer than ever to fall asleep even if I am so exhausted that I can't keep my eyes open. I proceed to toss and turn all night. I usually wake up in the middle of the night to go to the bathroom. Actually, I wake up several times while I am sleeping; and each time I do so, I am in the middle of some kind of terrible dream. For instance, last night I woke up three times. I went to bed at 10 p.m. hoping to get eight good hours of sleep, but I woke up at 3 a.m., 4:30, and 6. And then when I tried to get out of bed after my alarm went off at 6:45 a.m., I had a hard time doing so. I was dreaming something different each time I woke up last night. From my psychology classes, I learned that everyone dreams, but I also know that not everyone remembers these dreams. I think it [i.e., my waking up] means I am not completing my sleep cycle, and this is what is making me remember all of the dreams.

I am not sure about any of this. All I am sure about is that lately I have been starting each day in a crappy mood and that my day only proceeds to get worse when I go to work. I spoke with my sponsor about this last night and she completely understood all of it. We talked more about my job than about the dreams or my sleep patterns, but I guess that it is the job—along with my addiction—that is causing these dreams and is preventing me from getting a good night's sleep.

And so when I told her I just can't seem to stand working here any more, she recommended looking for a job with the federal government. She has a research position as well, and she told me that she might know of a few possibilities for me. I hope something works out, because I am miserable here right now. And like I said above, I can't imagine things getting better around here, but I *can* envision my attitude getting worse.

I want to stop writing about this now and move on to something else, but I guess I should start working now. Boy, am I looking forward to this day. I can't wait until 5 p.m. Later!

MARCH 30, 1989

Today, work wasn't as bad as I expected it to be. I got a lot done and I also got along with everyone in the office. None of us got on each other's nerves. Couple that with a smaller amount of pressure, and my day turned out pretty well.

Life for me is better today than yesterday. In fact, it is better than it was all week. It was supposed to rain today, and it didn't.

MARCH 31, 1989

Relationships. Tonight I want to talk about [the subject of] relationships with men because it was on my mind most of the day. I just got back from a meeting at the hospital where I saw a guy in the program whom I have a serious crush on—but I have yet to reveal my feelings [about this] to anyone. Before I went to the meeting, however, I thought about this guy and what it would be like if the two of us were together and were in love. And immediately I started thinking intimate thoughts—thoughts about how close the two of us would be and what we would do if we were in love.

Imagine being in love right now, Katy. Imagine being in a loving relationship with this guy. We would have arrived at the meeting together and we would have sat together. I probably would have wanted to touch him. In fact, I feel this strong urge to touch him as I am sitting here. Too bad he's not here. And we would just look at each other every once in a while; and I would be able to see in his eyes the love he has for me, and could feel it in the warmth of his touch. He would turn to me and say something sweet—something that would let me know I was his and he was mine.

Upon leaving the meeting, he would put his arm around my shoulders and would draw me close to him, and I would respond to this by putting my arm around his waist. We would proceed to leave the meeting together, arm in arm, and would get in a car to drive home. And when we got home, I would just turn to him and would place my hand on his face and would run my fingers through his hair, pulling him close to me so I could kiss him. And I would kiss him ever so passionately. I would kiss him this way because I loved him. I can feel the kiss right now. I can feel his lips on mine and I can feel the passion between us.

Eventually we would make love. Maybe we would make love all night and maybe we wouldn't. It really doesn't matter. What does seem to matter the most—and what I know would feel the best—would be lying in his arms and just looking at him. And it wouldn't matter what he looked like or what I looked like. It wouldn't matter if his hair wasn't combed or if my makeup was smudged. The only thing that would matter right at that moment would be that the two of us were in love and that we shared something very special. The fact that our bodies might be locked together at this moment would only indicate how close we were, would only show us how special our love was, and would only prove to us how inseparable we were.

And it would be at this very moment that I would probably feel something I have never felt before in my life. I say this because I have never felt this way about anyone in my entire life, but have wanted to feel this way so many times. I know I only wrote above about the intimacy of a relationship, and left out all of the other stuff that a loving relationship features. I wrote about the intimacy because it is what I am missing the most in my life right now. I have all of the other stuff that a relationship features. I have friends in my life who give me compassion, understanding, heartache, and headaches. I have friends who make me happy, sad, angry, and ecstatic. I have friends who are giving, compassionate, and thoughtful yet stingy, indifferent, and self-centered. I have all of the other stuff that relationships bring, but these relationships are relationships with women or male friends. Relationships with women or male friends give me everything that relationships with men give me except physical intimacy. And that's what I am missing today.

Lately, all I do is long for someone to hold me in his arms and tell me that he loves me. I want so badly to be intimate with someone, and I want that intimacy to be in the form of a loving relationship. No longer do I want one-night stands with men whom I hardly know. I want a lover, friend, playmate, boyfriend, and husband all smashed into the same human being. And I want the reassurance that, once I find this person, we'll be happy together for the rest of our lives.

Is this too tall an order to have filled? I don't think so. I am so long overdue for this. I haven't had anything like this in my 26 years of life, and the closest thing to it was over nearly three years ago. I am ready for it now. I think I can handle it, and I know I definitely want it. So why am I not getting it? Why am I not in love, and why do I not have this type of a relationship with a man? Beats me.

For an 18-month period of my life, I had almost forgotten what intimacy was all about and what it felt like. As a matter of fact, when I was using cocaine, I know I forgot what intimacy felt like and really didn't care about it anyway. There was just no time for intimacy while I was using cocaine. I just wanted to be around my cocaine friends and away from everyone else who was not partying. I can remember time and time again meeting many men, potential dates, but refusing to expend the energy in consummating a relationship with any of them because I was too concerned about cocaine. I did not need a man while I was using cocaine. I had a love of my life: cocaine.

This is where the relationship with Ricardo comes into play. I thought the two of us had something special. So sure was I that we shared something very special that no two other people [had ever] shared. I thought he and I had the neatest relationship. Today when I look back on the relationship the two of us once shared, I see we cared about one another a great deal, would have done anything for one another, and loved one another. The important point to make here is that we weren't in love with each other and so there was never any intimacy between us. Of course, there might have been some intimacy between us if we weren't constantly doing cocaine. Cocaine really takes your sex drive away when you get heavily into it like we were.

Anyway, I am glad we never shared any intimacy. I am glad we never slept together, and I am glad we never took our relationship any further, because it would have been too difficult to leave him. It was difficult enough leaving him as I did, because I thought I was turning my back on him and was refusing his friendship. I hate to imagine what I would have felt like if I had been in a loving relationship—like the one I described above—with Ricardo.

The point is, when I surrendered on April 24, 1988, I knew right then I would have to terminate the relationship I had with Ricardo. Many other people thought the two of us could remain friends, and he even thought we could do so. I knew differently, however, and I have proceeded to make the choices and set the tone since April 24th. I have only seen him once in the past year and have talked with him only a handful of times on the telephone. I won't deny that I miss him at times; but for the most part, I am very happy that he is no longer in my life.

Well, it is a year after that decision, and I find myself in the same place concerning a relationship with a man. What to do? I don't know and I am getting tired of writing about it all. Maybe one of these days Mr. Right will come walking down the street and will sweep me off my feet into eternal happiness. Until then, I guess I will keep living this life of mine. It gets lonely here sometimes, but that's okay. Things are better today than they have been in a while; and I know, if I stay clean and sober, things will probably only get better as the days pass.

So cheer up, Katy. Feel safe knowing you like yourself and your life today and that's quite a bit more than you liked last year. And remember—you may be alone right now; but for the most part, you seldom feel lonely. Most importantly, however, make sure you fully understand that you cannot force things to happen in your life at certain times. You have to come to accept that you can only live life on life's terms and not your own. Maybe if you come to believe this one day, you will stop blaming yourself for all the things that have happened to you and maybe you'll find happiness. Maybe!

APRIL 5, 1989

When I got to work today, one of the secretaries handed me a message from Geraldine. The message informed me to call her as soon as I got into the office. Figures, she *would* catch me on a day when I was an hour late to work. Little does she know I am staying late at work tonight to make it up.

I returned Geraldine's phone call as soon as I got here, and I almost wish I hadn't. As it turns out, she wants me to go over to her house this evening to talk about some things because she is concerned about me. Just let me tell you right now that I have thought about nothing else all day. I have been stressed out all day anticipating what might happen at Geraldine's tonight. I gave her some of my journal writings last night and I know this is why she called me so urgently this morning. She said she had read the writings and was worried about me.

Naturally, I immediately called up my journal on my computer to review the writings to see why she might be concerned about me. As soon as I started paging through the journal, I was able to see why she might be concerned. For the past few months, most of my writings have been about painful or troubling issues in my life. The struggle I am going through right now, and have been going through for a while now, is illustrated in my journal. I guess it is really not too difficult to guess why she would be concerned with me after reading these writings.

The problem is, now what do I do? What do I do to reassure her that I am okay? Am I supposed to do this? I don't know what the answer is. All I do know is what I plan to say to her this evening. I am going to tell her what I have been going through and am going to say only once to her that I am okay and things are going to get better in my life. But I don't really know any of this. I hurt right now. There is no doubt about it. Things are not going well and I'm very upset about it all. I am not good at hiding my feelings, especially from those people who are so close to me. I do know one thing, however: I am tired of having to prove myself to people, and that is what I will probably have to do this evening.

Proving myself. This is something I have had to do throughout my entire life. It goes way back to my childhood when interacting with family members. It was always like this: "Dad, watch and see what I can do." My father would reply, "You better not try that—you'll fall and hurt yourself." Or he would say, "No, don't do that. You probably can't do it anyway." And then there was my mother. I would say, "Hey, Mom, I've decided to go to college to study sociology." And she would reply, "Where do you think you are going to get the money for that?" I would tell her about college loans and financial aid and she would insist I would not be able to do it, would never be able to afford college. I would say, "I can work this summer and save money. I can get a job at school to help pay for the tuition"—and she would reply, "Don't get your hopes up, Katy."

Every fucking year I would struggle harder to make that money to go to school, and every year I made it. But I didn't make it without going through the frustration of dealing with my parents' doubts about it all. They complained about filling out the financial aid forms. They told me I shouldn't go to main campus, but should settle for a less expensive school. They couldn't understand my wanting a better education.

Four years later after I graduated from main campus, they started understanding me, but it all proceeded to get worse when I moved down here to D.C. Their doubts about my life goals mounted, and their worries about my success eventually became my own. After I received my master's degree, I said to my mother, "I did it, Mom. I am making things work down here in D.C." And she replied, "I knew you could, but I was just being cautious for you so you wouldn't get your hopes up too high." And that's the philosophy with which I have learned to live my life. That pessimistic philosophy that assumes the worst and hopes for nothing. That "I know I can't do it" philosophy and "so I might as well not try" attitude. And when I did try, I caused a lot of commotion because I did things that Hendrickses just didn't do.

Well, the doubting of Katy didn't stop with my parents. Geraldine doubted my skills and abilities when I first got here to the university, and I proceeded to prove my worth to her through hard, diligent work. And then I fucked it all up. I did the same thing with Ben. I have felt all throughout my graduate education that I have had to prove myself to my professors and colleagues at the university. And now as I entertain this position as research analyst for my office, I have to prove myself to even more people. Now that I am an addict, I find I have to continuously prove to people I am not using cocaine and am not headed back down that path of desolation and destruction.

The reality of this all has little to do with *what* I have been trying to prove. It has more to do with *why* I try to prove things to people. I think I know the answer to this question. I want acceptance. I want to be accepted because I feel that nobody significant in my life accepts me the way I am—or is it that I don't accept myself the way I am? I think the answer lies in the second part of that sentence and not in the first.

My cocaine friends definitely accepted me for who I was—at the time, I was a very generous cocaine fiend who always shared. Ricardo was different. I truly believe he accepted me for who I was. I had no barriers with him. He saw me exactly how I was at the beginning, but then I started hiding from him at the end. I hid the fear of my escalating addiction and how I thought it was a by-product of our friendship.

This is all just too much for me to sort through right now. I probably need help with this one. I better stop writing because I don't know where to go from here. It just all brings me to the possibility that there may be something wrong with me. And you see, the self-doubt comes back to me right there. Self-doubt. Is that what this is all about?

APRIL 7, 1989

Sometimes I wonder what life is all about. What is life, and what is living? Just when I think I have it figured out sometimes, something happens that throws me for a loop and I soon find myself confused about my existence. How do I write about this all right now? I am experiencing some very strong feelings, and I don't even know where to begin to start writing about them.

I just got off the phone with my mother. Money always seems to come up in conversation with her. [No.] Money just doesn't come up in conversation with my parents—it is always the primary topic of discussion. Ever since I left home for college, conversations with my parents always seemed to center around money. When I was financially secure during 1985–86, conversations about money stopped because I had no financial problems. Things have drastically changed in my life. I am financially insecure right now and can barely function. And now that I have totally fucked up my finances because of my addiction, my parents are once again active in conversations about money.

Money, money, money. Is that what life is about? I'm beginning to think that it is. So idealistic was I when I was in high school and at main campus. I thought life was all about doing what you wanted to do, helping others, saving the world, and enjoying yourself. I was wrong. Life is about money. These days, it seems as though you not only need money to live—you need a *lot* of money to live. Some places in this world require a little more money to live than other places. I happen to reside in one of those expensive places and am busting my butt right now to make ends meet.

I am living from paycheck to paycheck and am bouncing checks along the way. I can't get the creditors off my back, and I can't pay Uncle Sam either. Someone keeps breaking into my car, causing hundreds of dollars of damage; and my insurance company tells me they will drop me if I make another claim. I don't go out to eat for breakfast, lunch, or dinner. I pack my breakfast and lunch and frequently have popcorn for dinner. I don't even go to movies anymore, and I don't rent videos because I cannot afford a television.

Singing the blues I am, and depressed about doing so. I cried on the phone with my mother because I hate to admit to her that I am miserable. I hate for her to have to hear me cry. I want her to think I am doing just fine; but the reality is, I am not doing well today and she can certainly detect that in my voice over the telephone.

What do I do? This life of mine is so turbulent. I am up one day and am down the next. Things go well one day and then they fall apart the next day. I am still trying to control it all, and I am failing at doing so. I just thought things would get better if I gave up the drug. I guess I was wrong.

Maybe it all has to do with growing. Maybe life just has to do with growing. Hurry up and teach me the fucking lesson because I can't bear this pain much longer. Who am I trying to kid? I am still trying to control life. What is that program slogan—"Living life on life's terms"? What does that slogan mean? How come life deals better hands for some people than it does for others?

I am making no sense at all here. I want to believe that life will get better. This hope is the only thing that is keeping me going right now, except for this journal—but I don't know if life will get any better;. and if it does, I don't know when it will happen. I guess I can't control life, now can I? I can't control my cocaine use and I can't control life!? What do I do then? Do I just sit back and watch things happen? I am not a spectator in the crowd and have never been. I am an actor. I make things happen. I want to make a difference. Along with all of that comes power. I want the power to change things, the power to control my life; and right now I am having a difficult time trying to sort out the things in life I can and cannot control. I am having a hard time figuring out what I can and cannot change.

Please help me with the serenity prayer right now because I don't know what it means. God, please grant me the serenity to accept the things I cannot change, the courage to change the things I can, and the wisdom to know the difference. I need the wisdom to know the difference right now. Please answer this prayer. I know I don't talk to You often, and I barely know who You are and what You mean to me. But if there is a Higher Power in my life right now, please hear this prayer.

Well, at least I am not crying anymore. I am grateful for that. I know why I picked up that first drug and I know how I became an addict. At the time I was doing those things, I just didn't realize that all of this was going to happen. This entire year has been spent dealing with the results of my extensive cocaine use—and boy, has it been a difficult year! Can't wait to see what is in store for me next year! I trust in the program, so I know things *will* get better for me. I am just glad I made it through today without drugs and I hope I make it through tomorrow the same way. Until that time, I guess my life will just have to stay like it is. I guess I'll just have to be happy with my life the way it is. Later!

APRIL 8, 1989

I just read over the last entry I made and realized I feel nothing like that today. I guess my life is pretty turbulent right now—full of its ups and downs. I guess that this is what the recovery business is all about. I hope recovery brings me something different this next year, but then again I know I shouldn't really expect anything. If I *could* expect something, however, I would want to be able to count on less mood swings, less turmoil, less tears, and less fear. It is almost useless for me to write about these things, though, because I simply cannot control what is going to happen in my life.

This control issue has always been a difficult one for me. I have operated my entire life under the motto that I am the master of my own destiny. I can make things happen in my life, I can control the outcomes, and I am responsible for every decision I make. Basically, I have always felt and believed I am the one who is responsible for everything that happens to me. No one else is in control of my life and is responsible for things that happen to me. Only I am in control and am responsible. I am the master of my own destiny.

And it is this type of thinking right now that is making acceptance of addiction hard for me. Acceptance is hard because I want to do one of two things. Either I want to say I am different from all other addicts and can do recovery my way, or I say I will never forgive myself for fucking up so badly and hate myself for becoming an addict. Both lines of thinking conflict with the "master of her own destiny" motto, and both cause me difficulties in accepting my addiction.

It is this issue of control that I am struggling with right now. The program tells me I am powerless over people, places, and things. Does that mean I am powerless over the things that happen in my life and cannot be the master of my own destiny? Does this mean I am going to have to change my lifelong motto and adopt a more passive way of living life? What does this all actually mean for me? I have been experiencing problems lately with the serenity prayer—acceptance, powerlessness, and all of that other stuff that acts as an indicator of loss of control.

You see, last April I admitted I was powerless over cocaine, but I didn't realize at that time I was going to become powerless over all of these other things. Am I making any sense right now? I guess I am confused as well. What I do seem to realize, however—and what my sponsor seems to realize—is it's time for me to do some step work on character defects. And so, this is what I think my second year of recovery is going to bring me: step work on character defects.

I feel okay about this, but I have no idea where to *start* working on character defects. When I have difficulty starting something, I usually go to someone and ask for directions. I'm glad I have a sponsor in my life now because she is the one I will ask for these directions. She has been very helpful lately, and for this I am extremely grateful. There are other people in my life that will also be able to help me out with these things, and I will probably also call on all of them. And of course, I will need the help of my favorite 12 Step programs so I might be able to do some of this work on my character defects.

I started this entry at my office and now I am finishing it at home. I want to run a half marathon [13.1 miles] tomorrow at 8 a.m., so I need to sign off and go to bed so I am well rested for the race. However, I have just a few more things to say today before I close.

My life used to be better than it is today. I know that very well. I also know that my life is not so bad today as it was at this time last year, and for that I am very grateful. It is time for me to realize, however, that I stand to gain absolutely nothing by dwelling on how good my life was before I found cocaine and how miserable it has been since I have given it up. I have spent this entire year regretting every line I did, every friend I made, and every dime I spent last year. Basically, I have spent this entire year regretting my life, and it is time to stop doing so. Instead, I think it's about time to start focusing on my future and stop dwelling on my past. No one needs to tell me that I will have to deal with addiction for the rest of my life. I already know that. I don't, however, have to keep punishing myself for what I have done.

I am an addict and that's that. I have to remember this day by day and have to fight the battle of staying clean day by day. I do not, however, and will not keep hating and punishing myself for what I have done. Life is so difficult for me when I hate myself and punish myself for becoming an addict. I want life to become easier, and I think it *can* become easier if I just come to accept that I am simply human and can make mistakes just like anyone else. With all of this said, I think it's time I sign off for the evening. Good night!

APRIL 10, 1989

I received this letter from my mother today with $40 in the envelope. My mother claims she is going to help me out financially by sending me $100 a month until I get my feet back on the ground financially. In the letter, she said she wants me to tell no one about the money she is sending me, she thinks my future is worth the investment—and if I spend a dime of it on drugs or on people who are involved with drugs, she will stop sending the money. She also gave me a lecture about handling my money and about staying drug free.

I love my mother. I really do. I am not just saying this because she is going to give me money. I am saying it because she cares about me. She cares about me a great deal. So many times we get into arguments about finances, my work, or school and I end up getting very angry at her. I don't stay angry very long because I realize that, if she didn't care about me so much, then we wouldn't argue so much. You see, my family members and I express love by arguing and fighting with each other. We don't go around saying we love each other, miss each other, and are happy for each other very much. Our love for one another surfaces when there is a crisis in someone's life. And when things are going just fine, we all know our love for one another goes without saying.

My mother doesn't like to see any of her children suffer, and that is what she sees when she looks at me right now. I have discussed this before in this journal. My mother has been permanently scarred by my experience with cocaine. I can still see the look of worry on her face when I am around her; although the look is not so serious as it once was, she still has that worried look on her face. I am almost positive that she panics when I go through a crisis, because she probably thinks I'll go get some cocaine and will overdose.

I would love to reassure her that I will never do cocaine again, but I can't. She has to learn to deal with my sobriety one day at a time just like I do. I can only imagine how hard this must be for her, because I know how difficult it is for me. I must admit it hurts me when she questions my sobriety. I guess I sometimes expect her to trust me, to trust that I won't get high again. I realize this is an unrealistic expectation, but nevertheless I sometimes wish for it anyway.

I really don't know what my father feels or thinks about my addiction, because he never brings it up in conversation and I never talk to him about any of it, either. Sometimes I think he would like to forget it. I wish he *would* forget about it because I don't want him worrying like my mother. He probably thinks about it just as much as my mother, however; he probably just keeps his mouth shut.

My parents are just very protective of their children. They hurt when we hurt. They may not always say the things I want them to say or do the things I would like them to do, but that is their prerogative and I love them for it. I love them for being themselves. They have always been there for me when I have needed them in the past, and I know they will always be there for me in the future. What else can I say? I love them both very much. I never want to lose their love, because it is the most special thing in my life today.

I am not nuts about accepting this money my mother sent me, but I know she wants me to have it because she wants to help right now. I'll take the money and will keep track of every dime she gives because I will pay her back one day even if she doesn't want me to do so. I haven't said this one in a long time—but I am one very fortunate young lady. I am fortunate to be alive, healthy, loved, employed, and educated. I have many things other addicts don't have. I have many things other *people* don't have—and for that, I am very grateful today. I must go get my laundry. See you later.

APRIL 18, 1989

I just tried to pull up my journal on another floppy and I discovered a disk error. I am pissed right now because I lost about a week's worth of journal entries. These entries were good ones. This entire month, I have been reevaluating my life and my addiction and have made some good discoveries and progress. I have written about this a lot lately, so I am angry I have lost them—they are crucial to my frame of mind right now. I am not going to bother trying to recapture what I wrote in those entries; instead I will just write as though I never lost them.

My boss just came in, so I can't finish this thing right now. Tonight is my anniversary [celebration] and I am excited. Later.

I never got a chance to finish this entry today at work, so I was unable to talk about how I was feeling before the celebration of my anniversary tonight. I just got back from the meeting—hence, celebration—and I feel pretty good. A lot of people were there tonight and a lot of people congratulated me. I didn't mention it at the meeting, but I am very grateful for being able to have the opportunity to celebrate at the church tonight with all of those people. I feel like thanking everyone who was in that room, but that is probably impossible. It feels good just saying that.

I am sitting here trying to think about where I was last year at this time. Last year at this time, I was in the worst place in my entire life; and now I find I am no longer in that horrible place, but am rather in a good place. I am very grateful for where I am today. Basically I am grateful for everything today.

Gratitude—man, how it comes and goes! It's like, no matter how hard you try, you simply can't be grateful for everything all of the time. It just happens that sometimes you are ungrateful or spiteful, adamant, demanding, and obnoxious. How do you keep from becoming ungrateful, spiteful, adamant, demanding, and obnoxious? And how do you stay grateful? How do you stay grateful for recovery as the days pass? How do you stay grateful for good health, friends, family, and other stuff? How do you keep the scale tipped in your favor?

I should know the answer to that by now, and I think I do. To stay grateful and to keep from becoming all of those other negative things, I have to keep practicing the principles of the program one day at a time in all aspects of my life. Honestly speaking, I don't practice the principles of the program in every aspect of my life, but I am practicing them more and more as the days pass. It is becoming easier to practice the principles of the program as the days pass because I don't have as many obstacles in my life anymore. The obstacles that used to stand in the way of my program included the lack of acceptance of my disease, and self-hatred—along with all of the other obvious things like dangerous friends and social habits.

Setting all of these obstacles aside, I find this recovery bit is relatively easy most of the time. I don't mean to sound cocky when I say that, but I just want to say that recovery is easy for me when I practice the principles of the program. And I know very well that I have to practice them day by day and will not be cured of this disease after a certain amount of clean time. It's like—I know what I had to do to stay clean this past year; I willingly did it day by day, and have done it successfully for a year now. The trick to all of this—and the secret message that is waiting to emerge—is that the question or task I must now face is what I must do to *keep* clean.

What do I have to do to stay clean? I know I may have asked this question before, and I know I may have answered it before. What I am trying to get across here is that recovery is going to be a bit different for me this next year. I plan to work on the steps so I can get rid of some of my character defects. This recovery bit is a long process and it features a lot of change. I am going to have to keep making changes in my life not only to stay clean, but also to grow—grow toward peace and happiness.

I am grateful for all of this today. I have a lot of people to thank for this, but I also have myself to thank. You are coming along, Katy. Keep your chin up, do what you gotta do, and things will get better. Yeah! Feels so fucking GOOD!

APRIL 19, 1989

Life is full of surprises. Tonight, my brother came over to tell me he is separating from his wife of eight months and is moving to D.C. because he is gay. He says he has been gay for a long time, but has been denying it to himself. He says both he and his wife knew he was gay from the day they met. I just want to know right now if I am dreaming or if this is all real!?

Like I said before, life is certainly full of surprises. Christopher wanted to know how I felt about it all, and I told him I hurt for him, Nancy, and myself. Actually, I didn't feel much of anything; and I still don't, as I sit here writing. I probably won't know how I feel about it all for quite some time. All I do know right now is, I have had a very rough day and I want to go to sleep because tomorrow is only going to be rougher. And to think I said at my anniversary last night that I am looking forward to peace during my second year in recovery. Ha ha!

APRIL 29, 1989

I have purposely been avoiding this journal because I haven't wanted to deal with my feelings about my brother's situation. I have spent these past ten days brooding over the fact that my brother is gay and is leaving his wife. Many other things have come up these past ten days as well, but none seems as important as my brother's situation.

Right now I am pretty angry at my brother. I am angry at him for leaving his wife and causing her so much pain. She is absolutely devastated right now. She feels like an abandoned woman, and I really feel for her because I know she is hurting very badly. And to think that my brother is the cause of it all. How could he do this to the woman he claims he loves? The only woman he has ever loved and been attracted to is what I have heard him say this past week and a half. Yet he is living comfortably down here with his gay friends.

Wait a minute. Christopher is not really comfortable right now. As a matter of fact, he is pretty vulnerable and insecure; but knowing that about him doesn't make me any less angry at him. He has left Nancy in Pennsylvania with something she doesn't want, and he is down here chasing something he says he has always wanted. What does she do now? What about the life she planned with him? What about all of the financial matters left undone? Who pays for them?

Christopher doesn't have any job to speak of, and so Nancy is looking at a lot of bills conjured up by both of them. It's all so complicated and sticky. You know, the money might come between them. It might increase their anger toward one another. I don't want to dwell on money, but I just wanted to get those feelings off my chest.

What else am I angry about? I am angry that my brother had an affair with a man while he was living with Nancy and while she thought everything was fine between them. From what Christopher tells me, things haven't been fine for them for quite some time. He says they have been in therapy since October—the same time he started seeing this male friend of his, who lives down here.

And that really pisses me off as well. My brother talks about that fucking affair. He describes it as this incredibly loving relationship and tells me he was in love with this guy and misses him dearly. Get this one—he also says this guy has broken his heart and has devastated him so very much. I don't want to hear this! I mean, really, does he think I want to hear about this homosexual affair? I mean, he's my brother. He is not some flaming faggot.

I guess this is where I start to kid myself, and I guess this is why I am so angry. I have spent all my life thinking that I know my brother, only to find out this past week I don't know him at all. Who is he? What have our lives together meant? What about the time Wayne and I went to the beach with him and Nancy? Was that all a lie? Was he pretending then? What about all of the times the two of them came to see me at school? I thought I saw love between them, but now I find I am reevaluating those times. I find I am reevaluating my entire life—and that's not fair.

I want them to be together. They are perfect for one another. I want them to be together because they help me to understand things better. They have been my role models and I have always looked up to them both. When I look at them, I see success and happiness. I see what life is supposed to be like, and I keep tucked in the back of my mind that my life will be like theirs one day. And to think it has all been a lie—that what I have been seeing and feeling these past 20 years was false and was never really there.

Selfish. As I sit back and read over what I have written, I realize I am being very selfish about this whole thing. I can't help this. This is where I am with this issue today. He can't expect me to accept this situation right away and become accustomed to his new life. I have too much anger, denial, and all of that other good stuff right now. I am also tired of writing about this.

You know, all I can think about is what this situation is going to do to my family and how it will affect all of our lives. I am not thinking about my brother at all right now. I know I should be thinking about him, but I just can't do it right now. I do love him, but I find his news has placed a strain on that love. I guess this is one of those life instances my program tells me I will have to face. I know what I have to do. I have to keep my love for my brother out in front of all of this other stuff I feel. I wonder if that will work? I hope everyone can do this. Just think—my parents have one daughter who is an addict and a son who is gay. At least we are alive. Later!

MAY 1, 1989

I have had a few cravings for cocaine these past two days. I am trying to figure out what triggered them, but I can't seem to come up with an answer. I was at Rebecca's yesterday to celebrate Billy's birthday and had an okay time. Rebecca asked me to help her out in the kitchen. I was pouring sugar into this bowl so we could set up a coffee tray, and thoughts of cocaine entered my mind. The sugar looked exactly like cocaine, so I said to Rebecca, "Funny, how some things remind you about other things, huh?" She just smirked and said, "Yeah."

Rebecca told me last week she had some really strong cravings for cocaine a few weeks ago and was scheming to go out and get some. She said the cravings bothered her so much she eventually had to tell Jim about them. Jim hates to discuss things in Rebecca's past. She said she got over them, but couldn't really understand where they came from. She did say she notices the cravings when she is under a lot of stress or when she is really bothered by something.

I don't know what works for Rebecca, but I do know what works for me. When I crave cocaine, the only thing I can do to effectively deal with it is to call Karen, my sponsor, and go to a meeting. I realize I must be sounding more and more like the program as the days pass, but the reality of it all is that the program has become a major part of my life and staying clean is becoming my top priority in life.

Why is this happening now, Katy—after you have resisted it so long? I sit here and ask myself what has changed to allow me to structure my life around the NA and CA fellowships and what has caused me to place treating my addiction as my top priority. I know the answers, and they are relatively simple. The program has showed me a new way of life. A way of life that is functional and good. The program has showed me how to find serenity and happiness. It has showed me how to deal with issues and problems in my life without falling apart. And the best part about it all is, it will continue to show me these things and more. The program will help me to constantly grow.

You see, today I both want and need more from the program than to just stay clean from drugs and alcohol. I need to learn how to live life on life's terms, to roll with the punches instead of waging a war I will never win. I need to sit back and learn how to accept the things life brings me as well as the things it doesn't. I need all of this so I can live life happily, so I can be at peace with myself.

You know, I think I have grown quite a bit since April 24, 1988. I have gone through a lot of shit these past two weeks concerning my brother's situation and other troublesome issues in my life, but I am okay about it all. I am not moping around mourning my brother's situation. It hurts knowing that Christopher and Nancy are no longer together, that Nancy will no longer be a part of the family, and that my brother is gay. And I am sure it will continue to hurt for a while. However, I'm in a better place today to be able to deal with it all, and I really owe it all to the program. My finances are still screwed up and I am just getting by. The pressure at work is still tremendous and I am in the midst of finals at school, but what I have today is the ability to deal with all of this without falling apart and without turning to cocaine.

It's neat feeling this way. Funny, how I used to write about how neat it was to do cocaine and how good it felt. That seems pretty trivial right now. Guess that I was writing about artificial feelings that were drug induced, instead of real feelings from the heart. In other words, I guess I was writing from my head instead of my heart. I know I have written a great deal from my heart during this last year, and I don't mean to take away from those writings. All I am trying to say is, I wouldn't trade what I have today for any amount of cocaine because what I have today is so much better than anything cocaine could ever give me.

I am one fortunate young lady. Today—May 1, 1989—I am one happy motherfucker. I am just sitting here enjoying it all. Maybe if I am lucky, and maybe if my Higher Power has a say in it, I just might find that tomorrow is just as good as today. That's what I want. I want to feel tomorrow like I feel today; and if I don't, then I just don't. I can control my feelings. I have the ability to do that. I cannot control things that happen in life, and it is the acceptance of this basic fact that helps me stay in touch with my feelings and have good days like today. Later!

MAY 2, 1989

I want to go to the beach. I am ready for the summer and the warm weather. I am ready for a vacation. I am in desperate need of one. I wish I could have about two weeks off so I could go to the beach and relax, work on a tan, and run all day long. Wake up, Katy. You won't be able to do that this year. Oh well!

Maybe I'll be able to get away for a few long weekends here and there this summer. That would be nice. Right now I am thinking about how easy my life was when I was an undergraduate. I would go to school both fall and winter terms at main campus and then I would go home for a four-month summer vacation. I had so much fun during those summers. The only worries I had were getting enough money to return to school and keeping in shape. I worked so many jobs during those summers, but it was all fun work. Guess those were the good old days, huh?

May 3, 1989

I never finished what I started writing yesterday, but that's okay because I didn't know what I wanted to say. What do I want to talk about today? I guess I want to talk about dreams again. I have remembered nearly every dream I have had during these past two weeks. Many times during this past week, I have woken up in the middle of one when my alarm went off. I am saying this right now because it is not common for me to remember all of my dreams and to be in the middle of one when I wake up in the morning. What do all of these dreams mean?

This week, I have been dreaming about all of my brother's old girlfriends. I can't remember specifically what happened in any of these dreams; all I do know is, I have dreamed about a different one of his old girlfriends each night this week. I think these dreams have something to do with my attempt to reevaluate my brother's life over the years.

I don't know how I am going to deal with his homosexuality. I know it matters very little what I have to deal with, and I know I should only be concerned about his welfare and the love I have for him. I know exactly what I should be doing and saying in order to deal with his homosexuality, but I just want to feel what I am feeling right now instead of doing what I am supposed to do.

Today on the Metro, I saw this gay guy I usually encounter at the Dupont Circle station. I can basically tell this guy is gay by the way he talks, walks, and dresses. He walks with such a fucking cute walk, with his ass tucked tight. And his hair is perfectly combed, and he holds that head of his the way gay men do. His voice sounds effeminate and he uses a lot of "rights," "wows," and "supers" when he talks. There is no doubt about it—this man is gay. It bothers me looking at this guy now because it's like looking at my brother. It's not so much that my brother looks, acts, and talks like this guy; it's just knowing that he is one of them.

I sound horrible right now and I know it. I sound like a very prejudiced and arrogant heterosexual female. I don't want this life for my brother. I can be perfectly honest about that. I don't want him bringing home men, hanging out with "the boys," going to gay clubs, and living with homosexual men. I basically don't want my brother to be gay. It's too hard to deal with. You know, before all of this I used to say I wanted to marry a man just like my brother. What does that mean now? Will I be able to ask for his advice about intimate relationships I have with men, or will I hesitate to ask him because I think he may be interested in the men I want, as well? How do I ask his advice in relationships at all? Do I talk to him about sex like I used to, or will all of those conversations end?

The issues and concerns go much deeper than this. I am just too frustrated to write about them all right now. All I can clearly write about right now is how I feel my brother is testing my program. All of that talk I do at meetings about living life on life's terms, rolling with the punches, and being happy and serene is being tested right now by his homosexuality. I just have to admit right now that I am angry about this. Part of me thinks it is unfair what he has done to me, Nancy, and the rest of the members in our families; and then the other part tells me I have no business feeling and thinking this way. But who's to say that life is fair, anyway?

Is this where I am to say, "Oh well, that's life; and since I am trying to live life on life's terms now, I have to accept this as it is and must move on"? I can't do that yet because I have not lived the reality of his homosexuality. I haven't really interacted with him much since he has been down here, so I don't know what to expect. I don't know how I am going to handle things. Maybe I just don't know exactly what I am thinking.

One thing is for sure: I do know I cannot change my brother or control his life. I also know he doesn't live his life for me or according to my standards. I don't want him to do any of this, anyway. I love my brother and I always have and always will. I am just confused about who he is right now. Is he someone different from the Christopher I have known for 26 years? And if he is, how difficult is it going to be to get to know *this* Christopher? I am struggling with all of this right now, but I am not letting it tear me apart or come between my brother and me. What I am doing is dealing with my own feelings about his situation as best I can. I am trying to work it through and understand it. And God knows, I am trying to accept it and live with it to the best of my ability.

All of this is what I am dreaming about at night. It's common for me to dream about stressful things in my life. Luckily, I know how to deal with these dreams now. I didn't always know how, but I do know now. The dreams don't tear me apart. It's the reality of them that bothers me. I am going to close by saying the serenity prayer. Good night.

MAY 7, 1989

Something incredible happened to me this weekend. Something so incredible, it is almost beyond me to describe. Thinking about it just mesmerizes me. I can hardly believe this has happened to me. What is it I am talking about? I made a contact with God this weekend and have made a new discovery in my life. I have discovered God. Here is how it happened.

I was watching this show on television late Saturday evening at my parents' house. The show was about these young drug addicts. I want to skip describing all of the details of the show and get right to the part that affected me the most and caused me to make this discovery with God.

One of the addicts in this show shot some cocaine into his veins and was sitting on the floor overdosing. He started having a heart attack. He was gasping for air, holding his chest and complaining about the pain he felt. He cried out for help, but everyone in the room just laughed at him. His pain continued and he began jerking his head around. He kept saying with increasing difficulty that he was experiencing so much pain in his chest; and as you sat there and watched him, you could see him having a heart attack and you could see him overdosing.

I sat there and watched him go through that, and I found this guy was taking me back to the three times that I overdosed. I could feel the pain in my chest that he was feeling. He looked exactly how I looked when I had overdosed. He made me feel pain in my chest and the nausea in my stomach. I could see my head jerking from one side to the other and could see my body shake just like his was. I could feel the words slip away from my tongue as I struggled to gasp for air because I could not breathe, just like this guy was doing.

But I kept waiting for this guy's pain to stop, and it didn't. I kept waiting for this guy to catch his breath again, but he couldn't. I kept waiting for this guy to stop shaking and sweating, but he didn't. And I kept hoping he wouldn't have a heart attack, but he did. I kept waiting for these things to happen because this is how it happened with me. The pain in my chest went away after a few minutes, and I regained my breath. The nausea and the sweating stopped. I didn't have a heart attack because the symptoms went away. They were removed from me. They simply stopped.

And so I was scared and confused as I watched this on the television. I knew what was going to happen in that show and with this guy. I knew he was going to overdose and die, and I didn't want to watch it. But I found I couldn't leave the television. My eyes were glued to it. It was so painful sitting there watching this guy overdose and go through what I went through. My tragedy of overdosing was reenacted by this guy in this show, and I have never dealt with this before. I really wanted to get up out of my seat to leave the room so I wouldn't have to witness this overdose and so I wouldn't have to think back to the times I overdosed and go through that pain again, but I found I couldn't get out of my seat.

It's like something or someone was keeping me there and was forcing me to watch this guy overdose.

The show ended and I attempted to get another channel on the TV to watch something else because what I had just witnessed upset me so much, I knew I was going to have nightmares if I went to sleep right away without watching something else. But I couldn't find anything else to watch on TV, so I went up to bed, knowing I wasn't going to have a good night's sleep. And as I was lying on my bed, I found I could not keep the thoughts of that show out of my mind. I began to cry because I was just realizing what had happened to me when I overdosed, and I started dealing with those feelings about those overdoses that I have been suppressing for the past year. The tears just poured out of my eyes, and the pain all came back to me.

It was at this time that I saw what it all meant. The guy in the show overdosed just like I did. God, it all looked so real to me. But the guy in the show had the heart attack and died, and I didn't. I kept waiting for his pain to pass and for him to regain his composure, but he didn't. I did. I did this when I overdosed—but as I was crying in my bed, I couldn't figure out why. Why did the pain in my chest stop? Why did the nausea go away? How was I able to regain my breath, and what prevented me from having a heart attack and dying? Why did the guy in the show die, and why did I live? Why did I live?

It was at the very moment when I asked myself these questions that I also found the answer. The answer was God. It was God Who took my pain away. It was God Who helped me breathe again, and it was God Who stopped me from having a heart attack. It was God Who kept me alive those times I overdosed. I had nothing to do with it. It was all His doing. He was watching over me those days I overdosed, and He breathed life back into me when I tried to terminate it. It was God Who wouldn't let me kill myself with cocaine.

There is absolutely no other explanation for any of it, but still I find I have questions. Why *didn't* I die during those times? Why did You spare me? Why did You keep me alive? Is there some unfinished business I have to take care of here on this planet and during this lifetime, before You take me away? Is there some purpose I must fulfill throughout the remainder of my life here on this planet? Why did You spare me? Why did You force me to watch that show, at that time, on that day, in my parents' house? And why did You put me through that pain of overdosing again? Why did You make me confront the pain I have been trying to suppress for months? Why? Why? Why?

I just don't know. I can't even think about any answers as I sit here.

Must I spend the rest of my life trying to figure them out? Why do You care about me, God? You know, I can't even believe I am writing any of this—but after this weekend, there is no doubt in my mind that You exist and are watching over me. And even though I sit here crying, I find the tears are not for sadness in my life; instead they are tears of confusion and fear. I am confused by this discovery and I am frightened by it as well, but there is no doubt in my mind that You exist and that You were with me those times I overdosed and You kept me alive.

Furthermore, I know You were with me this weekend when all of this happened, because I had a wonderful night's sleep. I didn't have any nightmares, and I slept straight through the night. I know You were there with me because I would have been awake all night with nightmares if You hadn't been there. Why are You doing this for me? What have I done to deserve it? And what do I do now?

I started this journal [entry] writing to the reader, but finished it talking to God because I believe in Him now. My life makes sense now. I have God in my life now because of what happened to me this weekend. God has probably always been in my life, but it is only after this weekend that I have come to realize that. What a wonderful feeling! I have many of my answers now. I have Someone watching over me now and I feel okay with that.

PART FOUR

May 8 through December 31, 1989

The last eight months covered by this book begin with my attempt to establish a relationship with God—my Higher Power. I started talking to God during this time and asking Him (Who is male to me) to help me deal with people, places, things and feelings (that is, toward family, friends, men and in particular boyfriends, as well as self-love and acceptance).

I entered an incredible period of introspection during this time, and I realized many things about myself I did not like. Defects of character kept emerging, but I knew 12 Step and my Higher Power could help me change. And I was grateful for that. I was grateful that I could find a way out of the self-destructive behavior that dominated my life.

I became more and more entrenched in 12 Step as the days and weeks passed. I compared early months of recovery to later months and noted some progress, but I knew there was still a ton of work to do. Not only did I continue to deal with thoughts and feelings about cocaine and alcohol during this time, but also I was coming to terms with the things about myself that I did and did not like—mostly things I did not like.

By the end of this period (the end of this book, but not of my ongoing recovery journal) I had fully realized that self-acceptance and self-love are the keys to sobriety and happiness. And I knew I had a lot of work to do to get there. Self-acceptance and self-love seemed so far away—almost too far away—but I did have some hope that I would get there.

May 8, 1989

Today was a good day. I made it through the entire day without getting upset with myself or anyone else. This is a major accomplishment for me. Each day usually brings some tragedy or pain to me, but today was different. And boy, let me tell you that it is a welcome change.

I started the day off with a prayer. Actually, it was more like a conversation with God. You know, one of those get-to-know-you conversations. And I told Him I believe in Him now, but still had my doubts. And I admitted to Him that I thought it was kinda silly to be holding a conversation with Him after years of denying His existence; but nonetheless, the conversation ensued.

I don't know how my relationship with this God of mine is going to develop. I have never been any good at having relationships with things I can't see, touch, feel, or hear. But maybe I can see, touch, feel, and hear God now. I saw Him this past Saturday evening and I felt His presence in my house. Will I always be able to feel His presence and see Him work miracles in my life? Probably not, but I guess this is where faith comes into the picture. Faith and trust are what I need [in order] to develop this relationship with God. I suppose I need patience as well. I guess I need a lot of things.

Who ever thought all of this addiction stuff would have turned out like this? Not me! Someone at a meeting once said that becoming an addict was the best thing that ever happened to them. When I first heard that I laughed out loud and shook my head in disbelief. I could not understand why the person said that, but now maybe I do understand. Maybe things are getting better for me and maybe I am headed down that path to happiness. I don't know what lies ahead for me. All I have is today. I do know, however, that I have a program and a God today, and they will help guide me toward happiness. And it is not that either of these things will find happiness for me; it is I who will find happiness for myself by allowing the program and God to guide me. What a neat feeling!

May 13, 1989

Good news came in the mail today. I received my student loan check for $1,380 and my income tax check for $360. And just think—payday is only two days away! Anyway, I am so excited about getting this money. I just got back from the bank and the grocery store. I deposited the funds and purchased $50 worth of groceries. I paid ten bills today that I have been putting off for a while because I didn't have the money. Paying those bills felt so good! It was like a burden had been lifted from my shoulders. Ahhhhhhhh! What a relief!

As I was running this afternoon, many thoughts went through my mind about how I could have spent the money if I didn't have so many debts. (I actually still have many more than the ones I paid today.) I thought endlessly about what I could do for my apartment with that money. I thought about a vacation to the beach or about not having to pinch pennies for a while. One thing I didn't think about was cocaine. Well, that's not entirely true.

I did think for a minute about buying some cocaine with that money, but the thought left my mind without much work. I didn't keep thinking about spending the money on cocaine. Believe it or not, I actually got a lot of satisfaction out of knowing I paid those bills. I remember feeling like this when I admitted I had a cocaine problem. Of course, the feeling is nowhere near so intense; but by paying those bills today, I felt like I had lifted this incredible burden from my shoulders, and this is how I felt when I admitted I had a problem with cocaine on April 24, 1988.

There are a lot of similarities between these debts and my addiction. Maybe this is a bit far-fetched—but think about it for a minute. I will always have bills to pay, just like I will always have my addiction to treat. The two are related, therefore, in the sense that they are both permanent conditions in my life. Also, if I am not careful in keeping tabs on my expenditures or recovery, I may lose control over my debts or addiction and find myself heading back down that path of self-destruction. The two are definitely related in another sense as well. Part of the reason I am in such financial trouble today and have so many debts is because of my using. I lost all control of my money when I was using. I didn't care about any other bills, for the most part. I just spent my money on cocaine.

I am glad I don't have to finance a habit today. I don't think I could do it and keep the things I have and live the way I want to live if I were trying to finance a cocaine habit. Not having the money to finance a habit is really irrelevant to why I am not using today. I am not using today because I basically don't want to do so. I don't want the lifestyle back, I don't want the personality back, and I don't want the self-destruction back. I have been living a good life lately, and I want to keep it like that. I can't have any of these things if I pick up again.

I guess I've changed quite a bit since last year. I am clean and sober today, I am happy with my life and who I am, and I have real relationships with the people in my family, my friends, and a Higher Power. Not too bad for a recovering addict, huh? I am very grateful today and, God willing, I will have another day of sobriety tomorrow so I can be grateful again. Later!

MAY 15, 1989

I took the day off from work today because my sister was visiting yesterday and today. Consequently, I didn't get all of my work done this weekend, so I needed to take the day off from work to catch up. I feel like a real dope fiend when I do things like this. I feel irresponsible, lazy, and uneasy, yet I still find I do it quite often. I probably call in sick to work about once every three weeks, and I am never sick. I am one of the healthiest people I know. I just call in sick because I don't want to go to work.

I wonder if other people do this kind of stuff? I know they do. I'm not that naive. I'm just talking to myself here. Maybe these worries of mine are unfounded or maybe they are real. I guess I am the one who has to decide that. Oh well!

Kellie and I stayed up until early this morning talking about our brother's situation. We did a lot of talking and got some things accomplished. One thing we didn't accomplish was getting rid of our anger. In fact, Kellie and I are more angry at Christopher now than we were before we started having the conversation. Kellie, however, is definitely more angry than I am. I can understand this because she has spent time with Nancy since this all happened and I have only talked to Nancy on the phone. My sister has seen the pain Nancy is going through, and I haven't—and it is really tearing her [Kellie] up inside.

Fuck! Such a messy situation that is going on here. When will it all end? Maybe it never will. All of it is out of my control, and there is not much I can do about any of it but deal with the way I feel. It never ceases to amaze me how this powerless thing seeps into every part of my life. Does this have something to do with taking life on life's terms? And does it mean that I just sit back and watch this situation get worse? I don't know what it means yet. I'm still trying to deal with it all.

My brother has left his wife because he thinks he is gay. He is living here in D.C. with two other gay men and is working part-time at a restaurant. He seems perfectly content with all of this. His wife Nancy is living alone in their apartment in Pennsylvania, mourning his absence. She is devastated about this all and is falling apart. My family is confused because they can't understand why my brother would want to leave this wonderful woman who loves him very much. Only Kellie and I know

Christopher is gay. Beth and Paul don't know, and neither does the rest of my family. And if my brother has it his way, they will never know.

I know all of this. Everything in the above paragraph is a fact. What I don't know is what is going to happen now or in the future. I don't know what it all means. I don't know how my feelings will change about this as the days pass, and I don't know where Nancy will be in my life if things stay the way they are. And I don't know how she will get through this.

May 16, 1989

I kinda ended yesterday's entry abruptly. I must have been doing something important to pull me away from this journal. Instead of trying to finish what I was writing yesterday, I just want to talk about today.

I had a great day today. Many things are happening in my life right now that are making me happy. The program is responsible for all of this. It never ceases to amaze me how much my gratitude for the program keeps growing as the days pass. Thanks go out to the program and all of the wonderful people in it.

May 21, 1989

I could write about so many things today. I actually do not know where to start. I shared at the hospital tonight about the great weekend I had and how I thought it was a product of the program. The best part about tonight's meeting was not being able to share about things in my life right now, but [being able] to listen to what everyone else had to say.

Several people at the meeting tonight picked up one-day chips. These people had about one day sober. I listened to the horror stories they told about their recent using experiences, and I found these stories made me rather uneasy. Part of me wanted to tell them to stop talking about the drugs and the misery, while the other part of me wanted to listen so I could remember what it was like for me.

The newcomer is the most important person at any meeting, for obvious reasons. What the newcomer does for me is not so much remind me of what using was all about, but instead remind me of the feelings that went along with it. Stories of using bring back those painful memories of how I felt while I was using and just getting clean. I never want any of those feelings back again. Those were the most painful feelings of my life.

I know getting high will only bring back that pain once again, and it terrifies me to think about going through that pain again.

Yet, just like any other addict, I often find myself thinking about cocaine and wanting to get high. Despite knowing the consequences, I still find I want to get high sometimes. Sometimes I can actually feel my nose at the glass and I can taste the coke on my tongue. The cravings are strong enough to do this to me. Strange how I never seem to forget how cocaine feels or tastes. Some fucking powerful drug! To think that I haven't had any in 13 months yet can still remember how it feels and tastes is utterly amazing to me. Oh well.

None of this is new to me. I knew how powerful cocaine was as soon as I surrendered last year. So when I get frustrated with people who are constantly relapsing, I try to remind myself about how powerful the drug is and how I can understand why some people relapse. I guess I just wish more people would stay clean and the program would turn out more people with lots of clean time.

All of this is beyond my control. I can do nothing to bring this about. I can just keep a close eye on my program by doing the things I know I have to do. I could go on about this, but I am tired and tomorrow is Monday. I should go to bed so I am well rested for the week's work. Good night.

MAY 24, 1989

I had a hell of a day today. Work went well because everyone was in a good mood. After work, I went for a great run out around Haines Point and then I came home. I walked past my car on the way home from work—to check on it—and that's when I discovered it: the BOOT! Ha-ha! Katy got the Boot. The sign on the car said, "Warning! Please do not try to move this vehicle because doing so is illegal and will damage your car." I couldn't help but laugh. Despite knowing how much money it would cost me to have the Boot removed (about $150), I still laughed and got a kick out of it. It didn't really upset me.

Walking back to my apartment, I decided the new clothes I just bought would have to be returned so I could pay to have the Boot removed. There is no excuse for getting a Boot on my car. I should have paid those tickets months ago; but I just kept putting it off, thinking the city would never catch up with me. Wrong, wrong, wrong! What is that famous saying—"Everything you do comes back to you in time." I am living proof of that one.

That last saying, proverb, or whatever followed me right to my mailbox, where I proceeded to pick up my grades from school. I took an incomplete last fall term because I couldn't finish a paper on time, and I recently just turned the paper in to the professor for a grade. Apparently he thought the paper was shitty because he gave me a C for the class. (The paper was the main part of the grade.) I know I did a half-ass job on the paper, and I expected to do poorly. What I didn't expect was a grade this poor. Getting a C in graduate school is like failing a class. C grades are usually unacceptable, so I don't know if I have to take this class over again or not.

I really don't want to have to take the class over again, but then again I don't want a C either. It's too late to say I should have done a better job, because the fact is that I did a shitty job. I don't really have the time or the money to take this class over again. It will cost me $1,200 and about six hours a week during the fall term.

Amazingly enough, none of this is upsetting me right now. I am okay with it. Basically, I deserved everything I got today. I chose to take the easy way out of both situations by avoiding the parking tickets and by putting that paper off until the last minute, and I was rewarded accordingly for doing so. Now it's time to face my responsibilities. I have to pay the tickets and try to work the grade out with the professor. It is no more simple or complicated than that.

I am glad I am clean today because I never would be able to handle anything that happened to me today if I were still doing cocaine. Just think, Katy—you are not angry, upset, or devastated by any of this. You must be growing up, maturing, and becoming responsible. Oh noooooo! Not all of that stuff. Just kidding. It really feels good knowing I am a responsible person today; but as you can tell, I still have some work to do and some progress to make. Thank God I have a program and Higher Power to help me. Later!

May 31, 1989

I guess I haven't written in this journal for a while. Not much is new in my life since the last entry. I haven't gone through any crises. My life has been rather quiet during these past few days. In fact, I feel my life is pretty normal right now, and I feel at equilibrium.

Equilibrium. I ask myself what I mean by that, and I find I don't really have an answer I can easily put into words. I can remember so clearly what my life was like last year at this time. I was absolutely miserable. I was an emotional wreck, and my life seemed to make little sense. I used to change moods at the drop of a hat. I was happy one minute and sad the next. Actually, I don't think I was happy last year at this time. When I said in the previous sentence that my moods changed so rapidly and abruptly, I meant to say that some of those moods and the emotions guiding them included anger, resentment, sadness, frustration, and deprivation—not happiness. I can remember feeling all of those things so clearly last year, and what a painful year it was.

It was the mood changes that killed me. I just couldn't stay focused at all. I would be walking along feeling no particular way, and then I would see something that reminded me of cocaine and soon I fell apart. Life was so turbulent for me last year. I just couldn't seem to get a grip on my emotions. It was like living on a roller coaster that had more downs than ups. I was on an emotional roller coaster last year at this time, and I had no idea when I was going to feel depressed or happy. The only thing I knew for sure was, the good feelings didn't last as long as the bad ones.

But things are different this year. I don't seem to go up and down as much anymore. That is, my emotions don't fluctuate as much. I feel as though I can stay in a particular mood longer without disruption. It has taken quite a bit of time to get to this point, and it certainly has taken a lot of work. I have even developed some coping mechanisms to help me deal with bad feelings and replace them with good ones. What a major accomplishment! I know I have a lot of work to do, but today at least I know how to do the work. I didn't know any coping mechanisms last year, but I know a bunch now. I have learned them from the program.

And so I guess this is what equilibrium means to me. Once, I was on an emotional roller coaster and was in a state of disequilibrium and emotional chaos. I was on a roller coaster while I was using, as well. Goddamn, does it feel good to be off that roller coaster! I can look forward to days filled with just a few emotions and not a million. I can see and do things today without falling apart, and I can reflect on my past without breaking down in tears. I guess the most important gem of this state-of-equilibrium thing is the ability I have right now to stay in a good mood, to be happy, and to not let my day be ruined by some useless thought or feeling that crosses my mind or heart. I can be happy today for longer periods of time. The good feelings last longer than the bad ones right now. Thank God!

You know, the thought of cocaine is not appealing anymore. I haven't had a craving for a while, but I keep myself prepared in case one comes along. Maybe I haven't had any cravings because of the lifestyle I lead today and the way I handle recovery. I don't know the answer. I do know

I don't want to get high today, and that's all that counts. The state of equilibrium I find myself in today is a product of my sobriety, which has been given to me by the program. I know not to take any of this for granted; but because I am human, I find I do sometimes. With that, I will close. Thanks!

JUNE 5, 1989

Here it is two days later and I never finished the last entry I made. I have been very busy lately; and whenever I sit down to write or think about writing, fatigue usually settles in and I miss writing. No excuses need be made. I simply have been a bit lazy lately.

What I wanted to say was that my life was controlled by cocaine long before I ever realized. I gave Meg my car that evening so she could get home from class. I would run home later, after work. This was our agreed-upon usual Wednesday night routine. I can remember this one Wednesday in particular because I had copped some coke and couldn't wait to get home to do it. You see, our favorite smut show—*Dynasty*—was premiering that night and we wanted to get high to watch it. Meg and I got into a fight because she wanted the dope so bad she didn't want to wait until I ran home from work, but wanted to come pick me up. I told her repeatedly that I wanted to run home and that I would be home by about 9–9:15 p.m. I couldn't believe how unreasonable she was being about my running. She had always known how important my running was to me. I guess that's what cocaine will do to you.

Anyway, I ran home with a gram and a half [$150] in my backpack and must have stopped every half mile to see if my sweat was penetrating the bag and soaking the cocaine. It turned out to be a miserable run. I should have taken the ride home with Meg, but I was too stubborn and [on the other hand] paranoid about damaging the cocaine. But do you see the point I am trying to make? The cocaine was already affecting my life and controlling it by coming between my best friend and me, by altering my running patterns, and by infiltrating my work and academic lives during the week.

And to think I thought it was all okay at the time. So blind was I to the power of cocaine. I am some kind of addict. Looking back on it all right now makes me realize that I planned just about everything around getting high. I worked hard during the week so I could get high on Fridays, and then I started getting high during the week and postponing work. I postponed workouts or cut them short. I cut myself off from friends who didn't party and fought with the ones who did. And at the end, I was alone, scared, high, and depressed. Some fucking love story, huh?

I used to say I loved cocaine, and then I started saying I hated it. The truth is, I still—oddly enough—love the drug and sometimes wish I could just try it one more time. Sometimes I wish so hard for a life that could include cocaine without destroying me, but I know that no such life exists for me. It is thoughts like this that continue to confirm the fact that I am simply a dope fiend, a cocaine addict. There is no other way to put it. And it is this fact that I deal with on a daily basis. So far so good. God willing, I get another sober day tomorrow.

JUNE 8, 1989

I am broke once again. I have $20 to my name and will not get paid for another five days. I have my last morsel of food on the stove right now. I wonder what tomorrow will bring? I am not depressed by any of this, but I do wish I had more money in the bank.

I spoke with a friend today I hadn't heard from in a long time. It was good hearing from her. I used to be best friends with both her and her sister; but as the years passed, we kind of drifted apart. We are still very close. I decided to write her sister a letter after I was done speaking with her. The letter I wrote was quite long.

I don't know if this is what I want to write about now or not. I am being an indecisive female right now. Lately I have been thinking a great deal about this guy on my softball team; and on my way home from work this afternoon, I prayed to God and asked him to remove the thoughts of this guy from my mind because I know I will never have him. This guy is currently involved in a very good relationship with another person. The two of them make such a good couple. I almost hate myself for thinking about him, because I like them both very much. This is a dilemma in my life right now.

JUNE 11, 1989

Hi. My parents and nephew will be here in a few minutes, and so this entry will be short. I feel good today. It's beautiful outside and I am looking forward to a nice day with my family. They are going to watch me play softball today. They haven't seen me play since high school. I hope I play well.

I want to talk about last night right now. I spent the evening with people in the program. One of my closest friends in the program celebrated a year's sobriety last evening, so I went. After the meeting, a bunch of us went back to her parents' house in Potomac to continue celebrating. The house we went to was gorgeous. I guess her parents have a lot of money. I didn't bother obsessing about the house and this wealth, but rather just tried to enjoy the evening with everyone who was there.

I had a nice time with everyone, but part of me felt as if I didn't fully belong there. Sometimes I think this recovery business is too good to be true. I look at the people in the meetings and I listen to their stories and I see what they are doing today. It is just an amazing process. I can see how these people have changed their lives around, because they recreate their lives for me at meetings or when we get together outside of the program. It is at that point that I begin to look at myself and compare myself to them.

No doubt I can identify with them about many things they have gone through and are still going through today. In fact, despite the different details of our lives, I find we all share a common denominator binding us together, and that denominator is addiction. The stories we tell about our days of using drugs may differ, but the feelings and end results of those using days are basically the same.

Yet still I find myself uncomfortable with them sometimes. They all looked as if they were so confident about their recovery last night. They looked and talked so good, so peaceful, and so confident that it scared me. I know that not a single one of them takes recovery for granted and that each works one day at a time to stay clean. But last night I didn't feel their stress of working the program, but only shared in their wonderful feelings. I was sitting there thinking to myself that recovery is just not so easy for me and that I don't always feel like these people are feeling tonight.

I am sure the people I was with last night don't always feel great and that everything in their lives doesn't always go great now since they have entered the program. But last night I felt as if I was the only one who still struggles with this recovery bit. And maybe that's just what my feelings were about—me struggling with my recovery. Sometimes I get so scared that I will get high again. Oddly enough, at times I believe someone will come along and will force cocaine up my nose, or I feel I will lose all control of my mind, body, and soul and will go get high. And so I had a cocaine dream last night because of these doubts.

Katy doubts her recovery and she is scared of getting high. I guess I am writing about this so I can reassure myself that if I keep working the program and take things one day at a time I will not get high. The doubts and fears stay with me, and I guess they will forever. I have got to learn to deal with them. I have got to remember that I am the only one who will make me get high. No one will force me to get high. The decision to get high is mine. Knowing this fact is sometimes reassuring, and other times it is frightening. Who ever said life was easy? Not me. Guess I continue to realize this more and more the older I get. Thank God for the program, because without it I'd have to do all of this coping alone—and I know what happens to me when I try to do that.

JUNE 12, 1989

I wrote with a lot of self-doubt yesterday about the confidence I lack in staying clean. And today I find I feel good about recovery and my ability to stay clean. What an interesting cycle this recovery bit is. One thing is for sure: Recovery never is dull, but rather is full of many types of surprises.

I stayed home from work today because I had a splitting headache. The headache subsided for a few hours, but now I can feel it reappearing. Guess I should go up to the drugstore to get some Advil or something. I wish there was another way to deal with physiological discomfort besides medicating it with some drug. You know, since I have entered the program, it doesn't really matter if drugs are legal, illegal, or behind the counter or over the counter. Drugs are simply drugs, and I wish I could stay away from all of them all of the time. I guess this is nothing but an unrealistic wish. I really don't have much against over-the-counter drugs like Tylenol and Advil. I guess I was just looking for something to write about.

What I really should write about today is the amount of time I spend thinking about Craig. Craig is this guy I play softball with. I think I might be in love with him or could very easily fall in love with him. There is one problem, however: He has a girlfriend already. I don't know if I want to get into this right now. Basically, he appears to be everything I want, and I feel this incredible attraction to him when I am with him. Shit, I even feel it when I am not with him. He makes me feel so much like a woman and even makes me feel beautiful. He simply makes me melt.

I like feeling this way and I can't deny that. I spend countless minutes recreating the feelings I get when I am with him, and often pretend he is here with me. Part of me feels lousy, on the other hand, for feeling this way—because I really do like his girlfriend. She is such a sweet young lady. The two of them look so good together and I can tell they care a lot about each other.

She doesn't realize how lucky she is to have him. Maybe she does realize this—I don't know. Craig is so much fun. And on top of that, he is kind, warm, and generous. He is also cocky and arrogant at times, and I think it is these qualities that draw me to him. He is a lot like me—tough on the outside, but soft on the inside. I just wish he were mine.

You know, I mentioned being tough on the outside and soft on the inside in the above paragraph. All of my life I have been like this. I put up such a tough exterior that sometimes I actually repel people, yet I am actually just a soft teddy bear with a paper heart. As time passes, I am learning that this dual personality is a character defect of mine and is nothing more than a defense mechanism to prevent myself from getting hurt or being rejected by others. I hope I continue to chip away this false exterior of mine and let the real Katy out. The real Katy—the one who hides inside of all the bullshit—is really a neat person, I think. Maybe one day when I finally get rid of the false exterior completely and let the real Katy shine, people like Craig will look my way and say, "Boy, is she a neat person!" Until then, I'll just keep coming back to work on me.

JUNE 14, 1989

Two days have passed since I wrote in this journal—and boy, has a lot of stuff happened! Craig has broken up with his girlfriend. I found this out by attending a meeting with his girlfriend, Beverly, Monday night. She shared about the breakup, and she and I ended up talking for an hour after the meeting.

I am a bit confused by this situation. I was happy about the breakup because it meant Craig was free. On the other hand, I was also sad because Beverly seemed upset by it all and I am beginning to develop a friendship with her. Needless to say, I feel like a schmuck for liking Craig. I felt as if I was lying to her while I was talking to her Monday night. I am just wondering what I should do.

Maybe my real anxiety about this situation with Craig has little to do with Beverly and more to do with what Craig will do now. I wonder if he'll ask me out and if he's interested in me. I feel like a little schoolgirl with a crush. Does he like me or not? I want to know right now.

Maybe I spend too much time obsessing about him. Karen, my sponsor, told me last night I was obsessing about this guy. I hate to admit a man could be dominating my thoughts like this, but the truth of the matter is that he is doing so. I am certain that I really do like him. And so I now find I am afraid of finding out what his true feelings are. He told me before—when I asked him out—that he would go out with me if he wasn't seeing Beverly. Was he telling the truth or not? I guess I will find out soon enough, and I guess this is what frightens me.

Funny how I wish I could write about cocaine right now so I wouldn't have to deal with these feelings. Isn't that just like me, though? When feelings like this came while I was using, I continued to use so I could suppress the pain and not have to deal with them. Now when feelings emerge that I don't want to deal with, I write about cocaine—and the thoughts of doing it take me away from my feelings. What is the difference, Katy? You are still using cocaine to get rid of feelings.

Knowing that I do this pisses me off. I don't always shut my feelings off by thinking about cocaine or something else, but I seem to do it often enough. Coping with feelings is difficult. Let me rephrase that: Coping with feelings while being sober is difficult. Painful feelings were so easy to deal with when I snorted cocaine. If something bothered me, I just called up my dealer and went to cop some coke. I got high and stayed high until I thought the pain had subsided. The truth of the matter is, the pain never subsided. It only got worse.

So now I have to deal with my feelings without cocaine. It's not so bad. My problem seems to be my blowing things out of proportion by coming to quick conclusions and overreacting to insignificant matters. I also have a tendency to sell myself short a lot of the time. Also, I am still too fucking critical of others.

I need to pray to God and ask Him to remove these character defects of mine, because they get in the way of my recovery. My character defects fuck with my serenity on a daily basis. Someone shared at a meeting tonight that the Big Book says we are not responsible for our disease, but are responsible for our recovery. I guess I better start facing my responsibilities. I am responsible for staying sober and I am responsible for living this life. I know I can't do it all alone, but asking for help doesn't mean I am relinquishing my responsibility. It simply means I am doing what I have to do—and that's pretty responsible, I guess. With that, I will close on this last note. Thank you, God, for being there for me, for putting my sponsor in my life, for helping me to find and work the program, and for surrounding me with many wonderful people who care about me—because with these things and people, the responsibility I must take for my recovery becomes easier to handle. [Ended on June 16]

June 23, 1989

I am going to the beach tomorrow with a guy in the program whose name is Nathan. I don't know exactly how I feel about this right now, but I am a bit nervous about it. It's not like this trip to the beach is a date or anything. I think he just wants a ride. I am not sure if his going along has anything to do with me, but I guess I'll find that out tomorrow.

Today I thought about this situation quite a bit. I called a friend [named Penny] at her office and talked about it as well; plus, Sarah and I had our usual morning chat session—where the topic was my beach trip. Needless to say, then, I have done a lot of thinking about Nathan and this trip today.

I can't remember when I last spent time alone with a man. It has been quite a while. For some time now, I have been complaining about the absence of a man in my life; and tomorrow I will have such company. How will I act? What do I do? And what will he think of me? I don't know. All of a sudden, I feel vulnerable, like I am both powerless and impressionable. I guess men make me feel vulnerable. Wait a minute, I *know* they make me feel vulnerable—especially the ones who attract me. I am very attracted to Nathan and, therefore, feel vulnerable when I am around him.

It is truly amazing what happens to me when I interact with someone to whom I am attracted. I get so nervous and excited around guys I am attracted to. Actually, I even start feeling silly and stupid and stuff like that. What is it about a man that makes me feel like this? Is it all physical, or is there some substance there? Why can't I relax around guys and practice the things I preach to the girls at the office about how to deal with a man? Is everyone like me, or are people different?

Boy, am I full of questions and insecurities today! Men bring out my insecurities. I worry whether they find me attractive, kind, likable, funny, and all that other good stuff. And I desperately fear they might think I am a fat, ugly bitch. I am very afraid of rejection, and I guess that is the bottom line. Maybe I am making too much out of all of this and should just try to be myself tomorrow and have a good time. Maybe I should take Penny's advice, after all. Later!

June 27, 1989

I spent Sunday and Monday in a shitty mood. Notice that I didn't write in my journal until tonight—Tuesday. I have been crying the blues about not being in a relationship. I miss a man, what can I say. I moped about it for two days, talked to a lot of people about it, and even cried about it; and now I find the whole subject is out of my mind. I am okay with being alone right now and with not being in a relationship. I had a good day today.

A lot of things are responsible for helping me to get out of the slight depression I was in during the past days. My girlfriends in the program spent time talking to me about it, Sarah had some good things to say, my sponsor helped, meetings helped (I went to a women's meeting last night and left with a lot of gratitude), and saying my prayers helped. I was finally able to turn it all over this morning. To be perfectly honest, however, I think I was able to turn all of this over because of the dream I had last night. The dream scared the shit out of me and pulled my head and soul back to my top priority in life: keeping clean.

I had a horrible cocaine dream last night. I dreamed I relapsed once again. In fact, the dream had the same pattern as most of my other cocaine dreams: I got the cocaine, but had trouble doing it. Things just kept getting in the way last night. I can remember copping the dope and being very concerned that I had so much of it. At first, I tried to tell myself I wasn't going to do any of it, but was going to sell it to make some money. What bullshit!

In the dream, my family was moving to a new house and I was supposed to help them move. In fact, all of my family members were home helping my parents move into a new house in which, oddly enough, all of us were going to live. I went to the old house with the cocaine, scared to death they might find out I had it and planned to relapse. Oh, by the way, I had started to get high on the way home.

I arrived at the old house after everyone else because I was late. They all asked me where I was, and I made up some excuse that I can't seem to remember right now. I went upstairs with Kellie to help her move things out of a room the two of us once shared, and I looked around desperately for a place to hide the cocaine. I finally put it under this table. Kellie went to move the table and I panicked and tried to distract her so she wouldn't move it. Finally, after a few unsuccessful attempts at trying to dissuade her from moving the table, I finally went over and stood in front of it so she could not move it or see what was under it. She asked me why I was doing what I was doing, and I confessed to her that I had hidden some cocaine under the table. I pleaded with her not to tell Mom and Dad, and this is where the dream fades from my memory.

[I do remember] Kellie did not say another word about the cocaine. I just picked it up and put it back in my pockets and walked out of the room. But the cocaine was too large to hide. You see, I copped about an ounce and a half and I just couldn't conceal that much in my pockets without drawing attention to myself. I still can't figure out why she didn't say anything about it.

Anyway, I started looking for another hiding place in the house, but it was becoming more difficult because the house was rapidly emptying. Finally, I got frustrated with trying to find a hiding place for my cocaine; I made up some excuse to leave so I could go get high. I left and went right to Ricardo's house so he and I could party. I was a bit ambivalent about going over to his house with the coke because I was afraid he wouldn't party with me because of my commitment to sobriety. I soon realized, however, that where there was cocaine there was Ricardo. And I also began to realize that my commitment to sobriety was slipping through my fingers.

I got to his house and approached him with the coke. He agreed to party with me, and so we did a few lines together. A few minutes later I wanted to do some more, but he didn't want to do the same. In fact, I soon discovered he didn't want to do cocaine as fast as I did, as fast as I needed. I was crashing and needed every line I could get, and he just didn't want to keep up with me. I had to party at his pace. I kept looking for opportunities to leave so I could go get high, but something kept happening to interfere with my leaving. Finally, after my arguing with him about the amount we were doing, he just screamed at me to slow down and try to control my use.

I tried my hardest to do this, but I just couldn't. I needed to do lines every few minutes, but I couldn't seem to do them. I was craving the coke so badly. I just wanted my lines. I just wanted to do it all. I didn't care about selling any of it and I didn't care if I had no one to party with. I just wanted to be alone to do my cocaine as I saw fit, as I needed it—but something was fucking with me and I couldn't do any of it. Why in the fuck can't I just do it the way I want to do it? Leave me alone. Get out of my way. Shut the fuck up and mind your own business.

And as I was walking out the door of his house, I walked past my family members and stopped. I awoke at this moment. When I awoke, I thought I had used. I actually felt high and on the verge of crashing. I began the day thinking and feeling I had relapsed and had lost everything that I have discovered during the past 14 months of my life. I awoke thinking that my life was slipping away from me. And boy, I can tell you for sure that I had to get up out of bed, wash my face, and look in the mirror for quite some time before I was able to believe that what I had just experienced was a dream and didn't really happen. It took me a while to realize I was still sober and had not relapsed. What a fucking dream!

It all makes such perfect sense. The dream was a reenactment of my last binge before I surrendered. And what the dream did for me was to remind me that my priority in life is staying clean. The dream reminded me that I am an addict who can never do drugs again, that relapse is my biggest worry and fear in life, and that I have a disease for which there is no cure. It took this dream to make me realize how silly I was for moping about not having a man in my life. It took this dream to make me realize how lucky I am to be alive and clean. It took this dream to remind me of how grateful I am for recovery. And so I asked God to remove my depression about not being in a relationship and asked Him to remove the thoughts of the dream from my mind so I could get through the day without using. I didn't use today. I had a good day. Thank you, God.

JUNE 29, 1989

I spent the evening with Ben and Sandy last night and had a wonderful time. They had me over for dinner before they left for a two-week vacation. I will be house-sitting for them during that time. What I want to talk about briefly tonight is how I feel about this house-sitting excursion. I truly believe it is a gift from my Higher Power because of recovery.

I first admitted I was having a problem with cocaine on April 24, 1988, to Ben and Sandy. At the time, I was a physical, emotional, and mental wreck who couldn't seem to do anything I was supposed to do. More serious than that, however—or at least I thought so at the time—I had exhausted the patience of Ben, Sandy, and Geraldine by not fulfilling my work obligations I had with them. Needless to say, each one of them was at the end of their rope with me. Basically, I had lost all the respect and trust I once had with these three people—the most important people in my life in this town.

No doubt about it, I put them through Hell these past two years. But they never left my side, irrespective of what I did or didn't do. Today, I feel confident in saying I have their respect back, along with their trust. Ben and Sandy are letting me house-sit for them for two weeks. They are trusting me with their house, food, swimming pool, and car. This is truly a gift of recovery. I would not be doing this if it weren't for my Higher Power and recovery.

It feels absolutely wonderful to be treated as an equal again. Better than that, it feels wonderful to be trusted and respected by the people I love. Geraldine is out of the country for five weeks and she has entrusted all of her correspondence and her office with me [to take care of] while she is away—plus, she is paying me $20 an hour for doing so. How could these wonderful things happen to me if I were not in recovery? They simply couldn't.

Thank you, God, for giving me nearly a year and a half of abstinence. Thank you for putting such wonderful people in my life. Thank you for being there when I needed you. Please give me the strength to make it through tomorrow without using, and help me do the best possible job for Geraldine and Ben and Sandy. No cocaine high could ever give me the things recovery has given me. I wouldn't trade this recovery bit for anything in the world. Thank you.

JULY 16, 1989

Here it is the middle of July and I have yet to write in my journal. What a dumb fuck I am. I have chosen to make this month difficult for myself by not writing in my journal, by not calling my sponsor as much as I should, by not praying, and by not attending many meetings. Basically, I have been running a real shitty program lately and it is about time that I get back on track.

I just got back from a meeting at the hospital where two friends celebrated one and three years of sobriety. I love both of these guys a great deal. Both have been in the program since I arrived more than a year ago. My sponsor was at the meeting tonight with her husband, and it was really good seeing both of them. Some really neat people were at the meeting. I'm just glad that I went, and am grateful for another day without drugs.

Lately, I have been taking my sobriety for granted. I get so cocky sometimes, thinking there is no way possible I will ever do cocaine again. I know this kind of thinking is detrimental to my recovery; yet at times, I choose to think this way irrespective of any consequences that may follow. I put myself through more shit than I have to. I am basically my worst enemy in recovery. What is it about me that makes me do this to myself? Why do I make things harder for myself than they have to be? And why do I consciously choose not to grow past the pain and on to a better life? Why is misery so appealing to me?

Sometimes I think I have the answers to these questions, and other times I realize I don't have a clue. I guess if I had all of the answers I wouldn't be writing in this journal and I wouldn't need the program to help me stay clean. I know better than this. Intuitively, I usually know what I have to do to stay clean and to deal with issues in my life, but I do not always know what it will take to make me happy. None of this knowledge of how to live life does me any good if I choose not to do what I have to do to stay clean and choose not to deal with issues in my life the way I should. I don't know everything about life. Sometimes I think I don't know what it will take to make me happy. What I do seem to know, however, is that I can't just sit around and wait for things to happen in my life. I can't sit around and expect to grow and get better. And for sure, I cannot sit around and wait for happiness to come walking through my door so I can live happily ever after.

Irrespective of what anyone else has to say about any of this, my [quest for] serenity, happiness, and sobriety takes work. It takes work on a daily basis. Shit, it takes work on an hourly basis. I don't get things for nothing anymore. In fact, I never did. I have to work for the things I have today. I don't buy the idea that happiness comes easily, sobriety comes with time, and pain subsides by itself. It all takes work for me. It gets difficult for me when I decide not to do my homework. It gets difficult when I choose not to work my program. It gets difficult when I try to do things my way and my way only. When I take control of my life and everybody else's life, I start fucking things up.

Don't get me wrong. I do have some power in my life. I am not powerless over everything. By choosing certain things and making decisions, I find I can control some things in my life. But I have got to accept that I am truly powerless over other people's lives and am powerless over many facets of my own life. I don't like giving up the power, and I don't like not being able to control the outcomes. I don't think there are many people on this earth today that would disagree with any of this.

I guess I am rambling right now and may not be making any sense. It just never ceases to amaze me how much work recovery is. Recovery takes work every hour of every day. And I am not just talking about abstinence from drugs and alcohol. What I want out of recovery today is a better way of life—a life full of self-love, happiness, and peace. I don't want to be the same person ten years from now as I am today. I want to grow to be a better person, and this takes work. I know some of the things I have to do, but am still clueless at most of it. My problem is not in knowing what I have to do. It's finding the motivation to do it. To sum it all up, Katy has got to get motivated and become willing to make the changes and do the growing that she needs to do so she can become that better person. This willingness and motivation does not come naturally and does not proceed naturally. It takes work on a daily basis. Get your lazy ass to work, Katy!

JULY 19, 1989

I went to two meetings tonight. I led the first one and am not entirely pleased at the job that I did—but isn't that always the case with me? I am never pleased with the work I do. I don't want to dwell on the job that I did or did not do at the meeting I led tonight. The second meeting I went to helped me forget about those selfish feelings. What I do want to talk about tonight is the frustration I am dealing with at work.

Today was a difficult day for me in sobriety. It wasn't difficult because I had cravings for cocaine. It wasn't difficult because of anything that anyone did or said to me. And it wasn't difficult because I had to deal with anything unusual. Today was difficult because I forgot to work the principles of my program. I was miserable at work today because I wanted to gain control over an impossible situation and, when I finally realized I couldn't get control, I chose to isolate myself in my office and complain about the organization I work for and the people who work there.

What I should have done was turn it all over to my Higher Power, but I just couldn't seem to do it. I am writing about this tonight because I don't want tomorrow to be like today. Time and time again I find myself fighting with this acceptance or powerlessness thing. Somewhere along the line, I forget that I must accept life on life's terms and that I am powerless over people, places, and things in life. Let me take time out right now to talk to God.

God, what is it about me that can't seem to remember this acceptance/powerlessness thing? Why can't I turn things in my life over to You? The program tells me in its third step that we made a decision to turn our will and our lives over to the care of God as we understand Him. Have I not done this with You? Days like today make me realize I probably haven't taken that step yet. I thought I took this step, but I guess I haven't. Does this have anything to do with my lack of faith in You or my struggle with acceptance and powerlessness? I know You will not send the answer down to me right as I sit in front of this computer talking to You, but maybe You'll give me the answer one day.

I have to admit that my lack of faith in You is very discouraging. When I discovered You that one evening in front of the television, I thought I was going to be okay after all. I took the second step that night and came to believe You could restore me to sanity. But what I am finding out more and more as the days pass is that the second step of this program is a discovery step and the third is an action step. Simply put, I have made the discovery, but am not taking the actions required in the third step to make that discovery real in my life. I don't turn things in my life over to You when I should. I take them on myself and try to solve them without anyone's help. I do this because this is how I can get my way, stay in control, and have power. I do this because I don't have faith in You.

Will my faith come as time passes? I guess not. Faith, growth, and all those other gifts of recovery have to come through work. They don't come naturally. Gosh! I just wrote about all of this two days ago, didn't I? Forgive me for being so stupid at times. Forgive me for my lack of faith.

I don't know what else to say. Perhaps I have said too much and am getting into my head right now. I am praying tonight to thank You for another day of life and sobriety, and I ask that You help me make it through tomorrow. I want to be able to have a good day at work tomorrow despite whatever may happen. Help me turn over any discomfort I may face tomorrow. I want to get the third step right, and I want my faith in You to grow. Thanks for listening.

Katy, your faith is lacking because you don't do what you are supposed to do on a daily basis: pray. You think you're different and you don't have to pray as much as everyone else. You say you forget to pray or don't have the time. And when you do pray, you don't even concentrate on a conversation with God. Instead, your mind wanders to this or that and forgets about what it set out to do. Get your shit together and start taking this thing—recovery—one hour at a time and no faster. Shape up, girl.

JULY 20, 1989

I have just finished cleaning my entire apartment. I feel really good when my apartment is clean. I consider myself a relatively clean and tidy person. I can remember how messy I was when I was using. My car was dirty, my apartment was dirty, and I was dirty. I can remember walking through piles of clothing on the floor, and not dusting for weeks. What a turnaround I have made this year! And boy, does it feel good.

Cleaning up my act is very satisfying. I feel good when I take care of my possessions and myself. I have been watching my diet pretty closely and have been swimming and running quite a bit. I am beginning to notice some changes in my body, and I like them a lot. I finally feel confident I will reach my physical goal shortly. The hard part of taking care of myself is not working on the exterior—cleaning house or car. The hard part is working on the inside.

For so many years, I have thought that looking a certain way, having certain things, getting certain degrees, and knowing certain people would make me happy. How foolish could I have been? People used to tell me all the time I was the one who had to make me happy. I had to find happiness within myself. I used to say to these people that I would not be happy unless I finished this degree. I said over and over again that my education was the most important thing in my life and I would not be happy if I couldn't fulfill my educational goals. I even used to tell professors, counselors, and people in the program that my education was my top priority in life and that, if it didn't take that [front] seat and if I had to postpone educational goals, I would go out and use drugs again. In other words, I made it clear to everyone that my education would make me happy.

This whole subject gets so complicated for me at times. How so? Of all the things I do in a day, I enjoy most learning about new things or practicing the things I have been taught. In fact, what I enjoy most in life is teaching other students about issues of crime and research. I am in my prime when I am learning, teaching, and interacting in an academic environment. This is the honest-to-God truth. The only other thing I enjoy nearly as much is running. There are many other things in life I love to do, but they are less enjoyable than my academic ventures.

And so I am happy when I am learning, teaching, or practicing what I have learned—because I enjoy it so much. This is what enables me to conclude that my education is the source of my happiness. On the other hand, I realize that my educational endeavors are something I do that happens to bring me joy, and are really not a source of internal happiness. I have got to stop thinking that my educational achievements and career success will make me like or love myself or will make me happy for the rest of my life. In fact, it is this notion of something *making* me happy that is fucking me up. I have to learn to find happiness within myself and must stop thinking that something or someone else will make me happy. I guess I am trying to say that I must learn to love myself for who I am and must not base that love on looking a certain way, having certain things, getting certain degrees, and knowing certain people. That's what's on my mind right now. It's time to go read my Big Book [12 Step manual]. Later!

JULY 21, 1989

He called me today at work and really surprised me. We actually had a wonderful conversation. It really was good to hear from him today. We reminisced about old times and laughed quite a bit. He told me about the trouble he is having with his girlfriend, and I told him about my social life or lack thereof and he just laughed. He said those sweet nothings to me today like he used to say when we hung out. I told him about my dissertation, and he actually wanted to hear about it. He wants to see me next week. He wants me to fix him dinner like I did one day two Februarys ago. I want to see him too. I want to fix him dinner and I want to talk to him, but I can't. Why does Ricardo have to be a drug dealer?

One suggestion I took seriously when I came into the program was to cut the "bad" friends loose. "Bad" is defined as those who have, use, or sell drugs or alcohol. And so I cut him loose and didn't talk to him or see him for a very long time—nearly a year, to be exact. But after today's phone call, I start to wonder if I really have to keep him out of my life and wonder why I can't see him just one time for dinner.

Constant dilemmas and problems are what I face in recovery today. Recovery does have a lot of good things to offer, and it has given me a great deal. In fact, I have received more gifts from recovery than from anything else in life. It just seems as though those gifts come with costs sometimes. Recovery costs me. It costs me certain friends, places, and things, and it alters my lifestyle. And times like today make me stop and wonder why there has to be such a rigid line dividing my past life from my present life.

I guess the problem is, I want everything my way. I want to be able to keep this friend, go to this nightclub, and still stay in the program. I want to be able to do anything I want and still stay clean. The reality is, I can't do all these things. I can't have everything I want, and I have to try to stop getting my own way. I need to say a prayer right about this point.

God, the call came out of nowhere today. I wasn't expecting him to call, but then again I asked for it because I called him on the 4th of July to wish him a happy holiday. Was I asking for this or what? What do I do now? I must admit I would like to see him, but I am afraid of doing so. I am afraid of the feelings he might stir up inside me. I am afraid he may look, smell, or taste like cocaine. When he sees me, he will hug and kiss me, and I will be able to tell if he is high right at that moment. Should I put myself through this? The answer is no.

I want to turn this all over to You right now. I want to lay it to rest and get it out of my mind. Thank you for helping me get through another day without using. I pray that You help me get through tomorrow without using as well. As far as my old drug dealer is concerned, I don't really have to worry anymore about seeing him tonight, and I know I won't see him tomorrow because I am going to the beach. Whatever You have in store for me concerning this situation, show me Thy will and help me see it through. I trust You will show me the right thing to do. Thank you!

JULY 25, 1989

I have been thinking about my past a lot lately. I haven't been thinking about my using past. I have been thinking about my childhood and adolescence. I have been purposely forcing myself to think back to my early years of life in order to gain insight on why I am the way I am today. Basically, I have been looking into my past in order to find meaning in my life today.

I am not sure if this is the right thing to do, but I am gaining quite a bit of insight from all of this self-reflecting. One thing always seems to surface when I look back into my childhood and adolescence: being different. I noticed at a very early age I was different from the other members of my family. From a very early age—as long as I can remember—I have always wanted different things, held different beliefs, and gotten involved in things other members of my family would never do. The things I wanted to do, the beliefs I had, and the things I got involved in were all "good" things according to most people. And so my family members began calling me special and continued to call me special and different when I began excelling in all of these good and desirable things.

None of this stopped with the members of my family. Teachers, classmates, coaches, friends, and other parents began telling me I was special because I was doing this or could do that, and soon I began to believe them. I started believing I was special. I started winning all kinds of awards in junior high and high school in almost anything I did. I excelled in very many different things. I was very popular in school. Everyone liked me—and if any, by chance, didn't like me, then I would do what I had to do to make them like me.

All of this just exploded when I went off to college. I was pissed off my freshman year of college: I had to go to a branch of main campus because my SATs were not high enough. I went to this godforsaken campus; and on the first day there, I decided to dedicate myself to proving to everyone

I was smart enough to go to main campus and was too good for this small school. After all, the people at this small campus were different from me. So, I started making the dean's list and found that all of my friends and my family were in total awe of me because I was excelling so well in school. But none of this was good enough for me. After all, I was making the dean's list at a branch of main campus—and we all knew branch campuses were easier than main campus.

And so the next year I went off to main campus to prove to myself and others I could cut it in a "real" school. I played superwoman for the next three years. I made the dean's list every term, while also working 30 hours a week and playing competitive field hockey for the school. Soon all of my new friends at main campus started thinking I was special and different as I got better grades than they did, as I lost all kinds of weight without any problems, and as I got in close with the people with whom I worked.

The years of my undergraduate education are very complicated for me to explain at times. I went through so many changes those years. I found I couldn't relate to the people with whom I was living because they were jealous of my grades, my job, my running and fitness ventures, or my appearance. By my senior year, I found I was much different from most of my friends, and so I was ready to move on to something bigger and better. After talking to a few professors, I decided to go get my master's degree at a much more competitive school because I had "conquered" main campus. Several professors at main campus actually told me to go to a better school for my master's degree because I had what it took to excel in my profession.

And so, after graduating magna cum laude, I applied to three top schools in my field and not only got accepted, but was offered an academic fellowship at each school. To make a long story short, I used my good old competitive personality to excel in my master's program and graduated in a year and a half at the top of my class. Everyone thought I was destined for greatness. After all, I was 23 and had a master's degree and was going to start a Ph.D. program in half a year. I was working for this professor and for the dean of our school. I was teaching my own class in a university at age 24 and had been to some very prestigious meetings in my field, presenting a paper I had researched and written. I was the shit! I had arrived.

Does it all sound good right now, or does it sound as if I am bragging and am conceited? I guess it doesn't really matter, does it? Because what happened in 1987 was, I had finally heard once too often that I was special and different. I was tired of my parents telling me I wasn't like them and was cut from a different cloth. I was tired of my family telling me I was out of their league. I just wanted to be like everyone else.

It was getting too difficult being special and different. I was competing in a new world that had people in it who were smarter, in better shape, and better looking, and who had more money than I would ever have. I found it harder and harder to live up to the expectations that others had for me; but more importantly, I found it impossible to live up to the expectations I had for myself. For it didn't matter what I had ever done in my life—I was never satisfied with any of it and I always thought I could have done better.

And so I started developing an inferiority complex, thinking I was not good enough to be doing this or that or to be with this person or that person. You see, I have spent my life with people who told me I was the best at this or was the best that; and if they didn't tell me I was the best, than I made damn sure I did what I had to in order to become the best. But in this town, I was no longer the best, no matter how hard I tried. And so I decided to just give up instead of fighting so hard to be second best. I decided that being second best was not good enough but was all I'd ever be. I started believing I was worth very little to everyone. And it is at this point that cocaine became a problem for me.

I once wrote that cocaine made me feel on top of the world and as if everyone in the world was at my feet. Of course, it did this: It fed my ego when I could not feed it myself. Cocaine filled the gaps and holes inside me that I only made worse. Cocaine made me feel better about myself. And so I continued to use, and my disease progressed. I soon found cocaine could not only make good feelings feel better, but could also make bad feelings and pain go away. So I continued to use. I used cocaine to make me feel better, to make things better—because, once again, nothing I ever did was good enough for me.

I have come to realize all of this in the past month of recovery. It is time to deal with all of this now, but I don't have the slightest idea where to start. I have so many insecurities, so much false pride, and so much arrogance at times, I can barely get through the day—let alone try to work on changing 26 years of my life. Maybe it will come with time. I don't know what is in store for me tomorrow. That is God's will. I am in touch with certain things about myself and I am grateful for that today. I am grateful for recovery and all of the gifts it has given me. I am beginning to see what I have to do to stay clean and am beginning to see the work I have to do and the changes I have to make in order to find internal happiness. I just hope and pray to God that He shows me His will on a daily basis and helps me live it. Please be patient, God, because I have a great deal of work to do. Thanks for listening.

AUGUST 1, 1989

My rent is due and I don't feel like taking it up to my landlord. I guess I'll do it tomorrow. Wouldn't it be nice if I didn't have to pay rent this month? What I could do with that $600 would be absolutely great! Just a thought.

I guess I want to talk about the meeting I led last evening. Last night, I got to lead the women's meeting I attend downtown. It was wonderful. It's a really neat experience to lead a meeting. I am going to lead a few more this month and am looking forward to doing so.

The best thing about leading a meeting is when people tell you they liked what you had to say and got a lot out of your sharing. Several people said things like this to me last night, and it made me feel absolutely wonderful. Oddly enough, compliments like this in the past would have inflated my ego, but today is different. I consider myself fortunate to have had the opportunity to share my story with all of those other women, and feel I am doing nothing different or better than anyone else has ever done while leading a meeting. Isn't this humbling disease wonderful? It is certainly a wonderful therapeutic tool for my often destructive ego.

I just really wanted to write a little bit today about my experience last night. Thanks go out to God for allowing me to do this and for preparing me to do so. I better get back to work on my dissertation. I have a feeling tonight is going to be a long one. So long!

AUGUST 2, 1989

I just got off the phone with a new friend of mine whom I am getting to like quite a bit. Her name is Margaret, and I met her through my other wonderful friend, Penny. Margaret and I always talk at great length about things. She told me tonight her father is a professor, and this amazed me. I like many things about her. I hope the friendship continues to grow.

Friends are a gift from the program. I have so many new friends today that I love dearly and care about quite a bit. I have tons of new female friends and a few male friends I met there. I used to shut out people in the program, but I don't anymore. Making friends is good and right today.

No longer do I have unrealistic expectations of friends. I am learning to accept what they have to offer and have stopped trying to make them into the people I want them to be. More importantly, however, I am no longer sacrificing my feelings to spare theirs. In fact, I no longer have to sacrifice any part of myself for a friend. Part of this has to do with the people I have as friends now, and the other part has to do with learning how to have normal and functional friendships.

I am glad I have all of this today. Thanks go out to my Higher Power and the program for showing me such wonderful new people. Thanks go out to my Higher Power and the program for helping me to become a better person. I feel myself growing as the days pass. I hope I continue in this period of growth because I do want to rid myself of my character defects so I may live a happy life. But I do know I will not be able to grow every day, friends won't always be so wonderful, and I may struggle with many different things as the days pass. One thing is for sure, however: I no longer have to drink and drug over any of these things. I have a Higher Power and a program to help me deal with anything. With that, I feel safe; and with that, I will close.

AUGUST 6, 1989

I almost felt like blowing off writing in my journal tonight until I got a message from Geraldine on my answering machine about a particular entry that she wanted to discuss. After receiving the message, I immediately came over here to look up the entry she was referring to and read it over. It was the entry about being lonely and looking to friends to fill the gaps inside me. It was about not being able to love myself and how I used cocaine to get rid of all these horrible feelings.

I made that entry almost five months ago and find I have changed quite a bit since then. The feelings I wrote about back in March—about being lonely, not loving myself, and having voids in my life that need to be filled—are leaving me. Today, I seldom feel lonely. The program has given me many new friends that care a great deal about me. But more importantly, the program has given me the ability to be content with myself. I actually enjoy being alone today. I don't isolate when I am alone. I just take some time to be by myself.

I am able to be alone today and happy about it because the program is helping me to grow. I am learning how to fill voids in my life with useful things instead of drugs. And I am learning how to deal with pain without trying to suppress it with drugs. All in all, these things are helping me to discover self-love. I have spent my entire life thinking one of two things: I loved myself when I actually didn't, or I hated myself and that was how I was going to feel forever. Well, it's just not like that anymore. I am very much in touch with how I feel about myself today, but must admit it brings me some discomfort at times. The key to all of this for me is, I can deal with the discomfort now without falling apart or turning to drugs.

Most of the time, I enjoy being in touch with my feelings because life becomes a lot easier. I know what to do with anger today. I know how to deal with stress, anxiety, and depression without harming myself. The thing I find more and more amazing as the days pass is that I seldom feel angry, lonely, depressed and all those other negative things anymore; and if I do feel them, they don't last long.

This program of mine is wonderful. Sometimes I think it is too good to be true; but then I realize this is a simple program for complex people like me, and it can work for anyone who takes the first step. I took that first step nearly a year and a half ago, and my life has never been the same. It has gotten progressively better. And to think that more will be revealed if I stick around! What a gift from God!

AUGUST 8, 1989

God answered my prayers today. I asked Him last night to help me to share honestly and to take a short time doing so, and that is what I did tonight at the meeting. I led a small women's meeting tonight and had a wonderful experience. I'd like to be able to go to this meeting every week, and hope I can arrange a ride to go. My Higher Power must really be with me today because there is a lady who was at the meeting tonight who offered to give me a ride every week. What luck!

I really want to change the subject right now. What I want to talk about tonight is the impossible situation I find myself in at work. After talking to Margaret and some of the other women tonight, I have reached the conclusion that I am basically getting two things from my job right now, and nothing more. These two things are a paycheck and an occupational experience for my resume. There is absolutely nothing else that my job is giving me, and I must learn to live with that.

Look, I don't want to sit here and explain the impossible situation I am in today. Doing so will take me away from what I need to do and will prevent me from growing. What I need to do today is to accept that I am in this situation and will be so for the next year. I must focus on how I will accept this situation on a daily basis and not on how I envision the situation or hope to change the situation.

I just read back over the last paragraph and don't really know if I made any sense. Actually, I don't even know if I want to write about this right now. What seems to be sticking in my mind right now is what Margaret said on the way out to the meeting when I was discussing my impossible situation with her. Margaret said my Higher Power really must want me to experience some humility right now. She also said He must want you to humble yourself right now.

Margaret's remarks are so true. I have been discussing for the past few weeks about how I have spent my life getting what I have wanted, excelling in everything I did, and wanting to be the best in everything. Also, I am beginning to realize that these things have been the blueprint of my life and I must rewrite this blueprint to remain sober.

Well, my Higher Power must have already figured this one out. At work right now, and in other areas of my life, I am not getting my own way, I am not excelling in the things I am doing, and no one believes I am special or the best in anything. What I am experiencing is a big piece of humble pie. I am eating from that pie every day and I am not used to doing so. I accepted the fact that this disease was a humbling experience for me quite some time ago, and I have no problem with accepting that fact today. I do, however, have problems being humble sometimes—but so do many other people. Like most others, I want to shine and be right and almighty. I want to be Master of the Universe at least twice a day, but I know I am not.

It is the humility of things I cannot seem to accept. Part of me really doesn't know what humility is. All I seem to know is what it feels like. It feels like shit. It feels like a lost battle, a defeat. And the reason work is humiliating for me is because everything that goes on there is a zero-sum game with a winner and a loser, and it just so happens that I am the one who is losing all of the time. Hence, I feel a great deal of humility at work right now.

How can I stop all of this? Can I redefine my perspective at work so as not to view it as a zero-sum game, and can I get my staff members to do the same? Yes and no! I can change my perspective of the job, but I am powerless over everyone else. How do I control humiliating feelings at work? Is this one that takes God's help? How do I continue to turn things over that happen at work when I feel as though, with each loss or point of surrender, I care less and less about the work I do? How can I do my best at a job I care nothing about?

I guess I have just defined this as a no-win situation for me; and to be perfectly honest, that is how I see it today. I don't have the insight to see how it will all work out for me. I am just confused and depressed. I just never guessed recovery would mean experiencing and dealing with things like this. Then again, I used to only want to remain abstinent from drugs. I didn't always want to recover from my disease and to find a new way of life. And because I want these "extra" things today, I must experience humility and eat humble pie. Help me through this, God. I need You more and more as the days pass. I can't do this all alone. Help me to use the tools You have put into my life, and help me to live Thy will. Thanks!

AUGUST 10, 1989

I am very angry right now. It is after 11 p.m. and I am just getting home from an 8:30 p.m. meeting—and [finally] back to my house since I left at 8 this morning. The reason I am so late getting back from the meeting and am so angry is because this guy at the meeting tonight locked his keys in his car like an idiot and the two people I took to the meeting decided it [would be] best to wait with this guy until the tow truck came to unlock his car. I had to wait outside of the church in the cold and rain for an hour after the meeting, and finally decided to leave after the girls told me they would get a ride home with the guy who locked his keys in his car.

What a fucking waste of time. Why didn't they tell me an hour ago they could get a ride home with this guy, and why didn't they just leave him there to wait by himself? I mean, after all, he's the idiot who locked his keys in his car. If he would have had a German car, this wouldn't have happened to him.

I know I sound horrible right now, but I need to vent this anger and be honest about my thoughts right now. I am pissed about having to wait on this guy tonight and about not having a nice time with these two ladies I think might become friends of mine. I was uncomfortable the entire evening and wasn't into the meeting at all. I don't like this meeting, and I don't know why I keep telling these women I will keep going to it with them. Thinking about it all just gives me the creeps.

One thing is for sure: I want to try to get rid of as much of this anger [as I can] before I go to bed so I can have a good night's sleep. God, I must really sound selfish. But I want to be selfish right now. I don't have extra time in a day to spend waiting around for someone to get into his car. Every minute of every day is occupied. I get to meetings, I work on my dissertation, I go to work, and I spend time with friends at meetings; but I don't have extra time in my life right now to spend on things like what happened tonight. My time is precious, and that is how I am really looking at this entire situation.

Tomorrow when I make a journal entry, I will probably read back over this and be mad at myself for getting angry tonight. Patterns, patterns, patterns! Play those old tapes, Katy. Get angry at others—and then beat yourself up for having those feelings, the next day. Kick yourself in the ass for being a schmuck tonight because you didn't want to help out a friend, and then draw a quick conclusion that you are not working your program.

I am a mess right now and I want to go to bed. I feel like an addict right now, but not a recovering addict. Have I lost the ability to deal with anger? I don't know. Later!

AUGUST 11, 1989

I just got back from playing softball all day and I am totally exhausted. I took a minute or so to read over last night's journal entry, and I must admit I really sounded like an addict then. It scares me to know that I get so uptight when things don't go my way and when I look at things the way I did last night. I copped the attitude that my time is too precious to spend on others' incompetence. In all actuality, I think I am just a bit irritable about things right now, and much of these feelings have to do with the busy schedule I have.

Breaking from these thoughts, I want to talk about men again tonight. I don't know if I've ever admitted this before, but I have a real inferiority complex around men. Basically, I just don't think any of them find me attractive and that any of them would be romantically interested in me. Lately, however, several men have been paying attention to me, and I think a few might actually be interested.

I don't know what has happened to change my luck with men, and I am not even sure the luck will change. I guess all I am trying to say is, it feels good knowing that men are attracted to me and might think I am a neat person. Irrespective of any of this, I find I am pretty cool about not being in a relationship right now even though I want one.

You know, I go to meetings and hear people talk about how wonderful their lives have gotten since they gave up drugs and alcohol and came into the program. And I look at my life right now and can see some of the same things those people are talking about. It just seems difficult to believe how powerful this program is and what it can do for people if they choose to work it. What did I ever see out there in that drug world? A quick fix to permanent problems? Probably so.

No amount of cocaine would have ever given me the confidence with men I have today. I can remember talking to men while I was high. I really didn't care what they thought of me because I thought I was better than them anyway. But as soon as the high wore off, or as soon as I began to crash, the low self-esteem would come back and my insecurities would shine. So, as I said, cocaine was just a temporary fix to a permanent problem: lack of self-esteem and confidence when it comes to men.

I am very tired right now and want to take a bath and go to bed. We have to play five games tomorrow starting at 11 a.m., so I need my rest. I just want to talk to God for a minute right now.

God, please forgive me for last night. There is no excuse for the way I behaved. Please show me Thy will and help me to live the best I can. What more can I say besides I have a lot of growing to do. Thanks!

AUGUST 19, 1989

I think it's the 19th, but I am not sure. Anyway, it is about 11 Saturday morning and I just got back from the grocery store. I made some fruit salad that I have to take to a pool party this afternoon, and it is really good. I hope Colin likes it. Oh, Colin is my date for this pool party. And I guess it's Colin I want to talk about today.

Colin is young and has two months in the program. These are two things about him that bother me. I guess his age only bothers me a little, but his clean time bothers me a lot. The program strongly recommends staying out of a relationship during the first year of recovery. My problem is, I am assuming a relationship will occur with this guy and will, therefore, present both Colin and me with problems. I guess I am being too anxious.

The other thing—his "youth"—bothers me as well. He actually knows students I have taught. He actually knows students I had last term. Scary thought. I told him never to mention to these people I am in the program, and he assured me he wouldn't. I hope he's a man of his word. I really don't know what else to write about him right now, and so I am going to get off this subject. I am just going to try to enjoy myself this afternoon. Yeah, Katy, now that sounds like a good idea.

LATER THE SAME DAY

Money, money, money! It is on my mind night and day right now. While I was grocery shopping, all I could think about was how the check I was going to write was going to bounce. And so while I was picking up items at the store, I tried my hardest to keep from spending extra money, so I would be less in the hole. I guess this is better than the attitude I had while I was using. When I was using, I would have thought, "Fuck it. I am going to bounce this check anyway, so what does it matter if I bounce it for $50 or $200?" Needless to say, I don't think that way anymore, but I do have dope-fiend thoughts regularly.

I was with Leslie last night, and we were joking about our cocaine days. And though last night I had no problem joking about those old times, today I feel pretty shitty about doing so. I feel shitty because I am paying the debt for it all today. I blew so much fucking money up my nose while I worked at the restaurant, and now I am fucking broke. Sometimes I don't think I'll ever get over how much money I spent on cocaine, and then other times I realize that brooding about it gets me nowhere and is a cop-out on what I need to do today.

What I need to do today to make it financially is to cut my expenses and to secure an additional source of income. My expenses are high because of this apartment and my new car (which I did not need!). I cannot get rid of these expenses. I am locked into a year lease, and I can't sell the car right now because I would lose my ass. And so the only things I could cut would be my American Express charges. I am making a conscious effort to not use the card, but it's hard when your other credit cards are at their limit and you have no other source of credit to use. My other credit cards are at their limit because of my using days. The Visa card is at its limit strictly [because I used it] for cash advances for cocaine. I mean I really didn't use the card for anything else.

You know, this is all boring me right now. I don't want to brood about it and ruin the rest of my day. I want to be able to leave this all here right now and go about my business. Please help me turn this over to You, God. I cannot do anything today to alleviate my financial problems, and so please help me to enjoy the day for what it is. Thank You for a sober week, and help me to get through another day without using. Later!

AUGUST 21, 1989

It's Sunday night and I just got back from a meeting at the hospital. My sponsor and her husband celebrated five years of sobriety tonight, and it was a great celebration! I am so proud to have her as a sponsor. She and her husband are great!

I guess this is not what is really on my mind right now. Colin is on my mind. He was at the meeting tonight and was looking rather cute as usual. He is so young and he has no sobriety to speak of, yet I find I like him. I don't know what it is about him that attracts me. I just know I like being around him. He is interested in me as well and asked me to do several things with him in the future. He wants to take me to an Orioles game and wants me to go sailing with him. I must admit I am a bit flattered, but am just as cautious.

I just want to say tonight I am enjoying the male attention and will keep it at that right now. I will wait to see what tomorrow brings when it comes. Thanks for another clean day, God. Oh by the way, if I should need guidance with Colin (and I am almost certain I will), could You please show me what to do and help me to do the right thing? Thanks!

AUGUST 23, 1989

I had a great day at work today. In fact, I have had a wonderful week at work. Life is pretty damn good right now, and it is not because of anything I am doing. It is because the program is working in my life today.

I don't really want to sit here and get into "programology" (ha-ha!). I just thought I would say that. I guess I mean it, but am not sure. I really can't pinpoint a particular source or reason for my happiness today. I just know I am happy. It must have something to do with my 16-month period of abstinence, increased faith in a Higher Power, and relationships with people in the program. Because it is these things that are teaching me how to live life on life's terms—that is, how to remain happy when I don't get my way and am not in control, how to change my attitude when it gets fucked up, et cetera.

Actually, I don't have any particular feelings right now, except fatigue. I was out with Colin last night until 12:30 a.m. and didn't get to bed until 2:30 a.m. Needless to say, I am very tired right now and want to go to bed. Speaking of Colin, I am amazed at how much fun he is and how much he can make me laugh. I truly enjoy being with him. Imagine that, Katy! Thanks.

AUGUST 29, 1989

I guess I haven't written in this journal since Saturday. Boy, did those two days fly by! I do have a lot to talk about tonight, and I am not sure where to start.

For two weeks prior to this past Monday, I was fantasizing about cocaine. It took a meeting on Friday and a long conversation with a program veteran to get me out of that period. I mean it was so bad that I was thinking about how wonderful it would be to get high, what I would look and feel like, and the whole bit. Not for one minute during this two-week period did I stop to remember the horrible things about cocaine like crashes, lies, fatigue, self-destruction, and that whole bit. It just goes to show me how cunning and baffling this disease really is.

Here I am with 16 months of sobriety under my belt, and I am finding cocaine attractive once again. It all just never ceases to amaze me how much I need this program and my sponsor, not to mention my Higher Power.

Work is going great and I think it's because I am getting better—better with my attitude. For, as much as I complain about the job, I have to admit I am very grateful for it because it has helped me to grow both personally and academically. In addition to that, my co-workers like me and respect my work. They have even started to praise me for my contributions at the office. Not too bad for a dope fiend, huh?

Colin. I really do like him. We kissed tonight and discussed our attraction to one another. I don't know what is going to happen; all I do know is how I feel about him. I really enjoy his company and often feel myself drawn to him. What to do!? What to do!? He is four years younger than I am, he has no time in the program, and—to top it all off—he has doubts about the program. He and I talked about his recovery tonight after the meeting, and he is going through the exact same things I went through a year ago when I had as much time as he does.

I don't know what is going to happen and I don't want to think about it. I trust my Higher Power will help me with this one. I will need His assistance more and more as the days pass. In the meantime, I am sitting here wishing Colin was beside me. Oh well!

I guess I should turn in right now. My things are all set for the class I am going to teach this term, and that comforts me. I am excited [about this chance] to teach. I feel as though I am being very responsible right now in my work and in my personal life as well. I have a lot to be grateful for today. After all, I made it through the day without a drug or a drink. Thanks!

SEPTEMBER 6, 1989

I had a great day at work today. In fact, I had a great day all day. It really amazes me that I had such a wonderful day, given that I have been away from my normal routine for a few days and have not attended a meeting in over a week. I guess this is what I want to talk about tonight. I want to talk about what happens to me when I don't go to meetings.

I know I have written about this before, but I want to write about it again because I find it very amazing. What I find amazing is how my addiction surfaces in my life when I don't attend meetings, write in my journal, and call my sponsor. I went out of town to visit my parents for a few days and didn't get to call my sponsor, write in my journal, or go to a meeting for an entire week. And don't you know—by the end of the week, I was dreaming about cocaine quite often. Like clockwork, man, cocaine thoughts and active addiction surface in my dreams when I don't do what I am supposed to do. It never fails! The first place I experience the negative effects of not working my program is in my dreams.

I guess I should consider myself lucky. After all, I didn't use while I was goofing off. But what seems to be most important to me—and what proves to be the most valuable lesson from goofing off—is that I begin to relapse, and the relapse starts in my dreams. Relapse for me begins at the subconscious level, which can be both a good thing and a bad thing.

The first dream I had (that I remember) took place Saturday night. I can't remember doing any cocaine in the dream and I can't even remember seeing any cocaine, but I definitely know it was a drug-related dream because it had a lot of old familiar drug scenes in it. The second dream occurred Sunday evening and I saw cocaine in this dream, but did not use any. In the second dream, I was in a room with a bunch of people who were partying and I was just watching them. By the time the third dream rolled around on Monday night, I had used cocaine in the same room with those same people and was incredibly high and miserable.

The third dream is most vivid in my mind right now—and it should be, because it is both the most recent and the most intense. I can remember copping a huge amount of cocaine and obsessing over it like I used to do while I was using. What stands out in the dream the most are the feelings of guilt that went along with the using. Throughout the entire dream and relapse, I was overwhelmed with feelings of guilt. This guilt superseded any of the feelings that the drug gave me. All I could think and feel while I was using was that I would have to start sobriety all over again, that I would lose my friends in recovery, that people at work and school would find out and wouldn't talk to me, and that my parents would find out and would be devastated. Basically, I thought and felt I had let everyone down in my life and that no one would want to have anything to do with me because I had relapsed.

This all just makes perfect sense to me, and it happens every time I choose not to do the things I am supposed to do in sobriety and [instead] opt to goof off. The relapse kept getting closer with each dream, and it only makes me wonder if the second or third dream could have been prevented if I had attended a meeting Saturday night like I was supposed to. I know the answer to this without even asking. I guess people in the program are quite serious when they say the relapse takes place long before you pick up the drug. And I guess this is where I am fortunate to be able to have these dreams and to be able to interpret them, because they clue me into what I am headed for if I goof off and don't do what I am supposed to do. On the other hand, I just hope I will always be able to remember these relapse dreams, because I might go out and use if I don't remember them.

I could write about many more things tonight, but I don't really have the time to do so. In fact, I feel as though I have rushed this entire entry and haven't really taken the time to talk about all of the things I need to discuss. Oh well! That's life! I teach my first class tomorrow night and have a long day ahead of me. I am going to bed right now and will not answer the phone if Colin calls. (What an asshole!) Guess I should discuss him tomorrow. Good night!

SEPTEMBER 8, 1989

I spent the evening with Colin and had a wonderful time. He came over around 7 p.m. and we ate Chinese and then went to a meeting. We came back here after the meeting and had sex. It was nice. The best part about it was lying in his arms and talking to him afterwards. I am really starting to develop some feelings for this guy. I wonder how he feels about me?

Life is pretty good for me right now, and I am not just saying this because I just had sex with a guy I like a lot. I really do mean that life is going great right now. Despite my perpetual financial problems, everything in my life is going well. I really have nothing to complain about, but have so many things for which to be grateful.

Recovery is giving me the ability to deal with life better than I ever could before I found the program. Perhaps the most special gift is the ever-increasing serenity I find in my life today. I don't get angry as much anymore. I don't get depressed as much anymore. I don't fight as hard as I can to be the best anymore. And when I see someone who does a job better than I do, is smarter than I am, and is better looking than I am, I might get a bit jealous—but I don't fall apart and become a spiteful bitch.

Tonight at the meeting (there were a lot of newcomers there), people were sharing about gratitude. Because most of the people were new, they talked about being grateful for still having their families, cars, and jobs. They were thankful for not having to hustle out on the streets, steal, lie, or cheat to support their habits. They even shared about being thankful for not having to experience a crash, a hangover, a car accident, an overdose, or even a sore throat or nosebleed. Not a single one of them talked about being thankful for everything recovery has to offer that I described above, and this is to be expected because they are so new to the program and have very little recovery right now.

I was the same way. When I first came into the program, I thought recovery was just about staying clean from cocaine and other drugs. I didn't know at the time that recovery was about a better way of life. So these new people are going through exactly what I went through when I first came around. They are thankful for being clean because that's what recovery is for them today. They don't know that recovery is about a better way of life, and so they can't be grateful for some of the same things I am grateful for today.

Don't get me wrong—I am extremely grateful for not having to worry about where the next gram is coming from, for not having to create another lie, for not having to experience those horrible crashes, nosebleeds, headaches, or the insomnia, paranoia, and insanity that characterize active addiction. I am grateful for those things every single clean day I have. But I want more than that today, and I am getting more than that today. I never would have guessed recovery would be this good, and I never would have guessed there would be these many gifts in recovery. And I surely never would have bet a dime on the fact that recovery could give me a way of life that was not only better than the life I was leading while I was using, but was also better than the life I have experienced in these past 26 years.

All I can think about right now is how this all connects. They say you must do a lot of changing in order to stay clean, you must get rid of destructive behaviors and character defects in order to stay clean. They go on to say that one day it will not be enough to stay sober if you simply don't pick up a drug or a drink. You must work on yourself. After all, recovery is an inside job. All this is where it all connects. Those people who shared tonight about being grateful to be clean were sincere. I do not doubt that. However, just as I came to see that staying clean and sober has a great deal more to do with making permanent changes in your life than it does with simply not picking up a drink or a drug, so too will these people have to see the same. For those who are fortunate enough to stick around long enough to discover this, they will find the gifts of recovery are never ending—and their gratitude for the program will continue to grow as the days pass. Those who don't stick around, or those who do stick around but don't make any changes, will eventually use again. Recovery is no more difficult than that. Later!

SEPTEMBER 11, 1989

Boy, a lot is happening with me right now and I don't know what to write about. My days are packed tight with so much stuff, and my mind is cluttered with so many thoughts, I can't seem to focus on any of it right now. I think I am going to try to change my writing strategy in this journal. I often talk about the events in a day and how those events make me feel, while other times I talk about past experiences and how they have made me feel at different points in my life. [However,] it takes too much time to write about events; and since my day is cluttered with so many events and things, I could spend a great deal of time just writing about what I did in a day and not about my feelings or the insights I may have had. What I am trying to say is that I am going to start talking more about feelings and insight in this journal, instead of discussing the day's events.

So right now I am feeling very tired as usual. I want to make this short because I need to get some sleep. Tomorrow is going to be a long day. What I want to discuss tonight are the feelings I have about this dissertation I am doing. I guess these feelings have to do with my work—my writing, in particular. I am having problems concentrating on the dissertation. I am running into creativity problems and, therefore, my writing is suffering. I am not taking the time to allow the ideas to come to mind, and then I am further complicating the matter by not focusing on the ideas that do come. I have got to learn to concentrate, relax, and develop my ideas.

I feel insecure about all of this. I felt as though I did some good writing this past weekend, and then Geraldine essentially told me on Sunday to rewrite what I had completed. I expect to have to rewrite this damn thing hundreds of times. This is not what upsets me right now. I am upset because Geraldine has pinpointed my problem and has forced me to deal with it. I should be thankful that she has brought the problem to the surface, because it prohibits me from hiding behind it. I am just feeling a bit inadequate right now.

Concentration. This is something I have struggled with my entire life. I know exactly why concentration is difficult for me. I simply try to do so much that I end up doing nothing to my best ability. Does this make any sense? The problem is, I want to do everything right now. I do not know how to limit my efforts and time to just one thing and, therefore, I cannot concentrate on any one task because I am so busy trying to get everything done that I never get one task completed the best I can.

Your inability to curtail your desires, to prioritize your tasks, and to just say no to certain people, places, and things is fucking up your concentration, Katy. You have got to slow down and limit your workload. I better take a look at the first step of my program right now, because the feeling of unmanageability is coming over me. My life is, essentially, unmanageable. I cannot manage the tasks I do and, therefore, my concentration is suffering.

How can I read that first step time and time again and not realize how well it actually fits into my life? Why couldn't I have understood the concept of unmanageability before? Is this disease cunning or what? I guess I know what I have to do and, to tell you the truth, I think I am about ready to make some major changes because I am tired of leading an unmanageable life. I have the rest of my life to do the million things I want to do. I don't have to do them all today.

God, please help me with concentration. If I continue to turn my life and will over to You, will You help me to manage my life? I desperately need your guidance because I am making no progress in this category. Thanks for listening. Later!

SEPTEMBER 14, 1989

I thought about Colin quite a bit today. Key West is on my mind as well. I am looking forward to the trip and the vacation, but I must admit I am a bit nervous about it as well. The real deal is, I want to talk about Colin right now, but am avoiding the issue.

I haven't spoken to him at all this week, and that really bothers me. I wish he would call. I wish he would call so I could tell him I don't want to see him anymore. But even if he did call, would I actually tell him I didn't want to see him—or would I ask him to come over? I don't know!

How do you feel about this guy, Katy? He is fun and he is cute. You enjoy his company. You love the fact that he thinks you are good looking and idolizes the ground you walk on, or at least he did when you first met him. And you can bet your bottom dollar that it is exactly this that is pissing you off right now. Colin used to be in hot pursuit of you, and now he is not.

I loved the fact that he pursued me. It made me feel special—like I was worth a bit more than I usually think I am. Actually, I guess Colin made me feel a little bit like cocaine used to make me feel—special and unique, just a little bit better than I actually was. Is this a healthy attitude to have about a relationship? Is this how a man is supposed to make me feel? Or is this just another incident of selfish behavior guided by character defects? I don't know.

Maybe I should ask my sponsor about this one. I have already talked to her about it—and to tell you the truth, I forget what she told me. I guess that means I can ask her again. Thank God for sponsors!

Lately, for the past few months, I have been fantasizing about turning people's heads. Believe it or not, I have been daydreaming a great deal about how everyone will think I am so good looking they will all turn to look my way when I pass by. I can't seem to go on discussing this, because it is incredibly self-centered. I almost hate to write about all of this.

I think I am relatively good looking, but I don't know just how pretty, beautiful, gorgeous, or sexy I actually am. And so I have been fantasizing about how different people are telling me and are showing me how pretty, beautiful, gorgeous, or sexy they think I am. I am really obsessed with my looks right now, and it is all just superficial bullshit. I think the real issue lies underneath this stuff, but I am afraid to talk about it.

Men sure do bring out my insecurities, and I know this is not the first time I have said this. Am I ready to love someone, or what? Is Katy ready for a relationship? Probably not, given the attitude I described above. I guess it's time to turn this one over to the big old HP and ask for help as usual. Thank God I didn't use today.

September 17, 1989

Here is what a man can do to me. Last night, my plans were to go to an anniversary meeting in Silver Spring and then go out with everyone after the meeting or meet my brother downtown so I could go out with him and his new boyfriend. I did go to the meeting, but I didn't stick to my plans afterwards because of Colin.

Colin called me last night while I was doing my nails and asked me what I was going to do. I told him I was going to the meeting and then I said, "I might go out with my brother afterwards." Colin told me he has been in a depression all week and this is why he hasn't called me. He says the pink cloud he was riding has turned black and he can't understand why. I talked to him a bit on the phone and asked him to go to the meeting with me, and he agreed to do so.

To make a long and boring story short, as soon as Colin expressed interest in doing something with me last night, I blew everyone else off without an explanation. And this is what a man can do to me today. Driving home last night, I realized I would have done anything he wanted to do in order to be with him. He was pulling my strings. I was simply his puppet.

This behavior kind of angers me, yet I haven't really written about what angers me the most. I had a nice time with Colin last night; but several times, I just wanted to take him aside and ask him what is going on between us. However, every time I got close to asking him what he thinks about us, or if he really likes me, or whether we are heading toward a relationship or not, I found I was tongue tied and couldn't ask him a thing. Why couldn't I ask him these things, and why couldn't I talk to him about us last night?

I think I know the answer to this. I am just too insecure about the relationship. I am scared I will jeopardize something between us if I start asking questions and talking about a possible commitment between us. I am scared I will scare him off, and I don't want to do that. And this is sick behavior. I know I should be very honest about what I want from Colin and should talk about all of this with him, but my insecurities and desperation to have a man in my life right now prohibit me from doing what I should. And so I end up being a puppet on a string like I was last night.

Tomorrow I leave for Key West for eight days and will not see Colin until I return. I'd like to say right now that this vacation will give me time to think about things between the two of us and will also give me the courage to come back and tell Colin how I feel, but I know it's unrealistic for me to think time away will change me or my behavior. What I need to do is to pray a great deal about this one and talk about it with my sponsor and other people in the program, because I am making no sense of the situation. With that, I will close for right now.

SEPTEMBER 26, 1989

I have returned from vacation in Key West. I got home about an hour or so ago and am exhausted yet irritable. I have a lot I want to write about the vacation in Key West, but don't really feel like getting into it right now. It was a good week overall, and I had a very nice vacation. I feel well rested, but am anxious to get back to work. I am supposed to have tomorrow off, but I think I'll go to work. I feel out of touch and also feel this need to jump back into things right away.

I guess one of the things I want to talk about the most was how my vacation made me feel about work at the office and my work on my dissertation. I missed work a lot and, ironically enough, am very eager to get started again. In other words, I guess I had enough vacation. I know for sure I have had enough sun to last me until next summer. I'll write more about this tomorrow.

What I want to write about now are the feelings I experienced on the airplane today. Every time I fly, I feel absolutely wonderful about life. I always ask for a window seat so I can look out into the sky to see all of the pretty clouds. It is the clouds that totally fascinate me, and it is the clouds that gave me some incredible feelings today and some interesting insights.

I was sitting in my seat today and was peering out my window into the sky. We were flying above the clouds as I could see them all beneath me. They looked so soft and fluffy. The sky was covered with them. I looked down on the clouds from my seat and could not see anything but them and the sun shining above, casting glorious light on them. And for several minutes I felt I was in heaven. I wanted to step outside the plane and onto those clouds. I wanted to feel their softness, grab a chunk of them and rub them against my face. I wanted to run through those clouds. It would be so easy to run through those clouds because they were so soft. I would feel so light on my feet because I would be running on air. Won't someone stop the plane and let me out for just a few minutes so I can play in these clouds? I'm sure that everyone would want to play in these clouds once they experienced it.

And it was at this moment that a familiar feeling came back to me. That good old cocaine feeling—the one that used to make me feel like I was in heaven, was walking on air, like the world was beneath me, and everything I touched was soft and weighed nothing. Did someone just shove a few lines of cocaine up my nose, or is this for real? Am I high on cocaine right now, or am I sober watching the clouds go by? I think I am sober and am watching the clouds go by.

What a wonderful feeling! And it was real. It wasn't drug induced. God, how I love that feeling. It gets a grip on me and holds on so tight. It wraps itself around me and won't let me go. It takes all my worries and pain away and makes me so happy. Why can't I feel this way all of the time? Wouldn't it be wonderful to feel this way all of the time? Flying above your worries, feeling weightless and carefree. Running through endless piles of soft clouds without a worry in the world. That is what I felt today up in that airplane.

I felt closer to heaven today and closer to the people in my life who have died. As I was peering out of my window into the sky, I wondered if I would see any of those dead people. Would I see my aunt or my great-grandmother? Would I run into Trish and Eric from my high school class? And would I get the chance to see Elvis, John Lennon, Emile Durkheim, or Benjamin Franklin? I knew the answer to this question—but somehow I felt I had a real chance of seeing those dead people up there in that plane, 45,000 feet from the ground.

There is no doubt about it. I was high today in that airplane. I was high on life. Being up in that airplane today—flying through those clouds—felt a lot like a cocaine high I used to experience a long time ago; but the best part about it all was that there was no crash. I experienced no crash from today's high and I always experienced a crash from cocaine, no matter how much I did, how often I got high, and what other drugs I used to bring me down. On the airplane today, there was no crash. I sailed through those clouds high on life, and experienced some wonderful feelings I haven't felt for quite some time. And I didn't crash. In fact, I am still a bit high from it all. I just guess I am high on life today. Thank you, God. What a wonderful way to end a nice vacation. Later!

SEPTEMBER 30, 1989

Today is the last day of the month. I don't really care much. Like I said in the last entry, September was a good month for me. My life went along smoothly and I experienced no crises. I have to thank God for this.

October is here, and that means that fall is in full swing and winter is right around the corner. I am looking forward to fall, but not winter. I hate being cold. Staying warm restricts my freedom. I hate having to take precautions to make sure I am warm enough. The only two things I like about winter are the snow and celebrating Christmas with my family. I have come to despise New Year's Eve and I basically think January and February are useless months. They are simply too cold for me.

I am boring myself with this seasonal discussion. I said, when I came back from Key West, I was going to discuss it all in this journal. Time has passed and I find my desire to discuss the vacation is sliding by. Don't get me wrong—I had a wonderful time in Key West and experienced some things I would like to discuss in this journal, but my heart is just not really into it.

Here goes nothing. The weather in Key West was perfect for me. I really think I could deal with that climate year round. Who needs the change of seasons when every day is bright, sunny, and about 90 degrees? I would love to walk around in shorts year round, although part of me would miss wearing wool sweaters and leather jackets.

Despite the attractive element of the weather, Key West is not some place I could live. The lifestyle there is too slow paced for me. People just move too slow, have little drive, and are not very goal oriented. They certainly are not very competitive at all. I need a fast-paced life full of competition. That is what I know and is what I want. None of this can be found in Key West. I guess I am trying to say I could not live in Key West, after all. Besides, I would not want to live in a place so densely populated with gays and lesbians. I was there in the off-season, so the Key West homosexuality was at a minimum. I hear it gets much worse.

Key West has 12 Step recovery, but it is very weak. I went to about five meetings down there, and they were populated with nice people who didn't have much clean time. The meetings are very small and are not prevalent. There are very few professional people who attend meetings because most of Key West's employment is "service-oriented."

I can't believe I am doing this. I am describing to the reader what Key West is like, instead of making a good journal entry about how I felt being on vacation and what it has done for me. I guess I should describe the feelings I experienced during the week, but I know it will take me a long time to discuss them because I experienced so many different emotions.

I spent the first five days with people from the conference; and to set the stage for the feelings I am about to discuss, let me just say that these people were very "party-oriented" and so was all of Key West. There was booze everywhere, and these people drank every possible moment. The drinking didn't bother me at first; but by the end of the week, my patience with drunkenness and the party atmosphere was ending. I was anxious to spend a few days alone, away from all of the bars and the drunks. I saw a lot of alcoholism down there and a lot of behavior that goes along with it all. Men were cheating on their wives; women were cheating on their husbands; people were sleeping with people they didn't even know, without "protection"; everyone had hangovers; and everyone kept saying that they didn't know why they got drunk the night before, they would never drink again—and sure enough they were drinking a few hours later.

It all sounded and looked a lot like me two years ago. And I was damn glad I didn't have to go through that shit again. Every time someone complained about a headache, I got some gratitude. Every time someone tried to rationalize their drinking, I got some gratitude. Every time someone felt guilty for doing something they shouldn't have done while they were drunk, I got some gratitude. In fact, I spent the entire week feeling very grateful for the new life I had and sorry for the lives of these other people. It was all a miracle for me. I no longer have to be a slave to alcohol and cocaine. I no longer have to play the pretentious game in bars and clubs. I no longer have to rationalize my drinking or my cocaine use to anyone. I no longer have headaches, one-night stands, and guilt to make me feel bad. I am just fine without any of this, and this is the miracle of the program. This is the miracle of taking the first step and admitting you are powerless over drugs and alcohol. What a wonderful life I have! Thank you, God. Later!

OCTOBER 8, 1989

It has been a few days since I wrote in this journal. I have been incredibly busy these past few days. So busy and active that I am feeling sick right now. I feel run-down, like I haven't had enough sleep or something. I know why I feel this way and I know what I have to do about it, so I am not going to belabor this issue. I just have to cut the workload back and get the proper amount of rest. More importantly, I just have to relax and calm down.

Christopher wanted me to go out with him and some of his friends tonight, but I called to tell him I am not going because I don't feel very well. This is true, but I must admit I really don't feel like going out with his gay friends to a nightclub. I'd rather stay home and do some work. I guess I'd rather isolate tonight.

I am isolating for many reasons, but only two are really salient. I could say I am isolating tonight because I have to work on the dissertation, the class I teach, or the book—but that is really not isolating. That's just doing my work. I am isolating tonight because I do not want to go out with my brother's gay friends and I do not want to be around alcohol tonight. The more I think about it, the more I realize that the alcohol thing is why I don't want to go out. I just don't want to be around alcohol tonight because I am feeling vulnerable about having a drink.

You know, ever since I entered the program and started recovery, I have had a reservation about drinking. Somewhere deep in my mind is buried the belief that I might be able to have a drink one day and will not have to give up alcohol for the rest of my life. Yet this weekend I finally realized that alcohol is no longer a part of my life and cannot ever be a part again if I am to remain sober and involved in the program. And this is what I am dealing with right now.

I am feeling sorry for myself because I can't drink, yet some people insist I can and wouldn't raise an eyebrow if I got drunk right now—because cocaine was my problem, not alcohol. You see, I bottomed out on cocaine, not alcohol. Most people, including myself, feel that cocaine is my problem and that alcohol is no problem at all. I can understand why other people think this way because they don't know that the substance is just a symptom of a disease called addiction. So it really doesn't matter if it's cocaine, heroin, alcohol, or Quaaludes; addiction is addiction, and the only way that your disease can be arrested is to remain abstinent from all mood-altering substances.

But it is me who forgets this at times. I don't understand the nature of my disease. Right now I want to overlook the fact that I have a disease, and I want to indulge in a drink. And the only reason I can't have a drink right now is because I have a fucking disease that is a permanent part of my life. Katy, this is what happens to you when you skip meetings. You start forgetting you have a disease that needs constant attention. You forget drugs and alcohol are mere symptoms of the disease and the hardest part of staying clean and sober is working on yourself. You think too often that cocaine is the only thing that has to change in your life, the only thing bad in your life that you must remove. You forget that you picked up the drug because things in your life were not satisfactory, not good enough for you to accept, and too painful for you to deal with.

Well, start remembering this shit, girl, because you are starting to get depressed. Get to a meeting and sit with people who are like you and feel the same way you do. Stop feeling sorry for yourself because you can't drink. Forget that you have to do it for the rest of your life and just do it for today. Get on with life, Katy. You can't waste your time moping about not being able to have a drink. There are certainly more important things in life than a drink—like living.

God, grant me the serenity to accept the things I cannot change, the courage to change the things I can, and the wisdom to know the difference. Later!

OCTOBER 10, 1989

My life is completely unmanageable right now. I do not feel as though I am working on recovery one bit. I do not feel I am working my program, doing any growing, or even living life. All I feel I am doing is working and trying to manage my unmanageable life. I can't even begin to fucking list what is going on in my life right now. I wouldn't know where to start if I could list the shit anyway. What is going on with me right now? Why are You putting me through all of this, God? Or am I doing all of this to myself?

I just can't seem to think clearly about much right now. For the past two weeks, my mind has been occupied with thoughts of one thing while I am doing something else. I can't stay focused on any one thing for any period of time. I am frazzled, confused, tired, wired, excited, bored, lazy, and energetic all at the same time. When will this insanity end?

You know, I can't believe I am feeling this way and this is happening to me right now. Funny thing about it all, I am not depressed or sad. I am actually very happy right now despite all of this turmoil. Does this make any sense? I don't know. I just don't seem to know much right now. All I do seem to know is, I have a million things to do before tomorrow and there are a million other things I need to do by the end of the week. I probably won't be able to complete many of them, and the things I do complete will be a far shot from my best work because—once again—I am trying to juggle too many things.

I can't even seem to concentrate on this entry right now. I have got to pray to God right now because I feel my life is a mess and I am only making it worse as the days pass. Maybe I'll be able to focus on my writing tomorrow. I hope so, because I have made shitty journal entries this entire month. Later!

OCTOBER 13, 1989

I am in a depression. That's what is going on right now. I am depressed and I don't understand why I am depressed. Why am I depressed and unhappy? Why now? Why now, after all of the things I have done to stay clean and sober? Why now, after I am finally succeeding in my work? Why now, when I am in the middle of my dissertation? I just don't know.

I want to sit here right now with this journal and try to iron all of this out. I want this journal to do for me what it has done for me so well in the past: help me to solve my problems and take away these horrible feelings. But the more I think about it, the more I am sure this journal will not be able to help me. I am losing faith in this journal, I am losing faith in God and the program, and I have almost lost faith in myself. What am I supposed to do?

It's like I am hovering above my life again and am watching it go by. I can feel I want to change things, but something just stops me from doing so. What is it? What is fucking me up so much? I go to work every day, I run every day, I work on the dissertation, I do consulting, I swim, I go to meetings, I do, I do, and I do. What is it that I am not doing? Working on me, I guess.

What in the fuck *is* "working on me"—Katy Hendricks—anyway? I thought doing these things was supposed to make me into the person everyone admires, was supposed to bring me happiness, was to keep me company, and was to take care of me. And Jesus, I am beginning to see that this is not the case at all. Nothing is bringing me happiness right now, and no one or no thing is taking care of me right now. I simply feel nothing. I feel empty once again.

Think about it, Katy. Your life gets fuller and fuller by the day, yet the emptiness inside you grows. Why? Still you are trying to fill those voids with external stuff. When will you understand that happiness is an inside job? You know that—you just forget it at times. Wake up, girl, and look at what is going on around you. You don't want to get up off the sofa right now because you are afraid of the work that you have to do. You sit and do nothing because you are scared of being so overcommitted. You are retreating once again, just like you did a year and a half ago on that last cocaine binge.

God, please don't make me go through that binge again. I don't want to. I couldn't bear it. I don't want to isolate on my couch in my apartment. I don't want to run from things and keep trying to escape. I want to settle down and find my place in life, but it just seems as though I get lost along the way. Why do I keep getting lost along the way?

Well, I simply can't do it. I am going to give up trying to pull myself out of this mood, mode, depression, et cetera. I need help. I need the program. Don't let me down. I'm just an addict in search of recovery, of sanity, of happiness. Why are these things so hard to find? Why do I get lost in the search?

God, grant me the serenity to accept the things I cannot change, the courage to change the things I can, and the wisdom to know the difference. I need the wisdom to know the difference. Later!

October 16, 1989

I am feeling much better today, but I am still a bit depressed and confused. I finally reached out for help Saturday night after a meeting. I went over to Kathy's new apartment with Michelle, and the three of us just sat and talked for about four hours. It was good to be there with them both.

After talking about fun things for most of the evening, I brought up the fact I was in a mild depression and was feeling rather lonely, confused, hopeless. The three of us ended up talking about my situation for an hour, and the two of them helped me to sort some things out. They basically told me I should quit my job and should concentrate on my dissertation. They told me this is not because they want me to place my dissertation first, but because they know that my job is making me miserable and that finishing the dissertation is a lifelong goal I want very badly.

And so I talked to two of my bosses today and asked for a two-month leave of absence without pay. The one boss totally supported my request, but the other one had reservations. William—the one with the reservations—wants me to work 16 hours a week instead of leaving totally. I do think William will [eventually] be supportive of my request. But the bottom line is, it's the director's decision and I don't think she'll be supportive at all.

I guess I am kind of scared right now. Actually, I have the attitude that I will quit if she decides to deny my request. I need and want to work on my dissertation. I have two comprehensive exams to take before the New Year and I have an incomplete to finish. I cannot afford to work 40 hours a week. Then again, I can't afford to not be employed at all. I do need to secure some income, and this is the reason I am confused right now.

Life certainly is hard at times, and being in recovery doesn't necessarily make it any more simple. Recovery is actually complicating my life right now by giving all of these incredible career opportunities, by putting me in the habit of living up to my responsibilities, and by giving me people who care about me enough to offer their help. What do I do now?

Thank God for recovery, because without it none of this would be happening to me. Just think what I have to complain about right now: too many jobs to choose from; completing my Ph.D. in one or two years; and borrowing money from this professor or from my family. I didn't have any of these choices to make while I was using. In fact, I had no choices to make at all. I was a slave to cocaine and could not function without it. I answered to cocaine only, and did whatever I could to satisfy my desire for it.

Well, my life is not like that today. Instead, I have choices to make, friends and family to love, job opportunities coming at me left and right, and a wonderful education that is helping me to achieve my lifelong goals. Thanks, God. Thanks for everything. Please help me to make the right choices and do the right things. Later!

OCTOBER 18, 1989

I have waited too long this evening to write in this journal. There are many things I want to write about tonight, but now I am just too tired to do so. The good news is, my office has decided to grant me the leave of absence I requested, the firm is allowing me to work when I want to work, I will have my loan money in two weeks, and it looks as though things will work out financially and academically for me these next two months. There is basically good news all around me—and boy, am I ever feeling much better.

Part of me actually thinks this change in schedule is what I really need. Another part of me is very hesitant about the disruption all of this might cause in my life. Basically I feel very confident about it all, despite any reservations that may crop up here and there. I have faith it will all work out for the best, and hope that—if I continue to pray and work my program—things will turn out just fine.

Life just keeps getting better for me. Recovery just keeps sending gifts my way; and I am not talking about tangible gifts, gifts of relationships with others, or gifts of career opportunity. The gifts I am talking about are the internal changes that are happening to me. I am changing internally—and these changes are not only making me a better person, they are helping me to gain self-love and find happiness. These are truly the most important gifts of the program, as far as I'm concerned.

You know, I pity the people who never get the chance to experience these changes. It feels like a rebirth, like a fresh start. It just feels good. The change comes slowly at times and often causes some pain, but I have a way that helps me to make it through these painful times: the program. And to think all I had to do was take the first step—admit I was powerless over drugs and my life had become unmanageable. Thank you, God, for helping me to take that first step. Thank you, God, for recovery! Thank you, God, for making me an addict! Later.

OCTOBER 24, 1989

The vanity trip I have been on for the past month escalated today to a very tumultuous point. I have called today's event "the smoking excursion." Here is what happened to me as a result of my ever-increasing obsession with my appearance.

On the way back from a meeting at the police department with Sarah today, I decided to get a pack of cigarettes and start smoking. I have been contemplating this idea for weeks now. I admitted to Sarah today that the only reason I wanted to start smoking was because I thought it was cool, it made women look attractive and sexy, and I wanted to look this way. In other words, my ego has been obsessing about improving my looks lately and thinks that smoking cigarettes will enhance them. (This is where I suffered my first point of illogical thinking.)

So I bought the pack of cigarettes and pulled one out and lit it up. Sarah, a previous smoker (one pack a day), was instructing me how to smoke properly. She helped me pick out a pack of cigarettes, told me how to hold the damn thing, showed me how to light it, and told me some of the dos and don'ts about smoking. Actually, Sarah really didn't want me to start this "disgusting habit" (as she called it), but said she wouldn't stand in my way if it was really something I wanted to do.

And so I smoked my first cigarette on the way back to the office and I got extremely light-headed. I coughed with each drag and choked on the smoke, but I finished that first cigarette. When I got back to the office, I felt high. I felt quite high, and this really scared me. In addition to my feeling high, my mouth was dry and I had serious cigarette breath. My hands stank and so did my breath. (Well, it must have, because my mouth tasted so nasty.)

I sat back down at my desk and was feeling totally out of it. As I was talking to people, I wondered if they could tell I had just smoked a few cigarettes and if they could tell I was high. And it is at this point that feelings of doing cocaine came back to me. I felt high, paranoid, agitated, yet anxious for work to end so I could try another cigarette. Am I an addict or what?

As soon as I bought those cigarettes, I could think of nothing else but smoking them. I kept thinking I couldn't wait until I got home so I could practice my new habit in the privacy of my own home. What a dope-fiend move! What a perfect illustration of my dope-fiend thinking and behavior. What perfect proof I am an addict!

Well—to make a long story short—I ended up smoking three cigarettes within an hour and got sick driving home in rush hour traffic. I actually thought I was going to pull over on the side of the road to throw up. I almost passed out in my car because of those cigarettes. Can you believe this cigarette excursion? Can you believe the vanity trip I am on—how it is so pervasive in my life today that it would force me to become physically sick over the pursuit of an image or appearance!? But most of all, can you actually believe, Katy, you felt just like a dope fiend all over again today when you were smoking those cigarettes!? Every single fucking feeling and thought you used to experience when you were using cocaine came back to you today while you were smoking. Those were the most painful moments in your life, yet you chose to recreate them today for the simple pursuit of vanity. What has come over you, girl? What is happening with you?

My program is weak. I haven't been attending meetings. I am slipping back into that dope-fiend behavior—and it is because I have cut my meetings way back, I haven't done any step work, and I don't communicate with my sponsor or my Higher Power on a regular basis. Part of me doesn't buy this as an explanation for my recent behavior and today's cigarette excursion, but then I know it really is the only explanation.

I really need to work some things out in my life right now. I have family problems, educational problems, financial problems, social problems—but most importantly, I have self-esteem problems once again. God, this road to recovery is rocky! Why couldn't I have just stayed an insecure, self-centered, Type-A jock in a doctoral program? Why did I have to go and become an addict and find out about the 12 Step road to recovery that gets rid of all of these things? I guess somewhere along the road, I decided I wanted a better life. What a fucking road to travel. I'm tired!

October 25, 1989

I just finished reading over this month's journal writings and am amazed at how often my moods changed. Rapid mood changing is one thing that has come with addiction and is one of the most troublesome things I face in recovery. I'd like to believe that my moods change so much because I am uncovering different parts of my personality and because I am dealing with things and issues in my life I chose not to deal with in the past. But I don't really know if this is the explanation or not. I just know that October 1989 has been a rough month.

But I feel okay right now. I am not sick today; in fact, I feel great. I couldn't help laughing about the cigarette excursion today. What a jerk I am to think I would like to start smoking and that it would make me look cool. Smoking has got to be the most disgusting habit around. In many ways, it is worse than a cocaine habit. At least with cocaine, your hands don't stink, you don't cough or choke on smoke, your clothes don't get saturated with the smell of cigarettes, and your car doesn't reek of smoke. No, with cocaine, you just get nosebleeds, headaches, cuts on your hands from razor blades, sweats, chills, heart palpitations, insomnia, and the ever-increasing possibility of a heart attack—not to mention self-destruction, an unmanageable life, depression, loss of job, loss of loved ones, et cetera.

I guess the point is clear, Katy. You should have seen this yesterday before you picked up that cigarette, but your vanity was blinding you. I guess I have accepted the fact that I will be just that much less attractive because I can't smoke. Actually, I don't really believe smoking will make me more attractive than I already am. I think it makes some people look sexy, but not me. Smoking does not fit into my lifestyle or image of myself. It just isn't me. I can't smoke and be a runner. I can't smoke and stay hygienically clean. I can't smoke without thinking I am a dope fiend. I just don't really want to start another disgusting habit—and for that matter, I will cease talking about cigarettes.

I want to go run right now. I started my leave of absence today and it feels very good. I need to develop a rigid schedule for my nonworking days (days at neither office) so I can be disciplined in my work. I'll do that later, but right now I am anxious to go running to see if the smoking has fucked up my breathing. Don't worry—I will not go get a pack of cigarettes if it has not harmed my running. The smoking excursion ended yesterday. Thank God! Later!

October 26, 1989

I said at the end of yesterday's entry that I was not going to buy another pack of cigarettes. Well, I lied. I bought another pack and have been smoking ever since. I just got off the phone with my sponsor after telling her about this smoking, and she straightened me out. She basically told me the smoking is indicative of a relapse. She told me that smoking is a horrible addiction and one can become both physically and psychologically addicted to cigarettes. And then she asked me why I started smoking, and that's when we both concluded I am headed down the road toward a relapse.

Why have I forgotten what it is like to be an active addict? Why did I have to go and forget the pain of active addiction? Why did I start to believe I would never relapse? Why did I start to believe I wasn't really a recovering addict or an addict at all? Because I am a mess right now—that's why. A couple of things are going on right now that I might explain.

Nancy has a new boyfriend, so I guess her marriage to my brother is really over. After all, she said in a letter that she was getting over my brother. My brother doesn't want her anyway. He has his own life and he likes it. In fact, he loves it. No more Christopher and Nancy. Guess I can't keep them together for me anymore. Guess I can't control what they do anymore. Guess I am finally accepting this situation.

My parents are depressed right now because of my father's job situation. He might be laid off for the first time in his life. But they have a daughter who voluntarily chooses to take a leave of absence from one job to start another one and to complete her dissertation. I have opportunities available to me they cannot comprehend. So they are unhappy, miserable, and pessimistic about their lives and about their children's lives.

My mother told me in a letter that all she ever tried to do her entire life was give us—her children—the best she could possibly give us, but apparently it wasn't enough. She says my father has done the same and he loves us very much, despite his inability to tell us so. The worst part of it all is, they blame themselves for the negative aspects of each of our lives and cannot even see—let alone take pride in—all of the good aspects that are a result of their guidance. They just can't see the good stuff in their own lives, in Kellie's, Beth's, or Christopher's lives, and in my life. They just can't see the good stuff in life anymore; and I keep hoping to restore their sight, but I just can't.

So this means I am powerless over my parents as well. I have tried to get them to see the good things in my life, in their lives, and in the lives of my brother and sisters, but they just can't seem to see any of it. Their pessimistic attitude blinds them and is causing their current depression. I want to change them and often think I can; but the data are in, and it looks as if they [i.e., my parents] are going to live the rest of their lives their way and not mine. And so I am dealing with acceptance again.

For some reason, I thought Kellie had stopped smoking pot. She talks about it like it is no problem, yet I hear from her friends and herself that she still smokes. She is full of self-doubt about her appearance, her talents, her intelligence—and, basically, herself.

Why does she do this? I have talked about it before in this journal. Why can't she do the right thing like me? Why can't she do things my way? Don't I know best? Bullshit, Katy. You are powerless again. You don't know what's best for Kellie; and even if your way was best, right, and good, you couldn't make her do anything she didn't want to do anyway. You can't change her outlook on life, her goals, her friends, her social habits, her substance abuse. You can't change anything at all. You are powerless over anything Kellie does, thinks, or says. So just accept it, you asshole. Just accept her the way she is.

All of this acceptance just hurts. I can't help but cry when I think about all of these things. God, why do things have to go so well for me but not for the other members of my family? Why do these things trouble me so much and hurt so much? Am I blinding myself to the good things about my family members, like my parents do? Or is it that I just don't want to deal with pain?

The cigarettes take my mind off the pain I feel. When I smoke, I can remember Nancy and Christopher as they once were, I can tolerate my parents' pessimism, and I can relate to Kellie's desire for a "deviant" lifestyle. The smoking just takes me somewhere else. It makes me into something I always wanted to be: a gorgeous brunette. So, in that sense, I guess smoking is doing for me now what cocaine used to do for me two years ago. I have suffered a mental relapse. I have suffered this relapse because I have forgotten the pain of addiction, the importance of acceptance, and the notion of being powerless over people, places, and things.

It's time to start remembering, Katy. Remember the pain, the powerlessness, and the acceptance before you ridicule Christopher's new lifestyle again, before you cry about Nancy again, before you complain about your parents again, and before you preach to Kellie about smoking dope. Most importantly, however, remember these things before the cigarettes turn into a drink or a line of cocaine—because that is some kind of pain you once said you never wanted to ever experience again. Turn it over to God now, and pray, and get your ass to a fucking meeting tomorrow! Later!

OCTOBER 29, 1989

I didn't write yesterday, and I should have. I didn't write Friday night, and I should have written then as well. I should have, I should have, I should have. How boring I must sound! If I had written yesterday or Friday night, I would have written about men again. Men. It's like they are a scarce commodity around here. Are there any single ones left who aren't gay, ugly, jerks, or losers? I am beginning to think there aren't any good ones left.

I was at a party last night with Jessica. The party was thrown by some program people—and so there were plenty of addicts and alcoholics there, but no alcohol. I didn't know if Jessica would enjoy herself at such a party because she is not an addict or alcoholic, but she seemed to enjoy herself anyway. All of my softball buddies were there last night, and the two of us stood around and talked to them for most of the evening. I haven't seen those guys in a long time, and so it was good talking to them. They are my buddies.

The guys absolutely loved Jessica. I mean, they loved the way she looked. It's utterly amazing how someone's appearance can totally color another's perspective. By the end of the night, two of my buddies were very interested in Jessica and wanted me to fix them up with her. They were convinced she was a very nice, sweet girl—not to mention a very good-looking, hot blonde. The deal is that Jessica *is* a nice girl, but she has a lot of hang-ups. She is a friend of mine, but we are not close. We aren't close because we have very little in common. She is often very snobby and has a very pretentious lifestyle. She knows she is gorgeous and plays on it as much as possible.

I know these things because I have known Jessica for a couple of years. My buddies don't know this, and given the extent of the conversation they had with her last night, they couldn't have known she is a pretentious snob. All they could see was her appearance: her blonde hair, petite figure, alluring eyes, and hot-looking outfit.

Why am I writing about this? I am not hitting the point. What I want to write about is how I was jealous of her because the guys were paying more attention to her than me. She turned more heads than I did and aroused more interest than I did. My ego was hurt a bit last night, and so I am writing about it today. Last night was a perfect illustration of why I have been obsessing about my appearance so much lately. To get the attention of a man, you must turn his head, look a certain way, talk a certain way, and dress a certain way. Simply put, you must be gorgeous.

I am not gorgeous. A few people might think I am good looking or attractive, but no one really thinks I'm gorgeous. And for some reason that is beyond my comprehension right now, I want to be gorgeous. I basically want to be something I am not. And that is a fucking familiar theme with me. The desire to be something or someone I am not has characterized my entire life, and I just can't seem to get rid of it. What do I have to do to be content with me? What do I have to do to be able to accept Katy as she is?

I don't know. Maybe I should call my sponsor and work this out with her. Maybe I should go to a few women's meetings and talk about this all. And maybe I should just pray to God. You know, the word "acceptance" just came back to me. What I am talking about here is accepting Katy the way she is. I really need to learn how to accept myself for who I am, but I get so caught up in things I don't even know who I am. Oh well, I am boring myself right now. I'll write again later.

NOVEMBER 2, 1989

It's 10 a.m. and I just got back from running about six miles. I realized when I was running that I have been clean for a year and a half now. It really feels wonderful. It has been 18 months since I have done any cocaine. WOW! There is a God.

I thought to myself the other night that God had put the program in my life to help me to change all of my destructive behaviors in addition to helping me quit cocaine. What I mean is, I believe God has allowed me to become an addict so I could discover the 12 Step programs, because these programs offer me a way to change my life. God wants me to change my life. I want me to change my life; and if I never had become an addict and found the 12 Step programs, I would have continued to lead a destructive, unhappy life for the rest of my years here on this planet.

How do I come to this conclusion? Drugs have not been a big part of my life. I used cocaine for a year and a half. While I was using cocaine, I drank more alcohol than I ever had, but I didn't have a drinking problem before the cocaine. Now I have a drug and a drinking problem that is a result of a year and a half of overindulgence in cocaine and booze. It was a short career and is not one that has rendered me totally dysfunctional.

What has rendered me dysfunctional and unhappy throughout my life are the personality characteristics and behaviors that fueled that addiction. I became an addict because of these destructive and dysfunctional behaviors of mine. I am an addict because I am constantly searching for happiness in external things, because I am never satisfied with anything I do, and because I try to fill my insecurities—which give me great pain—with drugs, alcohol, friends, clothes, degrees, et cetera.

These are the reasons for my addiction. These are the things that made me snort that first line. These are the things that fueled my addiction and forced me to hit bottom. And as far as I am concerned, these are the reasons that God has put the program in my life. He has shown me a way to change all of these things. He has given me an opportunity to free myself from these things, but the work in doing so is mine. God has shown me the road to recovery for more reasons than just remaining abstinent from drugs and alcohol, but it is me who has to walk the path. It is each addict who must walk the path to his or her own recovery.

Thank God we don't have to do it alone. Thank God for the 12 Step programs. Later!

NOVEMBER 3, 1989

A friend of mine is coming down from New York to visit me tonight, and I am anxiously awaiting her arrival. I haven't seen Meg in over a year. I have missed her on and off over this time. She is one of those friends I have kept in touch with despite any geographic distance between us. I continue to feel close to her because we are changing together. You know—maturing, and growing old, and stuff. What can I say besides I love her very much.

Meg and I used to do cocaine together when she lived here in D.C. In fact, she is the one who introduced me to cocaine. She was just as obsessed with it as I was; but when things got really bad for her, she moved to New York. Usually geographic cures don't work for addicts, but it has worked for Meg. She hasn't used cocaine since she left D.C. Meg can drink socially and can stay away from cocaine because she is not an addict or alcoholic. I can't drink socially or stay away from cocaine on my own because I *am* an addict and alcoholic.

Can you believe I called myself an alcoholic? I don't know why I said that, but I guess I meant it or something. I mean, why not? After all, I am powerless over alcohol because I cannot control my actions when I start drinking. I think about using cocaine when I am drinking—and so as far as I am concerned, I can't drink. Sounds like an alcoholic to me.

I really don't feel like continuing this discussion. Maybe it's just denial kicking up inside me. I am going to sign off so I can finish composing a reading list for my sociology comprehensive. I might get back here later.

NOVEMBER 6, 1989

What a weekend! I am just getting to the computer tonight—to write about the past few days. I really could write about a lot of things that happened and some feelings I had during the time, but I kinda don't feel like it. There is really only one negative thing that happened the entire weekend. For the most part, I had a wonderful weekend with Meg.

The one dark spot was the brunch I had here at the house on Sunday for Meg. I invited a few of my "old" friends over for brunch to reminisce about old times at the restaurant. Basically, I thought getting everyone together for Meg would be a nice treat for her. She enjoyed herself, but I didn't. I didn't enjoy myself because three of these people still have restaurant mentality and still consider drinking and partying as the right way of life. I really don't care if they think this is the right way of life or not. I just wish they would stop teasing me about my new way of life and would stop trying to analyze me and coax me back into my old way.

Why should they care that I don't drink, hang out in clubs, or do drugs? Why should they care that I attend meetings on a regular basis, and why should they care that I have a whole new set of friends? What I really can't figure out is why they feel this need to belittle me and criticize my new way of life. I keep my mouth shut about their lifestyles—so why do they openly criticize mine?

This subject is useless. It will never change. They will never understand my new way of life because they simply don't think I am a drug addict. And do you know what? I don't give a fuck whether they think I am a drug addict or not. I know I am a drug addict, and that's all that matters. That's about all I want to say about this subject.

My Higher Power was with me on Sunday, because this incident did not ruin my day. I am grateful for the third step of the program. I am grateful I can turn things over to God and let Him take care of them for me. Thanks for helping me out on Sunday, God. You allowed me to have a good weekend. I must go study now. Later!

NOVEMBER 12, 1989

It has been six days since I have written in this journal, and I have missed it. I spent the past four days playing mother to two beautiful children whose parents were away on business. I really enjoyed myself these past few days. The kids were wonderful, despite a few incidents. Parenthood is okay—or at least it was during these few days.

I have a feeling I am going to experience some feelings of loneliness this week. Since I have been on leave from work and have been studying for these exams, I really have cut off communication with a lot of people in my life. Basically, I am only taking time to talk to my friends and family on the telephone. I haven't been spending any time with many people at all. Basically, I feel as though I am sort of living in isolation. I don't have my office mates with me during the day, I haven't been going out with friends, and I haven't seen any family members for a month or so now. What I am trying to say is, I feel a bit lonely right now.

This weekend, I got to experience 24-hour-a-day company—the company of two beautiful children. I dropped them off at school, made them dinner, packed them lunch, and tucked them in at night. I made them take baths, clean their rooms, and go to bed when they protested. I laughed with them, yelled at them, kissed them, hugged them, and got very angry with them at times when they misbehaved. I guess I did what any other parent would do—but then again I don't really know that, because I am not a parent.

It was worth it. I didn't get a lot of work done, I didn't run as much as I wanted to, and I ate more than I should have. I didn't go to meetings, I missed a few parties, and I didn't sleep extremely well. But it doesn't matter, because it was worth it. I felt wanted and needed this weekend. Those two children gave me such joy. They hugged me back when I hugged them and even gave me hugs and kisses when I wasn't expecting or wanting any. I did for someone else this weekend, and it feels good.

Life alone is depressing at times, especially after you get a taste of what it can be like with others. I am not saying I am all alone in this world, but it sure does feel that way at times. I didn't feel alone this weekend. I actually felt loved by these two kids. What a neat feeling! I got accustomed to feeling this way in only a few short days. And now I will probably miss that feeling this week because I will be alone in my apartment studying for these damn exams.

I know I don't have to be alone if I don't want to be; but what I am really talking about is loneliness, not being alone. I have written about this before. I am alone quite often and seldom feel lonely. I like myself today. I like myself a great deal more today than I did two years ago. That is a fact! I am really talking about loneliness tonight. Nothing alleviates my loneliness besides the company of someone I love and care about a great deal. At times, I just want to share my day with someone I love, whether that person is a friend or a family member. Shouldn't I be able to do this?

Of course, I should be able to spend a day with a person I love. And maybe that's just what I need to do to ward off this depression I feel coming over me. I have taken the steps. I have invited two friends over tomorrow for dinner and to go to a meeting with me. I love these two ladies a great deal. I feel comfortable with them. I can be myself around them. They feel comfortable around me and tell me they love me and care about me.

I am tired and feel like ending this entry right now. I feel like my writing has failed me tonight, because I haven't been able to capture my feelings with words. Maybe it's just that I don't know exactly what I am feeling right now. Maybe I am feeling nothing more than fatigue.

One more thing before I sign off tonight. I watched a cocaine movie this weekend and really shouldn't have done so. It was the addict in me that kept me in front of that fucking screen when I should have walked away. I watched these two people become coke addicts and lose it all. I watched them climb onto that cocaine ladder that promises a never-ending trip up to heaven, but only delivers an escalator to hell. And in the end, the one guy was sitting alone in a room with nothing but the cocaine on the mirror in front of him. He was talking about getting it together, making it all right, and being victimized as he sat there cutting his coke—playing with the fucking lines on that mirror.

He was going nowhere, but he didn't know it. He didn't know it because he didn't know he was an addict. I knew he wasn't going anywhere and that he was an addict, because I have been there. I am an addict—a recovering addict—and I have been all alone in rooms with nothing but my pipe dreams, lame excuses, and a diminishing supply of cocaine. And do you know what? I remembered that part of my life vividly as I watched this fucking movie.

It all came back to me like it was yesterday. What pain. How disgusting! But it was just God working in my life to remind me I am an addict. I said a prayer before I went to bed and asked God to help me make it through the night without any nightmares. I thanked Him for another day of sobriety and asked Him to help me make it through tomorrow without picking up. And do you know what? God got me through the night without having any nightmares, and He gave me two more days of sobriety. My life is going somewhere today because I ask for help, because I work my program, and because I know I am an addict. People, places, my Higher Power, my program, and myself remind me on a daily basis that I am an addict. I can never forget this. I must keep the pain alive despite the discomfort it gives me. Keeping the memories alive keeps me clean today; but knowing and accepting that I am an addict helps me to change so that dreams can come true, so I can meet my responsibilities, and so I can live life happily.

Maybe someone should tell this guy he's an addict. Think he would believe any of them? I doubt it. I never believed anyone who told me. It was only after I had hit bottom and had enough that I was ready to surrender, to admit I was an addict. Maybe this guy just isn't ready to do this. Maybe a lot of people are just not ready to do this. Everyone has his or her own bottom, but the thing you have to understand is that your bottom is wherever you stop digging. I wish more people would realize this. Turn it over, Katy. Later!

NOVEMBER 16, 1989

Last night I went to my usual Wednesday-night meeting at 7 p.m. and ran into an old friend from home. I hadn't seen this woman for years, since high school. And there she was sitting in an NA meeting with me. Actually, I had seen her at a meeting before when I had about nine months of clean time. She was leading a meeting and was sharing about her three years of sobriety. I was totally amazed by the way she spoke at this meeting. It was hard for me to believe she had three years of sobriety. She sounded so peaceful. She sounded as if she had found a new way of life that was more wonderful than anything she could have imagined. At that moment, I knew I wanted whatever she had.

Well, after not seeing her for another six months or so, I ran into her last night and we actually talked. We stood outside the meeting for three hours and talked about the past and the present. Mostly, we talked about recovery. It was fascinating talking to her about recovery because the last time I spoke to her we were smoking hashish under a glass.

I always thought she would become an addict, but of course I never thought I would become one. I admired her so much in high school because she was so fucking intelligent. She scored perfectly on the SAT exam and had spotless grades in high school. She was in all of the honors programs. After we spoke last night about "our intelligence," she told me she only missed one question on the GRE exam and scored perfectly on the IBM entrance exam. This is what I have always considered intelligence to be: perfect scores without effort.

This woman is the kind that has "natural" intelligence—the kind I have always longed for. But when I was speaking to her last night, she told me she is just as insecure about her abilities as I am. She told me that she was jealous of me in high school because of my athletic abilities and she greatly admires me for pursuing my Ph.D. She basically told me *I* was the smart one, and we proceeded to discuss our ideas of what intelligence, success, and happiness were all about.

We just talked the same language last night. She has her good and bad points just like I do, and it's funny how two different types of intelligence could end up with so much in common: insecurities about their abilities. Part of me thought, "How can she be insecure about her intelligence and abilities?" I always thought people with natural intelligence had it made. That they were the ones who were most respected and were the ones who were most successful. But none of that seemed to matter last night, because she told me she always respected people like me who worked hard for whatever they achieved. She told me she has never had to work for anything and has just gone through life depending on her natural abilities and hasn't tried to improve herself through hard work. She therefore doesn't respect herself because she feels as though she is a lazy slob with poor study habits, a lack of motivation and discipline, and no direction in life.

I am thinking to myself as she is telling me this, "Well, that's not too bad. All you have to do is find the discipline and motivation to want to excel, and you will be unstoppable." After all, the woman is a registered genius according to the IQ test. But as much as I wanted to put her on this pedestal and place myself beneath her, she simply wouldn't let me do it. And it's not that she convinced me I was more successful or intelligent than she was, and it wasn't that I convinced her that she was the better person.

What we found out last night is that not only did we have addiction in common, but we had a lot of other things in common as well. I guess I learned a big lesson I probably should have learned years ago. Last night I learned I am the only one who defines myself and sets expectations for myself. People may think a certain way about me and they may expect me to do things, but none of that determines what I think of myself. We both have received thousands of compliments and criticisms about our intelligence and abilities throughout our lives, but nothing anyone said to us or did for us changed our definitions or expectations of ourselves. We both thought whatever we did was simply not good enough.

This life of mine has some interesting lessons in it, and it is only since I entered recovery that I am beginning to learn them. I realized, after last night's conversation with this woman, I am not such a bad person after all. I realized I am too hard on myself most of the time and have a lot of good qualities that shine through. Most importantly, however, I learned that any ideas, goals, and achievements I have had throughout my life have just been mine. I own them alone. I set the standards by which I am judged. No one else does that for me. And so now I can see the clear picture. I can go through life belittling myself through comparison to others, or I can start believing I am actually a decent person with some very good qualities. I can start believing in myself. Later!

NOVEMBER 19, 1989

This head cold is the pits! I feel as though I have walked into a brick wall. I barely have the energy to do any work because of this damn cold. But really, I am just not motivated to do any studying for my comprehensive exams at all right now and I am blaming it on the cold. I guess my mind is telling me I have been defeated by this professor, and I am allowing the situation regarding my oral comprehensive to render me totally useless this entire weekend.

I have isolated here in my apartment this weekend. Yes, I do feel under the weather. I went to bed last night at 9:30 and slept until 9 this morning. That's almost 12 hours of sleep. This is uncharacteristic of me, but part of me really enjoyed it. I felt like shit running today because of this cold, yet I beat myself up mentally because I only ran seven miles instead of ten. What's with me? I shouldn't have been running in the first place. I am sick. I have a sore throat, a runny nose, and a nasty cough. And I go running in the 40-degree weather. Sick for sure, Katy!

I am reading this book right now called *Passages* [by Gail Sheehy]. I am reading it for the dissertation, hoping I can learn how another author has discussed the notion of transitions in life. Yet while I am reading this book, I can't help identifying with certain crises she says are common to people in their twenties. She talks about being locked in, that people in their twenties often feel what they are currently doing is right and good and could never imagine doing anything else, or couldn't do it anyway if they wanted to.

I have often felt this way. I mean, I have often known that I have locked myself into a career, a lifestyle, a personality, et cetera. And I must admit it scares me to death to think I could suddenly change any of it. The author is accurate in describing me during these years of my life. I feel locked into my current career. I simply can't imagine doing anything else with my life besides becoming a professor. I have accepted the fact that I will always have my face buried in books to learn instead of to enjoy what's written. If I happen to enjoy a book, that's a fucking bonus. I read to keep up with the literature, I read out of curiosity, I read to do my work. I do not read to relax, but often the reading I do brings me enjoyment.

I will never have the life of a nine-to-fiver—a person who works during those hours and leaves the job at the office and comes home to vegetate, knit, or play golf. My mind works 24 hours a day. I need and want a job that constantly challenges me and demands my success, while offering me rewards. The rewards I want aren't extravagant. I want respect of colleagues and students, I want to publish, and I want to make a contribution. I'm not in this for money, but I can't deny that I get glory from doing this. Isn't that normal?

It's just I feel so locked into it all at times. Like right now. A colleague of mine told me the other day getting a Ph.D. took perseverance, and I am beginning to see what she meant by that. I feel as though I am in a no-win situation right now that will not work out to my advantage. I feel as though this professor has defeated me. I am in pain, but it never occurs to me to get out of it all. Despite any pain, crises, setbacks, or disappointments I have experienced in pursuing my education, it has never occurred to me to abandon ship. I have never seriously considered abandoning my studies and pursuing another totally unrelated career. I have never strayed from my lifelong goal of becoming a professor in the social sciences, despite the problems it has given me.

Why? Why have I held onto this desire, this career dream, this constant pursuit for a higher education? Looking back on it all now, I see I could have abandoned ship many times. I could have decided to never go to college after receiving my SAT scores. They were so low I was sure no school would accept me. Then I could have abandoned ship when transferring to main campus, because I was really unsure of my capabilities at the time. I hung in there, though, and graduated magna cum laude. I can't even remember doubting my skills during those years.

I could have abandoned ship upon entering my master's program down here if I would have allowed others' doubts about my abilities to become my own. No one down here at this school thought I would do well, because of my GRE scores. The only hope they saw for me was, I had graduated with high honors from a respectable school. And then my new colleagues tried their hand at intimidating me with *their* high GRE scores and private school educations. I simply pushed ahead, dead set on proving I was better and could be the best. And the best is what I became. I graduated at the top of my master's program and won an award for doing so.

And then I became an addict and nearly blew it all. I could have abandoned ship at *this* point; but once again I felt so locked into the life course I had chosen for myself, I simply pushed ahead despite this major setback in my life. You see, when I hit bottom with cocaine in April of 1988, I was at my lowest. I hated myself. I thought I was a worthless piece of shit who was trying to compete in a world that was way out of my league. As far as I was concerned, cocaine had defeated me and I thought everything else was going to defeat me as well.

Not until I got off that pity pot (only with a lot of help from others) and realized all I had was an addiction to a drug and not a death sentence to waste away on earth did I begin to regain my self-esteem. And so here I am 18 months into sobriety and actively involved in the hardest part of my doctoral education. Never have I considered abandoning all of this for a career that is less demanding, for a life that is more simple, or for a job that doesn't occupy my weekends. Why haven't I done so? Because I feel locked into it all. I feel as though I would not know what to do if I gave it all up. I feel as though I would be a failure if I didn't become a professor and get tenure at a nice university.

That's what I have wanted to do for most of my life. The pursuit of this career, of this dream, has brought me pain and turmoil at times, but there must be something about it all that keeps me actively pursuing it. I want to be a professor more today than I wanted to be one yesterday. The desire to do research increases on a daily basis. I want to contribute; I want to make a difference. This is my dream and I don't want to lose sight of it. This is why I am locked into this career. This is why I am locked into this lifestyle.

Maybe someone will read this one day and say I need help. Maybe someone one day will show me that this type of thinking is destructive. Maybe someone will tell me I will never find happiness if I stay so locked into pursuing this dream. But right now I am not thinking about any of that. I don't care if anyone finds a flaw in my thinking, in my life decisions, in my well-being. And I wouldn't give a damn if the author of this book [*Passages*] came by and said that, unless I loosen up, I will be doomed to a life of unhappiness and depression. Who is she, anyway?

I can't take breaks right now. I can't abandon ship any time soon. And what is really the point here anyway is, I don't want to abandon ship and have never really wanted to do so. My ship is academia and on it I plan to ride. It brings me great joy knowing I will be able to interact with students and mold their minds, I may get the opportunity to work with some of the most respected and interesting people in this world, and I might—if I am lucky—make an original contribution to a social issue that might affect one person's life and then one day a few people may come to know and respect my work. I can do none of this unitl I finish my Ph.D., and so I can take no breaks until I have completed the degree.

I don't know what life will be like after I have finished my Ph.D. I don't know if I'll burn out like this author says many people do who stay locked in during their twenties. I do not know what is going to happen to me in the future. The future is in God's hands, not mine. A few years ago I never would have imagined that cocaine could be so wonderful, and then I tried it. A year and a half later, it had me on my knees begging for help. It has been more than a year and a half since I used any cocaine, and that is a miracle. What seems to me to be even more of a miracle is, I have grown to like myself during these months of sobriety. I have learned many valuable lessons that have shed light on my life and have allowed me to change for the better.

I am convinced I will stay locked into this career I have chosen, but I do not plan to stay locked into the personality that has dominated my life. I want to change, to get rid of my destructive behaviors. I want to experience happiness like I have never known before. I can do these things with the help of my program, my Higher Power, and other people. And so, as far as I can determine, I am certainly locked into a career, but I am not locked into a way of life anymore. The program is liberating me. It is saving me from the bondage of self. It is the key to unlocking the door to my happiness. And to think all I must do is step through that door, walk into those rooms, and open my heart to others who are like me. Wow!

NOVEMBER 26, 1989

I was home for Thanksgiving and was unable to write in this journal for a few days. As usual, a lot has happened in these past few days that gives me a lot of material to write about. I kinda don't know where to start today considering I just woke up and my thoughts are a bit foggy. Wait a minute—I think the coffee is done. I'll be right back.

Okay. Thanksgiving was wonderful at home with the family. I didn't expect it to be so wonderful, because it was the first Thanksgiving in six years without Nancy. I did miss her, but not as much as I anticipated. We all had a wonderful time together reminiscing about old times and doing some crazy things together. At one point in the day, Christopher, Kellie, and I slid belly first down the steps like we used to do when we were children. The three of us proceeded to show our nephews how to do this slide, and they just loved it.

Thanksgiving Day was wonderful, but I was a bit perturbed because it ended with a cocaine dream. I had a relapse dream Thursday night. I can remember what happened in the dream, but not all of its details. I wish I would have written about it right away when I woke up Friday morning. Basically, I copped an ounce of cocaine and was doing major lines with others and by myself. About half of it was gone when I accidentally dropped the other half in the toilet and ruined it. I was quite upset in the dream.

What really bothers me about this dream is, I didn't have any guilty feelings while I was using cocaine. In past dreams I have often relapsed; but when I have done cocaine in past dreams, I usually experienced incredible feelings of guilt that usually acted to stop the dream or give it special meaning. There was no guilt in Thursday night's dream, so I don't know how to interpret it.

To be perfectly honest, guilt has always been the biggest impediment for me to get high. Of all the cravings I have had during these 19 months of recovery, I never went back out [relapsed, got high], because of the guilty feelings I knew I would experience from doing so. The reasons I would feel so guilty about getting high again are many. I would let all of these people down who are important in my life, I would fuck up my schoolwork and probably the job, I would worsen my financial situation, and I would definitely destroy my parents. All of these things act as sources of guilt; they act as impediments to relapse. These are the things I think about when cocaine becomes attractive to me. These are essentially the things that keep me from relapsing today.

But the dream is now telling me these things aren't good enough to keep me from relapsing anymore, because there was no guilt about any of these things in Thursday night's dream. What does this mean for me? Does this mean I have to not want to relapse just because of me, just because it is the wrong thing for Katy Hendricks to do?

A long time ago when I was in group therapy, one of the group members told me that staying clean for others was okay, but one day it wouldn't be enough to keep me clean. She told me I needed to learn to want to stay clean for myself—not for my parents, colleagues, friends, the job, or the education. And this is what the dream is telling me. It is telling me the possibility of disappointing my parents and friends, or losing the job or my Ph.D., is not a good enough reason to stay clean anymore. It is telling me this because I felt no guilt for getting high in Thursday night's dream. The dream is telling me it's time to really work on myself. It is time to stay clean for Katy.

This is scary. I mean, man, if I am left with myself to stay clean, I think I'll relapse. Wait a minute—that didn't come out as I wanted it to. I mean that staying clean for me doesn't seem like enough. I think I need to feel I am staying clean for others in addition to staying clean for myself. I can have this, right? Am I making any sense, God?

I do not want to get high today and, for the most part, I feel good enough about myself so I don't have to get high today. I have a life today that doesn't include getting high. It is a life I want. Using is simply not an alternative. Yet I get these cravings at times. Some show up in my dreams like Thursday night. When the cravings come, I say to myself, "You can't use today, Katy, because you have no money, you would disappoint your parents, Geraldine, Ben, and Jim and all of your friends, you would lose time in the pursuit of your Ph.D., you would fuck up at work, and you certainly don't have the money anyway." And I find these are the first things that come to mind when I relapse in the dreams. These things make me feel guilty about using and, therefore, keep me from using.

But according to Thursday night's dream, these things aren't making me guilty anymore; and so I guess they are not good enough reasons to stay clean anymore. I have got to start wanting to stay clean just because it is the right thing to do for Katy. I don't want to lose everything the program has given me in these past few months. I like myself today, and that is reason enough not to pick up and get high. I don't want to use today because I want to be around to live life tomorrow, happily and peacefully. And right now as I sit here in front of this computer, I don't feel as though I need to get high for anything today. There are no reasons to get high today. This is what God has given me and the program has shown me. This has to be good enough for me today—and along with this reason, the other ones will fall in line, I suppose. Later!

I want to talk about men later on today. I want to talk about living alone later today. I want to talk about being lonely. And I might want to talk about confusing thoughts, later today, if I find the courage to do so. I must go running now.

NOVEMBER 28, 1989

I took a day off from the journal—and what a day I missed! I should have written about it here. I guess I could recap the day's events and some of the feelings that went along with them, because today was rather boring.

Monday was great. I went to work at the office and actually had a nice time. The office could really do without a full-time research analyst—until they get these wild ideas of conducting complicated rigorous studies that usually require *several* well-experienced analysts. I guess they figure one full-time analyst is the solution to both of these situations. They have told me on numerous occasions that work around the office is feast or famine. Right now, they are experiencing a famine in terms of research, as far as I'm concerned.

But I don't want to talk about work. What I do want to talk about is my evening with Rick, the professor from Texas. We had a nice dinner together at a favorite restaurant of mine in Georgetown, and then we went shopping. I spent an hour with Rick in a clothing store, picking out things for him to wear to class. It was a lot of fun. I have always loved shopping for men. I love dressing them and acting like their spouse. I like that we appear to others as a "couple." What can I say besides it felt wonderful spending time shopping with Rick on Monday night.

He is warm and compassionate. I look at him and I see a male version of what I want to be. He is young, intelligent, and dedicated to his profession. He is a well-respected academician already, and this is his first year at a university. He is definitely going places, and part of me would like to go right along with him.

Make no mistake about it, I respect everything about him and could envision myself as his wife, but not at the expense of my career. Rick is not the type of guy who would make me choose, anyway. He is independent and secure. He is everything I wrote about in Sunday night's journal entry. He respects my independence and is not intimidated by my intelligence or achievements. Sounds like a catch, huh?

Only one drawback to consider. Well, maybe two. The first is, he lives in Texas; and the second is, I am not that physically attracted to him. It's not that I don't enjoy being with him and I don't feel good when we are together; it's just that there is no overwhelming attraction pulling me to him.

I do feel this animal-like attraction to Colin. I feel much more physically attracted to Colin than I do to Rick, yet that is the only thing Colin has over Rick. It's like this feeling—of physical attraction—is only one element on a scale of many dimensions. Rick beats Colin on the other 25 dimensions, and Colin beats Rick on only one: physical attraction. Why does physical attraction mean so much? Why does the feeling inside my belly tell me I like being with Colin more than I like being with Rick? And why is Colin pulling at my heart and Rick not?

Is it Colin I like? Do I like him because he is unavailable to me, and do I like Rick less because he is more available to me? Am I in my head right now or what? The problem is, I am trying to decide which guy I like better. My head tells me Rick, and my heart tells me Colin. Why does the heart have such a stronger pull? It has no logic, no rationality. The heart, it seems to me, is guided by the belly—or the motto "If it feels good, do it." That's not always logical to do, now is it? It can often be very painful. And so I am sitting here trying to figure out which would be better for me in the long run: follow your brain and go with Rick and hope the love comes in time, or follow your heart and go with Colin and pray he doesn't break your heart.

I don't know why I am writing about any of this, anyway. It's not like I have to choose today, you know. I'm not even in a relationship with either one right now. This is all so typically Katy. Project, project, project. The quest for control. The search for the right answer. The belief that I can figure it all out on my own. The desire to control others for my benefit. Man, do I need a meeting!

Thursday night after class, I am going to a co-dependency meeting with a friend of mine whose name is Nathan. Nathan could be a third figure in this love saga of mine. Just what I need, huh!? A third one to make things more complicated.

You know, I realize that two days ago I wrote about the lack of men in my life. I hope I made it clear that what I lack is a loving relationship with a member of the opposite sex and not just the company of a man. All of what I wrote then still holds true today. Right now, if my pattern with men persists, nothing will become of my acquaintances with these three men. Each will lose interest, and I will feel lonely once again and will continue to search for Mr. Right. Maybe I should just relax. Maybe I should get back to studying. After all, nothing is going to happen to me tonight anyway. Later!

DECEMBER 2, 1989

I feel awful right now. I am so tired of pretending I feel wonderful and I am fine, because I am not. Things in my life are going well, but I just feel bad right now and I think I know why. Before I get into the reasons behind these feelings, I just want to talk a bit about my coping mechanisms.

I always tell people I am fine when they ask me how I'm doing. Rarely do I tell them I feel shitty, lonely, depressed, or whatever. The only time I share my true feelings with someone is when I am on the verge of some sort of breakdown or crisis. A case in point was a month ago when I was contemplating a job change and was so depressed I was sitting on the couch shaking.

Yet I sit here right now on the verge of crying. Earlier today, I felt fine. What happened? All of this shit just kicked in when I came home from this party tonight. I went to a sober party after an AA meeting. I didn't know many people there. In fact, I only knew the two I went to the party with. At the party, these two women I went to the party with began talking to other people they knew but I didn't, and soon I found myself sitting alone hoping they would come talk to me. I felt out of place, uncomfortable, and miserable; yet when we left, I joined the other two women in saying I had a nice time and was glad I went to the party. I lied.

I feel like shit right now because I don't feel close to anyone down here anymore. I just don't have any close friends anymore. I don't have a best buddy, and I don't hang out with the people I was closest with for a long time. I just don't feel comfortable being myself around my new friends, my new office mates, and these few men I am dating. I don't even feel really comfortable around my brother, or not so comfortable as I would like. What in the fuck is happening to me?

I feel as though I have lost something. I feel empty. I have felt like this on and off for months now, but I have been blind to it all. Tonight at the meeting and that party, I realized I just don't have anyone in my life whom I can fully trust, be honest with, care about, and be myself with. Jesus, I am ending sentences with prepositions left and right here. Who gives a fuck right now, anyway? Not me!

I miss Rebecca. She was my buddy, my sister, my friend. She loved me, cared for me, made me feel comfortable, made me laugh and cry, and gave me many headaches. I don't really know if it is her I miss so much or having a friend like her in my life who is as close to me as she once was. I know how destructive that friendship was, and a while ago I learned it was better—for the most part—to not become so dependent on one person. But I just want to know if I can have a friend like her in my life today without becoming so dependent.

Maybe this is not even the issue. Lately, I just feel like I am pretending to be okay all the time when I actually am not. Maybe I pretend to be okay because it's what I think others want to hear about me. I just don't know. Maybe this all has to do with these fucking exams I am studying for. God, am I full of uncertainty right now. God, am I lonely right now.

And I almost feel as if the feelings of loneliness would stay with me even if I surrounded myself with my new set of friends. They just aren't close enough to me to take away my loneliness, but it's not their fault. It's just so hard for me to fully open up to another person. I am extremely insecure, I guess.

My insecurities never cease to amaze me. I thought insecurities passed as you grew older!? I thought we were supposed to gain confidence and wisdom with age!? Well, where the fuck is mine? Where is it going? Downhill like a bat outta hell, I guess.

The stuff that is going on in my life is fine, great, and almost wonderful. I am clean and sober for nearly 18 months now. I have a new job that is a step in the right direction for my academic career. I am progressing on my Ph.D. with some minor pain. I am even talking about my future with logic and confidence. I have plenty of friends who tell me they care about me. I have been out on dates with men. And I spend time with people I care about. So what's wrong with me? Why am I lonely, and why do I feel empty? And why am I so fucking reluctant to let people get close to me? How did these walls form around me? And when am I going to tear them down?

I just had a thought. Maybe I don't feel I can be myself around these new friends or anyone here because I myself don't really know who I am. Who is Katy Hendricks? In the past, it was always so easy to answer this question. I could get away with answers like, "Katy is a natural athlete, a hard worker, a magna cum laude graduate of this big university, the top master's candidate at this other university, a fuck-up of a doctoral candidate." Later the answers grew more arrogant. I would reply to questions about my identity with words like, "Katy is a hotshot computer specialist who is pursuing her Ph.D. and is destined for greatness. I am good-looking, I dress well, and I have wonderful taste. I am the master of my own destiny, and my destiny is to become a university professor who stays cool by continuing to party with cocaine." What an image I had—and this is the least of it. I believed I was this shit! I had arrived.

Well, all of that Katy was just image; it really wasn't me. I am not the best thing that has hit academia or the social sciences since Emile Durkheim. I am just another aspiring academician who has to prove herself through hard work and publications, just like everyone else. I am not Princess Stephanie—a 9.5 on a scale of ten. I am a slightly better than average looking brunette with a big body that will always be big despite a few fluctuations. I am not the queen of the social scene anymore and never was. I have little trouble getting dates, but have a great deal of trouble keeping them around. I am a loser at the "party" game, because I got addicted to cocaine and alcohol in a short bit of time. Basically, I am nothing I have professed to be throughout my life. I am not wonder woman. I am just Katy Hendricks.

Yet at times like tonight, I am not sure who Katy Hendricks is or how she feels, and so I play the old familiar game that I am someone else or feel just fine when I am actually in a great deal of pain. Why can't I just relax and be myself? I guess I just don't know exactly who I am. I am still trying to toy with the image of who I think I want to and should be, and in the meantime I am losing a grip on who I really am. Is it any wonder why I would feel uncomfortable around people tonight?

Once again, God, I ask for Your help in this matter. I am lonely and depressed right now, and I think it is because I am having a hard time being myself. Please help me find myself. Help me see who I really am, because I feel as if I will have no serenity or happiness until then. I am confused right now—confused about what's going on inside me. Do You think I should start seeing a psychologist? I might give it a try. I desperately need some help. I am tired of pretending I am okay when in fact I am not. Please help. Thanks!

P.S. I blew off a party tonight I was supposed to attend, and the hostess just called me. I screened the call and heard her voice on my machine. She sounded disappointed. I feel like shit. I guess I must call her tomorrow. I just hope I can tell her the truth about why I didn't go, instead of making up some lame excuse and taking the easy way out. Help me with this one too, God. Thanks!

DECEMBER 5,1989

I went to see a psychologist today. Actually, I just got back from her office. I have been toying with the idea of going to see a psychologist lately, and finally I just decided to go. Actually, the psychologist asked me why I chose to come now and not before, and I told her I am tired of feeling very lonely, unhappy, and depressed. I told her I just want to be happy and to be content with myself. I told her the pain of isolation and loneliness is more than I can bear right now. These are the reasons for my going to see a psychologist.

My dinner is ready now, so I am going to sign off. I hope to get back here in a few hours to do some more writing. I might not be able [to, though,] because I have to study and do laundry. Later!

DECEMBER 7, 1989

I want to talk about a lot of things tonight. I feel like doing a lot of writing. I could talk about so many things. I can't decide where to start. Here goes nothing.

I am lonely as shit and have been for months now. It has taken me countless attempts at trying to assess what is actually wrong with me to discover I am simply lonely. But I didn't come to this discovery on my own. In fact, this discovery has only come after talking to many people, being lectured to about my feelings, actions, and behaviors by many people, and finally consulting a psychologist on the matter. I have not made the discovery at all. It has been revealed to me.

And so I have started therapy this week with a female psychologist. I am happy about my decision to start therapy. I actually made this decision on my own, without the help of others. I feel better when I talk to her and have good days after I leave her office. I think our normal meeting time will be Tuesday evenings at 5:10 p.m. I am already anxiously awaiting our next session.

There are so many issues in my life that trouble me, that bring me pain and turmoil. Other people have these problems and issues, but it seems as though they have different personalities and values that just seem to get them through all of it. I have some major personality defects that keep me from growing; and to tell you the truth, I can't change them by myself. I used to think and have been told on numerous occasions by people in the program that working the 12 Steps will help me get rid of my character defects, that consummating a relationship with God will help me rid myself of destructive behavior and help me find serenity and happiness, and that working with a sponsor will help me make sense of it all.

But irrespective of what these people say and how much truth I know lies behind their words of advice, it just doesn't seem to be working for me. I need extra help. I cannot make it on faith alone in the program, God, and the people in my life. I am at an emotional bottom right now and feel the need for some profound direction. I feel I need someone to help me figure myself out, to help me put things back together when I feel I am falling apart, and to just listen when I am lonely, sad, depressed, angered, or resentful. What can I say? I need a therapist right now.

I have done some growing this past year. People tell me they see the change, and I can feel change. And for the most part, it is all change for the better. I am drug free right now and have been for 18 months now. I know what I have to do to stay clean, and I am doing it on a daily basis. I also know I can't take any of this for granted and that my disease needs constant, daily attention. Believe you me, I *know* I am an addict, but must admit I *forget* sometimes.

I also know I cannot control the lives of others; but the truth is, I don't really even want to do so anymore, anyway. I have given up the control over others' lives, and it feels good in the sense that I am not stressed anymore. I don't waste time and energy pursuing losing battles anymore. But somewhere along the line in doing this, I lost an attachment to others, a concern for them that kept me connected—and now all I find existing in my life is me. And this is scary.

I think it's all supposed to work like this: You learn in the program you are powerless over drugs, alcohol, people, places, and things; and you come to accept this. What makes the acceptance realistic, though, is that along the line you become attached to others in a good way and not a destructive way and you learn to be at peace with yourself by loving yourself. This is what makes the powerless things easier to accept and keeps people attached to others and, therefore, prevents them from feeling like I am feeling right now: detached from life!

I am just not making the connection, and I am getting tired of it. My daily schedule often prohibits me from spending time with others, so it is no mystery to me that I feel detached from people right now. When I say I am busy, I am *busy*. I do not like that I can't take a few hours each day to goof off with friends, can't relax and do no work on weekends once in a while, and can't be available for friends all of the time. I would often love to do all of those things, but what I want out of life most right now is to finish my Ph.D. so I can fulfill my dreams of becoming a professor.

Throughout the course of my addiction and recovery, I have come to understand that staying clean is my top priority, my primary purpose. Right behind recovery is my career, my ambitions, my dreams, my life. Never before did I have to choose between things like I have to choose today. I do not have a lot of time for social things in my life right now because I work to support myself, I go to meetings regularly, I teach, and I am a full-time doctoral candidate preparing for comprehensive exams and working on a dissertation. There is little time to go out to eat or to the movies, to go shopping, or even to enjoy the holiday season; and so I do not have close friends today, I do not have much of a social life, and I can't get into a relationship with a man.

The end result of all of this is, I am alone and lonely much of the time. When I am around people, I feel detached from them because I have not allowed myself the proper time to develop close relationships with any of them. And so this is my situation. I feel as though I am on a seesaw right now trying to balance all of it, but failing at doing so. This is why I need therapy right now.

I don't feel like discussing this anymore tonight. I will write tomorrow. I go to the dentist tomorrow to have two cavities filled. What a joy! Later!

DECEMBER 10, 1989

Today is my mother's birthday. I plan to call her from my brother's house this afternoon so we can wish her a nice day. Christopher and Tim are having a party this afternoon, and most of their guests will be gay men. I don't know if I am looking forward to going to this party or not, but will go anyway. I also must go over to a friend's house to decorate a Christmas tree. I should have a good time over there. I have the day planned down to the hour as usual, but all I can really think about is how insecure I feel about the study time I am going to have today for Thursday's exam. I just wish I could relax right now.

I was out on a date last night with a guy I recently met in the program. He is a lot like Colin—22 years old and new to the program. I know, I know, I know. His head is too mixed up for me right now, and I probably shouldn't be seeing him or talking to him on the phone. I just went to a movie with him. That's all. It's not like I slept with him or anything.

Like I said before, I don't seem to have a problem getting dates with any man. I just have a problem finding the right ones and then keeping them around. I really don't want to get into this right now because it is not really on my mind. I guess I just wanted to mention it today and reassure myself I can live with or without this or any other guy. Right, Katy—that's why you are so depressed right now. You are so full of shit.

Actually, what is on my mind right now is this test. I take a written comprehensive on Thursday and don't feel prepared for it yet. To be perfectly honest, I never feel prepared for an exam, despite any amount of studying I do. This time around, my studying has suffered from a lack of concentration because of this depression. In the past two weeks, I have found my thoughts wandering off to a distant place while I am studying, thus breaking my concentration on the subject matter at hand. What a fucking drag! These are the reasons I feel I will not do well on the exam this week.

I should have asked God to help me with my concentration sooner, and only plan to do so now. God, this exam is in four days and I feel unprepared. Please help me to concentrate as best I can during the next few days on the material. I am not sure if I am *supposed* to ask You to help me do my best on the exam or not, but I know this is what I *want* to ask of You. I need to pass this exam and another one before I can be formally admitted to candidacy and submit my dissertation proposal. I know that You probably already know this, but I'm just repeating it anyway. I've only ever wanted to get my Ph.D. in the social sciences and teach at a university for most of my life, God, and so I am asking You to help me achieve this goal. If I am appearing selfish right now, then I ask for Your forgiveness. Please show me your will, God, and help me to get through this week. Thanks for another day sober.

DECEMBER 11, 1989

The countdown for the exam is upon me, and anxiety is starting to dominate my actions. I am nervous about the exam on Thursday, but—

somehow and for some reason—I am not obsessing about the exam like I have done in the past. Instead, I find myself obsessing about men as usual. And so I guess this journal entry will be about men once again.

At tonight's meeting, I ran into Craig, a guy I used to play softball with and a guy I thought I was madly in love with. We talked for a few minutes, and the conversation was a bit uncomfortable. He was obviously there with a new girlfriend and was waiting for her to join him as we talked. Actually, he kept looking over my shoulder as we spoke to see where she was. I could tell by his actions and mannerisms he was uncomfortable talking to me, and the reason for this is because I told him a while back that I liked him and wanted to go out with him. He turned me down.

Before I expressed any interest in him other than friendship, Craig and I had a neat relationship. We were buddies. We had some things in common and we generally seemed to care about one another a bit. I interpreted his actions toward me as ones of romantic interest, and so I asked him out. He politely said he would if he could, but was in a relationship now and couldn't do that kind of stuff anymore. Well,Craig has since terminated that relationship and, from what I can gather tonight, he is on the verge of getting into one with another woman.

I kind of wish I never would have asked him out, because it has changed the way the two of us interact. We are no longer really friends and spend no time together. I just feel weird right now. I almost feel jealous of his new girlfriend, yet I never had a relationship with Craig to warrant any of these feelings. It was all in my head.

I don't even know why I am writing about this tonight. I know I am not his type, yet I find myself feeling rejection right now and feeling lesser than—lesser than this beautiful woman he was with, lesser than his group of friends, and not good enough for him. Why do I feel this way? I feel this way because he has told me no and because my self-esteem with men is really low right now and has been for some time.

I just got off the phone with Colin again, whom I let give me the runaround all because I want his attention. I'll take what he has to offer and settle for it. My self-esteem with men is so low right now. I am so fucking desperate and I just can't believe it. I just don't understand all of this and why it is happening now. Is this all a part of this loneliness thing? Am I craving men like I used to crave drugs? What is going on, God?

Tomorrow I go to my therapist and hope to get a chance to talk about all of this. I am emotionally vulnerable right now—so much, my concentration is being affected by the simplest of things. I don't like feeling this vulnerable. I don't like feeling this lonely, and I certainly don't like feeling inadequate—and that is what I have been feeling lately.

I can remember using cocaine when I felt this way before. Bummer! Can't use drugs to medicate feelings anymore. I guess I have to sweat them out. Please help, God. I can't do it alone. Man, am I starting to hate that word: alone. Yuck! Later.

DECEMBER 12, 1989

My boss from the office just called me and wants to know what my long-term game plans for the office are. I told him I wasn't sure what I wanted to do, but hinted I wasn't sure if I wanted to go back to work for the office at all after the beginning of the year. He was perturbed by this and said that the only honorable thing to do would be to come back for a few months and then leave for good. He says I would be burning my bridges if I didn't do it this way, and more or less hinted that any other working decision contrary to this would be unacceptable.

What do I do now? Nothing, I guess. I can't believe he made me talk about this two days before my exam. Why couldn't he have waited until next week to bring this up? How am I supposed to concentrate on my studies right now, knowing I have this dilemma to face next month? I am going to turn this over for today and try to get back to work.

God, please take this from me right now. I can't handle it at all. Please help me to focus on the tasks in front of me, and please help me to get through the day without using. Man, do I hate feeling this tense! Where are my cigarettes? Please take this from me, God. Thanks!

DECEMBER 16, 1989

I was at Ben and Sandy's house last night for dinner and had to spend the night because of the snow. I am pretty close to this family. I actually love them all quite a bit. Spending last evening at their house was a perfect way to end this week. I couldn't have asked for a better way to end the week and a three-week study period for the comprehensive exam I took.

I have some free time right now and feel like just relaxing. I am going to try to do as little work as possible today and am going to try to just goof off and do domestic and play things all day. It is going to be a fun day.

The exam went pretty well. I was not nervous Thursday morning before the exam; and as soon as I received the test, my anxiety subsided. I think I did okay on the exam, but I am, of course, not sure just how well I did. I do think I passed it. I am pretty sure of that. I wonder if I'll get a distinction, the highest grade possible. I want a distinction, of course, but don't really think my answers were that good. I guess I'll find out if they were in a few weeks.

I realized yesterday I am almost A.B.D. [all but dissertation]. I feel so good knowing I am a doctoral candidate. Never before have I felt this way about my degree or academic status. I actually feel pretty good knowing I am 26 and am nearing the end of my Ph.D. I love having this status and I like the respect that goes along with it. More than this, however, I finally realized yesterday I have accomplished quite a bit in these 26 years of my life and feel very good about it all. I am just very happy with myself today.

Today, I don't regret anything I have done in my life. In fact, I am quite proud of myself today. I am a happy camper and I am going to try to hold onto these feelings throughout the day. I am not going to try to project these feelings into tomorrow. I am just going to hold onto what I have today. That's a new one for me, huh? Feels good. Later!

DECEMBER 19, 1989

I had a really good day today. I was very busy all day and got a lot done. I felt really good about having the day off to take care of a lot of things at school. I have almost finished writing an exam for the class I teach, I did research on the reading list for my social psychology exam, I photocopied five months of journal entries and mailed them off to my editor, I went to therapy, I went to the grocery store, and I ran a few miles. It was a good day. I was very relaxed despite the busy schedule.

At therapy today, my psychologist and I discussed some of the issues that are going to arise when I publish this journal, and we also discussed how my life has been characterized by this unrealistic quest to have so much accomplished at such an early age. Basically, I left therapy thinking little about the journal, but a lot about why I feel this urgency to finish my Ph.D. and everything else I do in the shortest amount of time possible. And this is what I want to discuss tonight.

I have always felt an urgency in completing anything I have ever attempted to do. Simply put, I should have gotten everything done yesterday. What I mean by this is, I have spent my entire life setting expectations according to some unrealistic time clock. I simply must finish the Ph.D. by the time I turn 26, be tenured at a university by the time I am 30, be married by 30, and have kids by 32. I also have to be employed at a university by the time I reach 28 and should have several articles out by that time. My lifelong goals have been defined by a time clock, and it is I who have set the times of these events throughout my life.

I discussed this today with my psychologist, and she shed light on this subject for me. She basically told me that we had a lot of things to work on and that I have a lot of things going on in my life right now that are confusing me.

I can make no conclusions about this time clock today and how it has affected my life. And I cannot make any conclusions about what therapy, the program, or my Higher Power will reveal to me in days to come concerning this subject. All I can say tonight is, I can see I am beginning to uncover an identity—and that identity is mine. Every time I go to a meeting, get a message from my Higher Power, go to therapy, or just talk to a friend who cares, I find I can uncover something about myself if I just listen.

Listening. This certainly doesn't come easy for me. I hear what I want to hear, see what I want to see, and do as I please. I did these things until I entered recovery, until I *had* to enter recovery. And upon entering recovery, I soon realized I had to sit back and listen. I had to listen to things I didn't want to hear and from people I didn't care about. I also had to open my eyes to things I used to hide behind because I was afraid of what I might see. In recovery, I even had to do things I didn't want to do just because some other addict, friend, professor, or whoever told me to do them. I have had to do these things because I have wanted recovery from drug addiction, and now I find I am doing these things so I can get rid of destructive behaviors and character defects.

I didn't want any of this while I was using. I simply had my ears closed for two years. Today I realized my ears and eyes have been closed to a lot of things throughout my entire life. They have been closed for certain reasons. I don't know exactly what the reasons are, but my psychologist tells me we are going to find out what they are. The program, also, promises me that more will be revealed in time and things will get better.

I am kind of beside myself right now. I feel a bit like an iceberg submerged in water. The analogy to the iceberg goes like this: I was keeping my head above water while I was using cocaine. As my addiction progressed, I found myself gasping for air and almost drowning on numerous occasions. Somehow, the water receded enough around me and I was able to open my mouth to ask for help. Ever since I asked for help from the program, my Higher Power, friends, and now my therapist, I can feel more of myself emerging from the water. It's like the water is receding around me more and more each day; and I can feel, see, and hear myself discovering who I really am.

I don't always like what I feel, hear, and see as the water around me recedes; but I cling to the hope that, despite any pain I experience, things will get better. If I listen to others today, take a long hard look inside myself, and do what I am supposed to do, I think I may one day totally emerge from the water. I think one day after the water recedes I might find that not only have I uncovered my real identity, I might actually be something different—maybe a mountain instead of an iceberg. Who knows? All I do know is that this is all very scary right now. Later!

DECEMBER 20, 1989

Oh no! Five days until Christmas. Am I ready? No! Have I really even thought about it? No! Another Christmas and another three-day break, as I see it. Christmas never feels like a holiday to me. It rarely feels special; and the reason for this is, I am usually so consumed in my life I have little time to sit back and allow myself to experience a holiday. What is a holiday, anyway?

I shared at a meeting tonight about what I wrote in my journal last night. I shared about trying to find a middle ground in life, about finding some serenity, and about getting rid of my extreme behaviors and personality defects. I got some positive feedback on my situation and feel a bit better today. At least I can say I know more about these negative characteristics today than I did yesterday. I just don't know if I am ready to part with all of them yet.

I feel as if I am going to make little sense tonight. Actually, I just don't feel like writing much this evening. Maybe I'll write tomorrow when I wake up. As usual, I have a full day planned. I have the day planned from 7:30 a.m. until 12 a.m. Hope I have the energy. Later!

DECEMBER 27, 1989

I could have used this journal numerous times while I was at home for Christmas. This Christmas was hard, and it was hard because I needed recovery and could find none. I didn't have my journal to write in, I didn't have friends to talk to (well, I could have called a few long distance, but decided not to do so), and I didn't have meetings to attend. In fact, the only tool of recovery that I had in my hometown this time was my Higher Power, and He is what got me through Christmas.

There was drinking everywhere at home. In three days, I had four parties and three happy hours to attend. I decided, after the first party, I was going to blow off the rest of the parties and happy hours. I made a few people mad and even upset myself by not going to these functions. I experienced a lot of guilt from family and friends for not being more social over the holidays. Funny how the word "social" always seems to be defined by people who drink.

The big shocker of the Christmas season was when I decided to pass on Communion at church Christmas Eve. I realized as the members of my church were going up to the altar for Communion that our church served wine. So I decided not to go up and take Communion. I made this decision not so much because I didn't want to drink that little sip of wine, but because I wanted to send a message to my parents and family members that this drinking thing is as serious as the cocaine thing. I wanted to show them I plan to be abstinent from all mood-altering substances. What a foolish move on my part, for many reasons!

I will discuss this in more detail later. My dinner is ready.

DECEMBER 29, 1989

Well, it is almost 1990. 1989 is almost over. I don't know how I feel about all of this yet. Obviously I have no strong feelings or I would be writing about them now. A lot has happened this year, but I can't seem to find the energy to write about any of it. All I would like to mention is that 1989 has been a year of self-discovery. For the first time in my life, I have taken a look at myself this year. Basically, I do not like what I have found, but there are a few bright spots.

I guess 1990 will reveal more—or at least that is what I have been told. I hope I can really start to work on myself in 1990, because I have experienced a lot of pain this year. I don't want 1990 to be as painful as 1989, and there is no reason it should be if I just try to change all of the things about me that make me miserable. The problem is, this seems such a tall order. I have lived 26 years with arrogance, selfishness, false pride, and vanity. I have spent my life sacrificing my peace of mind to please others. I have manipulated people, places, and things in my life to try to get my own way. I have obsessed over everything I have ever wanted in my life; and when I got what I wanted or did something worthwhile, it simply meant nothing to me. Basically, I have spent my life pursuing desires I have often obtained, yet getting them still leaves me unsatisfied.

So what's in store for 1990? More of these kinds of behaviors and attitudes? I hope not. I am tired of living this way, but it's all I know. I am safe with this type of behavior. I know what to expect from it, and I know how to deal with the consequences of these things. Changing takes courage. It takes courage because I will not know what to expect from myself or others. I hate not knowing the outcomes, but I have got to start to take the chances involved in doing things differently.

1989 has been a problematic year. In every aspect of my life, I have experienced pain during 1989. I have been through so many emotions, moods, and states of mind. What's next? I hope something better, because I don't want a repeat of 1989 during 1990. 1989 did have its good points—after all, without it I probably never would have come in touch with myself and all of the defects of character I have. I just hope 1990 brings me courage and strength to change these things. The courage and strength don't just have to come from me. I have the program, my Higher Power, my sponsor, friends, and even a counselor to help me along. I just hope I don't forget to call on them. Later!

DECEMBER 30, 1989

The song says, "The party's over." And it certainly feels like it is right now. What's the party? The party is the obsession with drugs and alcohol and thinking they can make me someone else and take my troubles away. The party is the image I have of myself as Queen of the Universe, the image that I can do no wrong and am very special. The party is the role I play when I am around others. It is what I want them to think of me. The party is the charade; it is the charade that has characterized my life. And now that very charade is being revealed. People in my life are (and I also am) beginning to see that the charade is not me and that I have been hiding behind it for 26 years. For sure, the party's over!

And so the song goes on to say, "The party's over. I never thought you'd stay." The words "I never thought you'd stay" mean so much to me and are so relevant to my recovery today. At the beginning of my recovery, many people would have pegged me for a relapse and would have bet that I would leave the program. Shit, I basically felt the same way. I never wanted to be in the program. I never wanted to stay. I never wanted to stay around and do the work it took to stay clean. I didn't want to experience the pain of change, of acceptance, and of powerlessness. I wanted to leave many times.

Now I say it to myself: "I never thought I would stay." I never thought I would stick around and show up for life. Many times during these past 20 months, I have wanted to leave and go get high, leave and go daydream, leave and shirk responsibility, and leave to isolate in misery. And I have done all of those things except relapse. I should be grateful for that. My party is over, and I have definitely stayed around the program for 20 months now without picking up a drink or a drug—but it has been no easy task. The party is over, and the work has begun.

I am tired of this analogy—the analogy of my life to a phrase in a song. It's just that the song is so relevant and so beautiful. It's like the song just reveals so much to me, so much about my life. I love the song. It is my favorite.

I must go run. Tomorrow is New Year's Eve and I will be spending it with Christopher and David. I am looking forward to a good time this year. I mean a good New Year's Eve. Later!

DECEMBER 31, 1989

This is the last day of December, of 1989, and of the 1980s. During this decade, I have obtained three degrees: a high school diploma, a B.A., and an M.S. I had planned to finish my Ph.D. this decade as well, but then I became an addict. Oh yeah. During this decade, I went from a nonaddict to an active addict and on to a recovering addict. It has been an interesting decade, to say the least.

This song says, "Faith can move mountains; fire can cleanse your soul." What does this mean? Beats me! No, I know what it means, but don't feel like getting into it. I just heard those words on my stereo right now, and my mind drifted over there for a few seconds.

> Look at yourself; see how you lie. Your hands start shaking and you don't know why. Food for the saints that are quick to judge me. In my head there is a mirror—when I've been bad I've been really, really wrong. Food for the saints that are quick to judge me. Hope for a badman; this is a badman's song. [Tears for Fears, "Badman's Song"]

What a song. It kind of takes control of me when I hear it. Is everything in my life an analogy to cocaine? It seems that way lately. Maybe I'm just a romantic, looking for poetic phrases and metaphors to help make sense of my life. For instance, I was reading this book of poetry my brother gave me for Christmas last night, and I came across a poem written by Edgar Guest that had great significance to my life. The poem is entitled, "No Place to Go" and it goes like this:

> The happiest nights I ever know
> Are those when I've no place to go,
> And the missus says when the day is through:
> "To-night we haven't a thing to do."
>
> Oh, the joy of it, and the peace untold
> Of sitting around in my slippers old,
> With my pipe and book in my easy chair
> Knowing I needn't go anywhere.
>
> Needn't hurry my evening meal
> Nor force the smiles that I do not feel,
> But can grab a book from a near-by shelf,
> And drop all sham and be myself.
>
> Oh, the charm of it and the comfort rare;
> Nothing on earth with it can compare;
> And I'm sorry for him who doesn't know
> The joy of having no place to go.
>
> [Edgar Guest, "No Place to Go"]

This is the shit that I have been writing about all year. I have made countless journal entries about the pain involved in getting to know myself, in faking happiness to please others, and in making sure that every moment of every day is occupied so I can keep my mind off the loneliness I often feel. Oh, how I would long for moments to have nothing to do and be content enough with myself to just sit back and do nothing. But it doesn't matter if I do have moments when I've nothing to do or no place to go, I cannot enjoy them like Mr.Guest can. Mr. Guest said he was sorry for those who do not know the joy of having no place to go. He's talking about me, for sure. Katy Hendricks, this is a poem for you.

Maybe one day I'll reach this point. The point where I am comfortable with myself just having nothing to do and no place to go. I believe this will happen to me. Remember, I wrote above that "faith can move mountains." I meant it, and so did the composers of that song. Please, God, help me move these mountains that surround me and make me miserable. Help me move these mountains that prevent me from loving myself. I can feel my faith in You, the program, my sponsor, and my friends increasing as the days pass. And I can feel myself being more comfortable with it all as the days pass, as well. Does this mean I am starting to be comfortable with myself? I hope so, because I want what Edgar Guest wrote [about] in that poem. I want to know the joy of having no place to go.

God, thank you for the past 20 months and seven days of sobriety. It is a miracle!

"Katy Hendrick's" is a pseudonym. The author is completing her Ph. D. in sociology.

Barbara Sherman Heyl, Professor of Sociology at Illinois State University, is the author of *The Madam as Entrepreneur: Career Management in House Prostitution*, and has published extensively in the fields of deviant behavior and the sociology of law.

Norman K. Denzin, Professor of Sociology, Communications and Humanities at the University of Illinois, is the author of *The Recovering Self* and *The Recovering Alcoholic*, nominated for the C. Wright Mills Award in 1988.

KODAK BRANCH
Sevier County Public Library System
319 West Dumplin Valley Road
Kodak, Tenn. 37764